B-59
$2

A PUBLIC SPIRIT

A PUBLIC SPIRIT

George H. Atkinson's Written Legacy

Transcribed and with a foreword by
Donald J. Sevetson

PACIFIC UNIVERSITY LIBRARIES
Forest Grove, Oregon

A Public Spirit:
George H. Atkinson's Written Legacy

Selected, transcribed, and introduced by Donald J. Sevetson

Published by Pacific University Libraries 2015

ISBN 978-0-9884827-3-9

Pacific University Libraries
2043 College Way
Forest Grove, Oregon 97116

www.pacificu.edu/libraries

Published in the United States of America
Set in Georgia

Cover title/background font Mrs Saint Delafield © 2011 Alejandro Paul,
SIL Open Font License, Version 1.1

Bee Tree Books
An imprint of the Pacific University Libraries

*Our treasure lies in the beehive of our knowledge. We are perpetually on the way
thither, being by nature [...] honey gatherers of the mind.*
Friedrich Nietzsche

The "Bee Tree", an iconic ivy-covered tree that stood on the Pacific University campus
for many years, was already old and hollow when pioneer Tabitha Brown arrived in
Oregon in 1846. Mrs. Brown started a home for orphans that would grow into Pacific
University. According to the Forest Grove *News-Times*, the tree was "said to have
housed a swarm of bees who furnished the little old lady with honey which she sold to
buy provisions for her orphan children."

TABLE OF CONTENTS

FOREWORD

George (1819-89) and Nancy (1815-95) Atkinson arrived in Oregon from Vermont in 1848. Their first location was Oregon City. They moved in 1863 to Portland, where they lived the rest of their lives. George's primary contributions to life in the new region state were as a Congregational missionary and as a founder and early shaper of both public and private education. I recently published his biography (*Atkinson: Pioneer Oregon Educator*, CreateSpace, 2011).

Early in that work I described the way in which research caused a change in my understanding and appreciation of him:

> When I began my study of George Atkinson I thought that his main significance was as a missionary, and that his efforts for public education were an adjunct to that role. I was well aware that the Protestant Reformation had stressed placing the Bible in the hands of the laity. I assumed that that was what motivated him to advocate education for all.
>
> What I found was quite different. George Atkinson was a seventh generation New Englander. He believed that the church and the school are the engines that make the whole community moral and prosperous. He saw that schools had economic, social and political importance. I have concluded, as the title of this work states, that his primary importance in Oregon was in the field of education. Much of his pastoral and missionary life was a painfully difficult struggle.
>
> I also learned that his legacy of published work was notable for its volume, as well as for the range of things he both knew about, and was able to discuss in detail. He was an articulate, influential voice in his adopted region.[i]

---

[i] Sevetson, D.J., *Atkinson: Pioneer Oregon Educator*, CreateSpace, 2011, viii.

This publication is, from one perspective, a continuation of the biography. That work had been limited, of necessity, in the number and length of quotations from Atkinson's longer writings. This work reproduces much of his writing fully. The material found here will illustrate the breadth of Atkinson's interests, the depth of his knowledge, and the keenness of his intellect. Of equal, if not greater, importance, is that it offers a window into public discourse during the four decades of Atkinson's presence in Oregon.

Many of these writings appeared in the *Oregonian*, Portland's major newspaper. Two were also published in the Annual Reports of the Oregon Legislature. One is a letter sent to the secretaries of the American Home Missionary Society, which commissioned him, sent him to Oregon, and gave him financial stipends during more than twenty-five of his forty years of work in Oregon and Washington.

I am profoundly grateful to Pacific University, Forest Grove, Oregon for its interest in my "Atkinson Project." Special mention goes to three librarians at Pacific: Marita Kunkel, University Librarian; Eva Guggemos, Archives/Special Collections and Instructional Services Librarian; and Isaac Gilman, Scholarly Communications and Publishing Services Librarian. They have generously shared their outstanding professional gifts, while remaining patient, encouraging and enthusiastic. Without them this book would never have been completed. Thank you, Boxers!

My deep gratitude goes to my wife Mary Louise, who has tolerated and even supported my long and winding journey through George Atkinson's legacy. And we both thank Ann and David Munro of Portland, who gathered some thirty descendants of George Atkinson together one evening. That clan pronounced us honorary members of the family. We hope that this book gives them even more reasons to be proud of their ancestor.

I will admit that I still have a sense of awe over the sheer volume of Atkinson's work. I suspect that readers will experience it as well. A look at the earlier biography will increase that awe. During his forty year residence he made eight trips to New England as well as one to Alaska, and visited countless schools and churches. More than four hundred of his letters, some quite lengthy, are extant. He even found time, as will be seen in this work, to be one of the passengers on the first train to travel east through the Columbia Gorge on its way to Walla Walla and Dayton, Washington. He also took the time to write that event up and telegraph it to the *Oregonian*.

In my earlier work I cited Patricia Nelson Limerick's image of the 'sustainable hero', who does the right thing some of the time. She continues: "Sustainable heroism comes only in moments and glimpses, but they are moments and glimpses in which the universe lights up."[ii]

Welcome to the writing and the universe of George Atkinson, a "public spirit" who qualifies as a "sustainable hero."

Donald J. Sevetson
Portland, Oregon
October 2015

Note: All of the works in the book have been copied from original or microfilmed material. In a few cases [marked by (?)] words could not be deciphered. The only changes or edits made were done for clarity. All italics are in the originals.

[ii] Sevetson, 1.

INTRODUCTION

George H. Atkinson was not yet thirty when he accepted the invitation of the American Home Missionary Society (AHMS) to travel to Oregon to serve in their newly opening missionary field there. Only an accident of fate kept Atkinson from his original plan to serve in a foreign mission in Africa. This change of plans was hugely providential for Oregon. Over the next forty years, until his death in 1889, George Atkinson served as a powerful influence in the young state. He dedicated his life not only to his work as the leader and founder of Congregational churches in Oregon and Washington, but also to a much broader array of interests. And while education was foremost among them—and he is often called the "father of public education in Oregon"—education was not, for Atkinson, a narrow enterprise. It had economic and political importance, including language, history, science, engineering, business, and moral studies.

The rich and diverse quality of Atkinson's interests is evident in the collection of his writings, selected and transcribed by his biographer, Donald Sevetson, which comprise this book. Sevetson, himself a United Church of Christ minister (now retired), began his journey with George Atkinson over twenty years ago with a project to transcribe Atkinson's letters. That project soon grew into a more intensive study of the man and resulted in a biography, *Atkinson: Pioneer Oregon Educator*, published in 2011. After that publication, Sevetson felt strongly that many of Atkinson's original writings needed to be published in order to supplement the biography and to provide, as Sevetson writes in the foreword to this book, "a window into public discourse during the four decades of Atkinson's presence in Oregon." Thus, *A Public Spirit: George H. Atkinson's Written Legacy* came to be.

In the eight chapters of *A Public Spirit* we find evidence of the broad perspective that led George Atkinson to assume public leadership in subjects as diverse and significant as railroads, prisons, public and private schools, Native American relationships, agriculture, engineering, and commerce.

The writings include a report to the AHMS, exploring the Puget Sound region's potential for missionaries to be employed there. Atkinson is enthusiastic: "I had thought it (the western portion of the Washington Territory) unworthy of the noble name it bears, but my conviction now is that this rising state will be among the foremost in the union and worthy of him, who was first in the hearts of his countrymen."

Also included is Atkinson's 1866 report to the Oregon House and Senate, reporting on his visits to seven penitentiaries, including prisons on the east coast, the Midwest, and San Quentin in California. The scope alone of those visits is impressive, given the year, as is his 27-point summary, ranging from light and ventilation to the issue of inconsistent, unjust prison sentences.

In articles written for the *Oregonian* in 1876, 1877, and 1878, Atkinson advocated for the completion of the Northern Pacific Railroad, which had become a controversial issue; Atkinson accused one Oregon senator of attempting to sabotage the effort. Many of these articles were later republished by the Portland Board of Trade in a booklet, "The Northwest Coast." That publication is included in its entirety in chapter six of *A Public Spirit*.

Interestingly, it was not until the late 1870s that we find Atkinson turning his attention to Native American issues in a series of articles appearing in the *Oregonian*. His advocacy for policies of integration, while we see now as flawed, were expressed in opposition to proposed military solutions and show a deep respect for Native American lives.

Atkinson's greatest influence was on education in Oregon. He was tireless in his efforts to formulate and administer educational programs and institutions. The documents show that he believed that universal public education was foundational for a healthy, prosperous regional community. He saw secondary and post-secondary education, both public and private, as essential to the role and the contributions of education for the wider good.

INTRODUCTION

Pacific University was the early beneficiary of George Atkinson's commitment to education. It was he who called the meeting (in Oregon City in 1848) that established the Board of Trustees of Tualatin Academy. Atkinson served on the first Board of the Academy, and later served as a Trustee for Pacific University, until his death. His two histories of Pacific University, written in 1876 and 1888, comprise the final chapters of this book.

The subjects in this book vary and speak to the intellectual depth and civic engagement of this "public spirit." Taken together, this collection of George Atkinson's writings introduces us to his rich and important legacy. U.S. Commissioner of Education (1870-86) John Eaton understood the impressive capacity of George Atkinson when he wrote, "Dr. Atkinson was one of the most completely rounded men I ever knew, and I shall always be his debtor."

Pacific University is proud of, and grateful for, the vision and dedication of George Atkinson, who so influenced Oregon's history in the latter half of the 19th century. Likewise, Pacific University Libraries is pleased to publish *A Public Spirit: George H. Atkinson's Written Legacy* as the first book offered under our new imprint Bee Tree Books. We imagine Dr. Atkinson would have found this quite fitting, as do we. Bee Tree Books takes its name from a story about Tabitha Brown, who founded the orphan school that begins Pacific University's history. The story goes that she harvested honey from a tree on campus to support the young orphans she sought to educate. Bee Tree Books carries on this commitment of our early pioneers, George Atkinson and Tabitha Brown, to education and the sharing of knowledge.

Marita Kunkel
University Librarian
Pacific University
November 2015

ONE

Writings on Puget Sound

In 1847 George Atkinson was commissioned as a home missionary to Oregon by the American Home Missionary Society (AHMS). Among the several elements in the Society's initial charge to him was that he should report back to them on the territory as a whole:

> In order to keep pace with other denominations, exploring must not be lost sight of.
>
> (*Milton Badger, AHMS Secretary, to Atkinson, June 27, 1848. Pacific University Archives*)

A glance at Atkinson's life reveals him as a peripatetic man, fascinated by new modes of transportation and the places to which they took him. Hence Milton Badger's encouragement to explore was welcomed by eager ears. Within three weeks of his June, 1848 arrival in Oregon City Atkinson and Elkanah Walker took twelve days to explore the upper Willamette Valley.[i]

Eleven years later, in November, 1859, he undertook a survey of Puget Sound, one of the most ambitious of his journeys. Washington had been part of the original Oregon Territory established in 1849. It was granted separate territorial status in 1853. That original Washington Territory included present Washington and Idaho, plus some of western Montana.

The 1859 journey was three weeks long. Although his report does not provide a detailed itinerary, he describes the first part of the journey as by boat, from Oregon City down the Willamette and Columbia

---

[i] Sevetson, 46.

Rivers to the Pacific Ocean, thence north to the straits of San Juan de Fuca, with an initial stop at Port Townsend on the Olympic Peninsula. Other stops on Puget Sound were at Port Gamble, Port Madison, Seattle, Steilacoom, and Olympia. The return route took him overland through Monticello to Vancouver, where he crossed the Columbia and continued home to Oregon City.

This document is his full trip report to the AHMS, dated Dec. 1, 1859. The brief addenda include letters with recommendations, requests, and financial accounting.

Report of a Survey of Puget Sound for the American Home Missionary Society, December 1859

Source:
Archives, Amistad Research Center at Tulane University

Washington Territory
Oregon City Dec. 1st 1859

Rev. Messrs. Badger, Coe & Noyes, Secretaries, A.H.M. Socy

Dear Brethren—

I wrote you last from Port Townsend on Admiralty Inlet, at the finest of views of the Juan De Fuca Straits. I remained there two days after the Sabbath, and met with the "Dashaway Reform Club" one evening, and on the next addressed them and the citizens, on their invitation. The Concert house was full and good attention was given. This reform was and is much needed at that point. The citizens and strangers, especially the sailors, have suffered in purse, in health, and much in reputation from the use of intoxicating liquors. After a week of drunkenness, in the morning when their heads were aching and were apparently swollen to double size, with bloodshot eyes and trembling limbs about a dozen of the most hopeless inebriates took a solemn oath before a notary public that they would not drink or taste any kind of intoxicating liquors, whisky, brandy, (?) cider or beers, for six months.

Others joined them; in two weeks they numbered 25. The night on which I met with them their committee, appointed the previous week, reported a Constitution & Bylaws, which were well drawn up and fully guarded. They were adopted, being amended only to make them more stringent. Yet with the strictness of the law, they embraced also some of the Gospel, having a committee appointed to look up & provide for the poor & suffering, & to help the weak.

It was deeply interesting to see the clear working of their minds & hearts in this reform. Their differences of judgment were expressed in a manly way, and they, every one, yielded in a good spirit to the will of the majority. For three hours they worked over this Constitution & Bylaws, although only fifteen were present that eve, the rest being necessarily absent. It was (?) that several of them had seen better days. Though clad coarsely and looking rough, there

[6]

were beneath the marks of intelligent & noble men; such indeed as the Arch destroyer most frequently selects as victims of the Cup.

There is hope of the little Society. It is a spontaneous movement, an offshoot of the living temperance tree, and a mark of its inherent vitality and power. They take no slow steps up to the great principle of Total Abstinence, but spring to it at once, as the only true & safe course. One of their members died within four days after he had abandoned his Cups, and although the physicians said that he might perhaps have lived if he had left off gradually, his death & this inference worked no evil or hindrance to the rest of the Club, or to their influence. They are hailed as a necessity.

Two saloon keepers have joined them & they express the hope that the reform will stop their business. They do not agree to quit the sale or trade in liquors, but they all see and confess that this is to be the result.

There is a flourishing organization of the same kind at Victoria, and a motion for one at Olympia. Captains of steamers, who have been noted for intemperance, have joined in it. They are hard at work bringing in others. I left Port Townsend on Wednesday, in company with a very obliging friend, Seward Wilson, Esq., of Port Gamble. We took passage in a Plunger, a small vessel of five or six tons burden. These vessels afford safe passages on these waters, and they should be taken instead of whale boats, & in preference to anything except steamers or large sea going vessels.

We reached Port Gamble in four hours. I hoped to be there 36 hours before the Sound Steamboat came along, yet at the suggestion of Mrs. Wilson, we had an appointment made for a meeting that evening. About 40 persons came in. The little village is made and sustained solely by the lumber business. The mills saw regularly 60,000 ft per day, and when there is need they can saw 100,000 ft each twenty-four hours. Sometimes a dozen vessels are there at once loading lumber & spars.

The proprietors are very strict in enforcing a prohibitory liquor law, which they have enacted on their own account. They and their families are from East Machias, Me., and most of their employees are from Maine. The other mills adopt the same policy, yet they cannot keep all liquor away. The "Beach Combers", of the worst class, will steal along in the night & sell to their men. We passed a hut kept by one of these Whisky traders. His boat was hauled up for the day, ready to launch for the night.

I found five or six professors of religion at Port G. And a larger number who had been religiously trained. All these expressed a desire to have a minister come and settle among them. One truly devoted Mother in Israel, formerly from Danvers Mass., lately from San Francisco said, that this was her constant prayer. A few brethren were just then proposing to commence a prayer meeting. As well as perhaps a Bible class for the Sabbath.

The holy day is spent too much in giving and receiving visits. Officers of vessels come on shore to call & dine. The mill men go into the woods to hunt, or spend the day in washing or mending their clothes, or in idleness. They need a Sabbath. A faithful minister could, were he here, with the divine blessing greatly change this state of things. They want an <u>intelligent</u> man, who can instruct them, and a man whose whole life will correspond with his teachings. They express themselves as tired of untrained, ignorant preachers. In fact they have given such the cold shoulder so decidedly that they do not come any more.

I hoped to have a full day with the people at Port G. But the steamboat came at midnight. I was obliged to leave without saying good bye to even the few to whom I had been introduced.

Port G. as I have written before is a center, from which a minister can easily visit Port Ludlow, Sebac, Port Madison, Port Orchard, & Hulsilladilic Mills. I promised them that I would recommend the Society to send them a minister with his wife early the next year.

At sunrise we were at Seattle on the east side of the Inlet, having called at Port Madison on the way. Seattle is situated on a fine Bayou, one of the many which indent the land around this inland sea. It has a steam mill and besides a large farming region back to the Cascades, which will give the place business.

The Duwamish river enters the Bay here. Back of the town about two miles, is a lake 40 miles long, deep, abounding in fish, and surrounded by fine timber and farming lands. A navigable branch of the Duwamish flows from the lake. The Snoqualmie Pass, through the Cascades naturally leads to Seattle. The village has now only about 250 people; but it is gaining in the public favor as an important and permanent settlement. I had no time to go ashore but my convictions have been strengthening that we should have a man stationed there next year. One of the citizens remarked that an intelligent devoted minister would be well received and in part sustained.

We passed on through the narrows which are the dividing line between Admiralty Inlet and Pugets Sound, and reached Steilacoom in four hours, and Olympia in two & a half more.

Olympia is the Capital of the territory, & the largest town. It is at the head of Budd's Inlet. At low water long flats extend out from the town. At high water, large vessels can land at the wharf. The buildings of the town look rather dingy for recent erections. Yet the place has marks of considerable business. The town is spread out around the Inlet, and about two miles up there is another village, about a water mill. At high water vessels go up to get their cargoes.

At Olympia there are two churches, an O.S. Presby & a M. Episcopal. My impression is that the Episcopalians, also, have an organization here. The two former have buildings. The Methodists have also an Academy. As the field is fully occupied I did not stop in Olympia. The O.S. Presby have a church also on Chambers Prairie, seven miles from town, and a good house of worship. They have a smaller church at Grand Mound Prairie, 25 miles from Olympia, but no house of worship. Rev. J.M. Goodell has ministered to this church for a few years past. He died a few weeks since, leaving a large family to mourn his death. There is only one Presby minister now in Washington Territory, Rev. G.W. Whitworth, who ministers to the church at Olympia & who has the care of three other small churches. He informed me that he was expecting two or three ministers from their Board very soon.

The route from Olympia to Monticello[ii] on the Columbia, or rather on the Cowlitz near its mouth is for 60 miles most level and for 30 more rough, as the military road is now laid out. The settlements are scattered. On the Cowlitz Prairie are several old Hudson Bay farms, or farms which were taken by their Canadian employees. They are now selling out to Americans and moving to British Columbia.

We crossed the Chehalis twice, which is navigable for steamboats from Gray's Harbor up to these crossings, or about 120 miles. The valley of this river is now in process of settlement. The route across is the natural one for a Rail Road from the Sound to the Columbia, and the only way in which we can easily go from Oregon to the (?) portions of Washington.

As Monticello is at one terminus of the route, it becomes a natural and growing center of business as well as travel. I arrived there Monday evening, and having sent forward an appointment the day before, I found the people expecting me. The landlord kindly prepared a room which was filled, and good attention was given to my discourse, though I was much wearied by my long ride & walk over the frozen hills. I did not stop at Vancouver, as we can readily visit this place on our way up the Columbia. There are Methodist Episcopal and Catholic churches at V., and a Catholic school for boys & another for girls. This is their second attempt in what was formerly all Oregon. The seminary which they had at Oregon City was given up & the buildings sold. But they have begun again at Vancouver; and recently the Archbishop arrived with eight Priests and sixteen sisters of Notre Dame, to commence one or two schools in Portland and the female seminary again at Oregon City.

My tour of exploration around and through the western portion of Washington Territory has magnified my estimate of the value and importance of that portion of our national domain. I had thought it unworthy of the noble name it bears, but my conviction now is that this rising state will be among the foremost in the union and worthy of him, who was first in the hearts of his countrymen. It is not one thing, like extensive prairies or superior mines, which

---

[ii] Monticello was on the north bank of the Columbia River, south of today's Kelso.

will make Washington the home of hundreds of thousands. It is the combination of many advantages which must unite and combine multitudes of people for that rising state. First and most attractive now are its vast lumber interests. This portion of the territory has few prairies, but its plains, hills, and mountains, from the Columbia to the De Fuca Straits, and from the very surf of the Pacific to the Snow Line of the Cascades are all covered with the loftiest, largest and most useful kinds of timber trees.

I have already written you that the lumbering business, is the most lucrative. Probably more capital has been invested in this than in all other employments. An agent of the Port Gamble mill informed me that their company was assessed on $180,000 worth of property at that point. It may have been too high, for other places almost equal were set below these figures. But it is estimated that 30,000,000 of feet will be exported this year from the mills already in operation; 16,000,000 was the estimate for last year. The amount for this year is set too low, as can be easily seen from the amount sawed per day at each mill.

The next great advantage, and the one which gives value to the forests, is their proximity to navigable waters. Mr. Greeley remarks that the Sierra Nevada Mts. will furnish exhaustless supplies of lumber and timber not only for California but for the whole Pacific region, but those forests are far from sea, and among inaccessible highlands. The forests of Washington and many of those of Oregon also border on deep waters, which allow the passage of all manner of ships among them in all directions.

Capt. Molthrop, formerly of New Haven, who has navigated the Sound Inlet, and straits and bays of Washington for the past year, informed me this week that by careful estimates those waters afforded two thousand miles of shore line, including the inland shores. There are at least forty islands in this Archipelago, some of them large and valuable, nearly all covered with forests.

We may add to this estimate 130 miles on the Pacific, besides the small Bays, and to this the 40 miles afforded by Shoal Water Bay, and 30 or 40 by Gray's Harbor. We may add also 120 miles of steam boat navigation on the Chehalis into the heart of the country, and 130 on the Columbia, to the Cascades, besides all the facilities for sending timber & lumber to the sea which the smaller rivers, as the Lewis, Cowlitz, Whilapah, Queniault, Snohomish, Duwamish, and Nisqually afford. Indeed, the whole of this part of the territory is divided or surrounded by waters. All its wealth in forests and minerals can go into the great highways of commerce. And even now the small population has business with the great marts of the world, China, the Hawaiian Islands, Australia, the South American ports, France & England, besides our own Coast ports.

The waters abound in fish. Salmon, cod, hallibut, herring & sardines, and the flats & sand spits in oysters & clams. Wild game is abundant in the woods. The beaver, otter, mink & marten along the streams, and ducks & geese are everywhere. Beds of coal have been traced from Bellingham Bay, where they are worked, across the smaller islands to Vancouver Island, where also they are worked. This coal is becoming an important article of trade, being used in Victoria now instead of wood by many of the families.

East of the Cascades, Washington Territory has fine grazing regions, in fact, regions unsurpassed for these purposes.

The Colville and (?) gold mines are attracting miners with fresh interest and are becoming remunerative, if not alone at least in connection with those of Frasers and Thompsons Rivers, which lie in the same gold range still further north. Marble and lead mines have also been found within the same limits. The great Columbia affords navigation, it is now believed, through a large part of this interior basin. Every year develops some new and interesting feature of this interior country.

There are no very serious hindrances to the settlement of the whole country. The Indians west of the Cascades are mostly on reservations, and I am sorry to add that they are fast disappearing. Whisky and venery are decimating them. I know not what can or will be interposed to save this part of them. Some of the tribes east of the Cascades are in a more hopeful condition, and if Government favors the wise plans of Rev. E.W. Geary, the present Superintendent of

Indian Affairs for Oregon & Washington, some of the latter tribes may be saved—especially the Nez Perces, to whom Bro. Spalding begs to be again sent. He is near them now, often visiting them and watching over his little church there, but he has no means of support among them, and he cannot, therefore, give them his whole time. He wants to translate larger portions of the Bible for them & to employ two Indians, his former pupils, to help him, but he has no funds & no means to do this.

Settlers will find all the trials of a new country in coming either to Oregon or Washington, but they will find many compensations. People who reside here a few years have very little disposition to go East again or to abide if they go. A minister will find things some what rough, but with a spirit of adaptation and content he can do a great & good work.

Yours in the Gospel
G.H. Atkinson

Oregon City Dec. 2, 1859

Rev. Messrs. Badger, Coe & Noyes, Secretaries A.H.M. Socy

Dear Brethren—

We received, through you, authority to act as an exploring agency of the A.H.M.Socy for the current year, in Oregon and Washington. One of our members has accordingly spent three weeks in Washington Ty. Chiefly visiting the settlements in Pugets Sound & Admiralty Inlet. The information which we have gained of the state of the country and the character of the settlements leads us to the conclusion that three brethren with their wives can now be successfully employed a three stations there, viz. Port Townsend, Port Gamble, and Seattle, in preaching the Gospel, and otherwise extending the Kingdom of our blessed Redeemer. It is our conviction, from what we know of pioneer labors, that as many ought to be employed there by your Society. We find a readiness and a desire to have such laborers as you send out. They need to be educated & devoted men, versed in human nature & versed also in the Gospel. Eastern men are preferred by the citizens of two of the places, as they came mostly from the East. Men with wives are much preferred, as they will abide & grow up with the place, and exert a greater power.

A brother should take a steamer ticket to Port Townsend, and if he has goods ship them to San Francisco and reship either to Port T. or Port Gamble or Seattle, on one of the lumber vessels, which come up frequently. Messrs. Talbot, Pope & Kellar constitute the Port Gamble Co. And they have a house in San Francisco.

The people desire a minister as early in the year as possible.

Please to inform us if the Society accedes to our request, and how soon we may expect one or more brethren. We desire to inform the friends on the Sound as early as possible.

Yours very truly,
G.H. Atkinson
P.B. Chamberlain
P.H. Hatch—Committee on Destn & Supply.

Oregon City
Dec. 2 1859

Rev. M. Badger Secy. A.H.M. Socy

D ear Sir. Please find below a certified statement of my expenses, while on the late tour of exploration for the Society, and charge the difference between these and my draft on your Treasury for $100, to my account.

[14]

Fare for Steam Boats ½ rates	$41.00
Fare for horse full rates	5.
Meals & sundries	10.50
	66.50
Balance to be charged to acct	33.50
	100.00

Yours truly - G.H. Atkinson

We certify that the above is a fair and correct estimate of late exploration of Washington Territory.

P.B. Chamberlain—Committee on Destitution & Supply for Oregon Assn.
P.H. Hatch

TWO

A Report on Prisons

In 1865 the Atkinson family traveled to New England for a lengthy visit, leaving in April and returning in December. They sailed south on the Pacific, then by railroad across the Isthmus of Panama, sailing north on the Atlantic until reaching New York City. In addition to time spent with family in Vermont and Massachusetts, Atkinson attended a national meeting of Congregational churches in Boston and traveled west, as far as Moline, Illinois, for family visits and research on penitentiaries.

He had earlier accepted appointment as a Penitentiary Commissioner (one of three) of the State of Oregon. He understood that service as related to his work in education, since confinement provided opportunities for training and redirection. He visited seven penitentiaries: San Quentin, California; Charlestown, Massachusetts; Concord, New Hampshire; Auburn, New York; Columbus, Ohio; Michigan City, Indiana; and Joliet, Illinois. The three Midwestern visits occurred during a trip he made to see several siblings in and around Moline, Illinois.

The report on his visits was published in the collection of Oregon House and Senate journals for 1866. It was especially timely, since in 1864 the Legislature had appropriated funds to build a prison in Salem, replacing the earlier one located in Portland:

> The prison, operated by the Oregon Department of Corrections, has occupied the Salem site since 1866, two years after the legislature appropriated funds to build the facility. (*Oregon Encyclopedia*)

Report on Visits to Eastern penitentiaries

Source:
Oregon House and Senate Journals, 1866, Appendix, pp. 504-520
Oregon Historical Society

Portland
July 25, 1866

Messrs. A.C.R. Shaw and J.H. Moores,
Commissioners of Oregon Penitentiary:

Dear Sirs:

My brief report in December last, of a visit to the prisons of several states, at your request, may be properly followed by one more minute and extensive.

The structure of prisons and their discipline have of late years received much attention in England and in the United States. The great improvements made are comparatively of modern date, and Americans have been among the foremost to study the penal system and to perfect their penitentiaries.

As an illustration, in the 25th report of the board of managers of the Massachusetts Prison Discipline Society in 1850, they say: "The important points, which have been considered in the proposed extension of the state prison, of a general character, are *convenience, classification, light, ventilation, cleansing, solitary confinement at night, employment, instruction, humanity, discipline, order, security against fire, extension.*"

These points were supposed to include all the interests of the public, and also of the prisoner. They include not only the results secured in the new structure at Charlestown, Mass., but also those which should be attained in all prisons old or new, and as such they may serve as an important guide in our inquiries and discussions. Noting them in their order, I first speak of the *convenience* of a prison. This pertains to *location* and *internal arrangement.*

1. Although the location of the Oregon penitentiary has been settled by vote of the people, it may be proper to remark that it compares in most respects favorably with the sites chosen in other states for

these institutions. It has also the advantage of a stream of pure water for domestic and manufacturing purposes. It has a large area of land. Its vicinity to the capital, and to an intelligent, enterprising, moral and permanent population, and its nearness to a navigable river, favor both its discipline and its economical management. It is to be hoped that it will prove healthful, and that no reason will exist for a change of site.

The *internal* convenience of a prison depends upon a combination of advantages in its plan and structure, so that its operation can be conducted with system and thoroughness. The convict must be fed, clothed, and kept cleanly. But it was not convenient to do this, if the effort had been made, in the English prisons, where Howard found fifty or a hundred, or even two hundred prisoners in a single room, and where Mrs. Fry found three hundred women in two rooms. There they saw their friends, and kept their multitudes of children, and they had no other place for cooking, washing, eating and sleeping. It is not the most convenient to care for a dozen prisoners of all classes locked up in a single room, in which they sit, eat, converse, and sleep.

The time for such arrangements has passed. The modern penitentiary furnishes a cell for every convict. The room, though small, is sufficient for all his wants while in it. Two systems still prevail in taking meals—the old congregate system, in which all sit and eat together at tables with guards over them. This is the custom in the New York, Ohio and other western prisons. The other method, in which every convict takes his food to his own cell and eats it alone, prevails at Charlestown. While the convicts have their hour for meals, with doors barred, the guards and officers have the same hour, off duty, for their meals uninterrupted, and thus no time is lost in the establishment. To accomplish this, the kitchen, cell-rooms and guard-rooms must be conveniently and compactly arranged. To secure this, the prison at Charlestown begins with a central octagonal rotunda four stories high. The kitchen is in the basement, and being central, the food is passed through windows to the prisoners as they go from their shops to their rooms. From three sides of this octagon, wings extend for cell-rooms. From the fourth side the wing for the officers' quarters is built. Over the kitchen is the guard-room, open through gratings on all sides. The four other narrower sides are used for long grated windows. Standing at this center a single guard can see all the prison areas, the yards, shops, and officers' rooms, by simply turning round, and can go to any part through a grated door and down an iron staircase.

The chapel is over the guard-room, and the hospital is designed to be above the chapel, away from the noise of machinery, both having iron stair-cases from the corridors along the cells of all the wings. This compact structure permits the officer to have the oversight of the entire prison, day and night, without exposure. It gives to every prisoner the same light and air which the officer enjoys. The other prisons visited, had usually a central building divided into several rooms, each commanding a view of only a part of the cells or areas from a single point, and that through a gated door or a concealed aperture. In them the culinary and heating departments are usually kept separate.

At Charlestown the cooking and heating apparatus are in the central kitchen, from which pipes, conveying steam or hot water, radiate to all the wings. The cell-rows are in the center of the wing, three, four, and five stories high, double with broad, cool areas around, extending to the walls, high as the ceiling. In the walls are high, broad windows, similar to those in the penitentiary in Portland, affording an abundance of light and air. The cell-rooms of the New York, New Hampshire, Ohio, Illinois and other prisons visited, were similar, though not united to a central rotunda. The old idea of cells along the walls, and slots in the walls to each cell to give light and air has for the most part been abandoned.

2. Security is the next point to be noticed. This was, originally, the chief idea of a prison. It seems always to have been a problem with governments what to do with criminals. How to keep them securely. In the earliest times they seem to have been thrust into slimy dungeons. Under Roman law, free citizens, if convicted, were reduced to slavery and committed to the care of a master, or compelled to labor in public works.

The English early resorted to the transportation of convicts to America and Australia. At one time, their prisoners were confined in old hulks in the Thames. At another, they were huddled into close rooms, debtors, thieves, murderers, young and old; healthy and diseased, in one mass, to pollute and be polluted.

But the chief reliance has been upon strong walls of stone and iron; suggested, probably, by the old feudal castles, which were used for such purposes. Security is sought in most of the prisons visited, by having a system of cells of stone or brick, with iron doors, which are entirely enclosed in a stone or brick building. The prison yards are enclosed by thick walls of stone or brick, from twenty to twenty-five feet high. In addition, armed guards are constantly stationed in towers on the walls. As much reliance, perhaps, is placed upon the vigilance and courage of the guards as upon the buildings.

3. The supervision of prisoners when in their cells is gained on the rotunda plan more thoroughly than on any other. The turnkey or sub-warden can see any movement or hear any sound from any cell without moving from his place, or he can pass in his *felt slippers* to any part of the area or corridors unobserved. His central position enables him to give instant alarm to officers in the rear or to watchmen on the walls.

4. It has been felt of late years, that prisoners ought to be classified. This was one of the reforms proposed by John Howard in England and on the continent. The warrants and official visitors of prisons, assent to its importance. It is an evil to put a man guilty of larceny in companionship with a murderer, or a youth with an old and hardened offender. But the contract system seeks for workmen and makes no distinction among them. All classes mingle together in the shop. The evil can be in part obviated by having a watchman in every shop, as at Charlestown, Auburn and Columbus, who allows no conversation between the prisoners.

5. Solitary confinement at night is deemed exceedingly im-portant for the convicts as well as for all objects of justice. "If a man," says Mr. Buxton, "has the misfortune to be committed for examination to a London prison, guilty or innocent, he is locked up with perhaps a half dozen of the worst thieves, or at night he may find himself

in bed and in bodily contact between a robber and a murderer, or between a man with a foul disease on one side and one with an infectious disorder on the other." What was true there, has been true in every prison. The only remedy is a cell for every man, and to have every man in his room alone. This method assists the discipline, prevents corrupt communications and the concocting (of) plans for escape.

6. Employment of prisoners of all classes is essential to discipline and good order. In the earlier English and Scotch prisons convicts had nothing to do. Vulgar, profane and vicious conduct were the result. Then the tread mill was introduced, with no object but to compel work. Latterly, prisoners have been at once set upon some useful employment. The aim in Massachusetts is to give every one a trade, if he had not one before, so that he can earn his living, and also to discipline him to habits of labor, that he will earn it. The same general idea prevails in all our penitentiaries. To accomplish it large and airy work-shops are erected, various kinds of machinery are introduced, with good motive power, and the whole conducted by the state, or the shops are rented to contractors for periods of five or ten years, who furnish the machinery, and a definite number of men are furnished for the contractor's work, at prices varying from forty cents to one dollar a day. The wardens retained perfect control of the government of all the shops. All our late prisons have improved work-shops, in many cases they are two stories high. The convicts seem as earnest and skillful in their work as if they were free laborers. It gives them health, cheerfulness, and relieves the tediousness of their confinement.

7. Instruction has of late been found an important aid in prison discipline. At Charlestown no regular teacher is provided or regular times set apart for lessons, except chapel and Sabbath services. At Auburn and Columbus, teachers are paid to instruct the convicts after their daily tasks are done. Many who know not how to read or write have there learned. Libraries are provided for prisoners, and also writing materials, and lights are furnished until nine o'clock, P.M., so that they can improve themselves. The chaplain is usually the librarian. All letters to or from the convicts are first submitted to the warden or the chaplain for inspection. These means soften the

hardened offender and operate to restore the wanderer. Especial reliance is now placed upon religious services. At Charlestown the convicts have a choir among themselves and a melodeon. The choir spend half an hour every day practicing tunes for the next morning service. It has been found that a very small per cent of discharged criminals are returned for a second term.

In those prisons which give the least attention to ordinary or religious instruction there is more natural distrust and more insubordination, and more temptation to cruelty. Officers find the benefit of these means. We are to remember that prisoners are men, and that many of them have been untaught. A chapel and schoolroom are an important part of the structure.

8. Humanity is made a distinct consideration in the structure and discipline of modern prisons. The tendency of prisons is to promote inhumanity. It requires great self-control on the part of keepers to guard the convicts, and yet refrain from tyranny, and at the same time give them due care. Prisoners are considered, and they usually are, bad men—frequently the worst characters in community. Entering their cells under the force and restraint of law, they constantly feel themselves cut off, outcasts from society—banished, abandoned, and degraded. They naturally seek to form a society of their own, hostile to that outside their prison. They as naturally cherish revenge, and having no way to reach the public, they often vent their feelings upon their keepers. They soon show their corrupt and vicious characters. They expose themselves, by their violence, passion, deception and baseness, to receive the same in return. Some jailers at last consider it unwise to show them any kindness or special attention. They confess that their own feelings of humanity are changed toward prisoners by contact with them, and they distrust all attempts to reform them, or to benefit them. The public always share, to some extent, in these feelings, especially those who attend much upon our courts and who become familiar with criminal life. Both the prison and the prisoner are avoided, the one as hopeless of good and the other of improvement.

But to carry out the humane ideas of Howard and other philanthropists, it is ESSENTIAL not only that the hospital be suitable for the comfort and restoration of the sick, but that the physicians, the wardens, the guards, the watchmen and overseers, be humane, moral, self-controlled, as well as firm and courageous men. The Massachusetts and Ohio state prisons are good examples of the humane system as carried out in American prisons. It is often remarked that frequent changes of officers are injurious in this and other respects to the management of prisons. It has also been suggested that the appointed power be in the hands of the supreme court of the state, and that occasional visits of the judges to the prison might be highly useful.

9. *Light* is made a point of special importance in the structure of modern prisons. Light is found to be as necessary to health as food and exercise, and nowhere more than to persons confined in buildings. Nearly all the late prisons have long windows in both sides. The aim is to give the prisoner as much as the keeper enjoys. There are eight windows, each 22 x 8 feet in the external walls of the Charlestown prison, making the area around the cells almost as light as the open court. The cells have an open grated door of 6½ x 2½ feet dimensions. The sun shines in by day and the gas or oil lamps from the area at night. The prisons of other states have almost equal facilities for light.

At San Quentin, California, the buildings consist of a system of cells opening to the yard, without an enclosing prison. But the doors, being of iron plate, admit of less light than the grated doors in proper cell rooms. Besides, prisoners can have no light at night.

10. *Heat* is a more important consideration to prisoners than to those who have their freedom. It must be abundantly and steadily supplied or they will suffer. It is hardly less needed in our damp climate than in extremely cold ones. The method of heating at Charlestown is by means of pipes of steam or hot water extending round the area. In some other places stoves are still used. Furnaces are proposed in some places.

11. *Ventilation* is applied not only to the areas by means of long windows, and by apertures and gratings in the ceiling, but to every cell by a tube running to the top of the building, or by flues which extend to the top.

12. *Water* and *cleansing* are deemed very important to the comfort and safety of our prisons. By means of pipes and faucets an abundant supply is furnished in all the wings, and convenient to every prisoner at Charlestown, and every one is required to wash himself daily, and to bathe once a week. The opportunity and means for personal cleanliness are furnished in other prisons visited, but not to the same extent or thoroughness. An abundant supply of pure cool water is found to be essential to the establishment and to the health of the inmates of such institutions, if possible, more than in any other. Many prisoners are naturally uncleanly, while the restraint upon liberty perhaps destroys any self-respect and habit of cleanliness more quickly than any other condition. Were they neglected, and allowed to do as they please, doubtless their condition in these respects would become intolerable. Such was the case in English and continental prisons before the time of reform.

13. *Discipline*, though entering into every feature of a prison, deserves a separate notice. The structure favors or hinders it. All penitentiaries should be designed to impress the prisoner with the idea that he is *securely confined*, and *that any attempt to escape will be useless*. This is the first element in his proper control. Broken walls, defective cells and careless guards set convicts on the watch to escape and defeat all discipline. He has lived uncontrolled. He has broken law, defied authority, despised government, trampled upon the rights of men, and claimed impunity in the reckless gratification of his own appetites and passions. For his own good and the public welfare he must *feel the absolute and complete restraint of his liberty*. For this the massive walls and iron gratings must take the place of the majesty of law which he has defied. Rejecting the one, he must feel the other.

A third element of his discipline is keeping regular hours for sleep, for work, for meals, and for the recreation of reading or writing or study, and for religious worship. A second means is the constant supervision of an officer day and night. This, in several of our best conducted penitentiaries, is to prevent all conversation between convicts.

A fourth means is the single cell for every one. Convicts rooming together destroy discipline. Cliques are formed in prison which plot evil and involve newcomers, and cause much disturbance. A fifth means is punishment for refractory conduct. In some prisons, as at Michigan City, Ind., and San Quentin, Cal., a whip is used. In the latter, also chains and the dungeon.

In some prisons the shower bath and the iron collar are used. In others the solitary dark cell with only bread and water enough to support life, are the penalties for the rebellious. But the prisoner is allowed at Charlestown to come out at the moment he is willing to go to work and do his duty, and seldom does one stay in the 'solitary' twenty-four hours.

A sixth means of discipline is work, regular and steady, of some profitable and instructive kind. This is usually in shops, and the prison laborers seem like others in similar trades elsewhere. Work is now relied upon more than anything else to control and, if possible, to reform convicts.

A seventh means is the system of commutation for good behavior. In some prisons two days in a month are allowed, and these are increased to five days in long terms, so that a man sentenced for ten years may, by good conduct, get free in about eight years. But if he rebels, all his gains are liable to be lost. He is put upon his self-control. He forms a habit of it and of labor, and thus often is fitted to become a better citizen than ever before.

An eighth means of discipline is careful, attentive, experienced, humane, thoroughly temperate, well-trained keepers; not *brutish, passionate, violent, profane* and cruel men. More depends upon officers and guards than upon the prison itself.

A ninth means of discipline is some provision for discharged prisoners by which they can enter upon civil life again with hope of support and respectability. In Massachusetts, besides teaching the convict a trade, an agent is appointed by the state to see every convict before his discharge, inquire what he wishes to do, and then either send him to his home newly clad in citizen clothing free of charge, or to find a place for him to work at his trade, the employer only knowing his history, or to board him a week or two at a good place until he can find employment. Other states give discharged prisoners a few dollars and send them away without care. But the kindness shown him at this moment, when peculiarly exposed, is opportune, and it saves some a second fall. The hope of it imparts confidence to the mind of the convict that he has friends left, and it stimulates him to prove himself worthy of their regard.

14. The orderly arrangement of a prison ought to be simple, compact, complete and convenient for all the purposes of security, health, work, comfort and discipline. No prison has these points combined more fully than at Charlestown, though all have them to some extent.

15. For security against fire, the floors, walls, doors, galleries, stair cases, fastenings, grates, are iron, stone or brick, and there is nothing combustible in the structure except the window frames and the ceilings over the area of the prison at Charlestown, so that, although not absolutely fireproof, it is nearly so. The new prisons of the western states are made of stone, iron and brick and are nearly fireproof.

16. Extension is an important item in a prison in a new state. If it can be it ought to be done in harmony with an original plan, and without changing the mode of supervision. The central rotunda permits such extension by a wing on each of the four sides whenever wanted. The second wing will be as convenient and easily guarded as the first. On other plans the wings could be placed out of reach. The new buildings at San Quentin stand side by side away from the guard room. The plan of the prison ought to be a unit in itself, so complete and suggestive that all future additions will naturally grow out of it, as branches grow from a stock, and so that there will be no good reason to depart from it.

17. The comfort of the prison officers is an important element in the construction and provisions for a prison. It is coming to be understood that these officers ought to be gentlemen in the true sense of the term, intelligent, dignified, courteous, free from narrow prejudices, firm and kind, for they are to be entrusted with absolute

[29]

power over men, and over men who they will have some strong provocations to misuse and to injure. And if it becomes the state to choose such men as superintendents, wardens, sub-wardens, clerks, physicians, chaplains, teachers, guards and watchmen—men who will respect each other—it becomes the state to furnish them with good, comfortable, neat and tasteful quarters in the prison structure. They are sequestered from society; they endure a kind of imprisonment. At least one or more of them will have their family within. The head officer needs a room suitable to receive visitors. For this purpose one wing of the rotunda can project without the walls, and be equally convenient and safe.

Besides good quarters, these officials merit, if faithful, liberal salaries. They have great responsibilities. They are confined day and night to the same positions. They are subjected to insults and exposed to dangers from the vicious and reckless, who would murder them in an instant for the sake of escaping, and yet the utmost vigilance, prudence and courage are expected of them. The state which exacts so much of its servants for the public good, ought to regard them with a fair compensation, such as their standing and similar duties would elsewhere command.

18. The expenditure for a prison will be considered by every citizen. In order to a fair estimate of this subject, it is important to keep in mind the cost of crime before the prison is reached by the criminal. Consider the damage he has done to person and property—to the public peace and prosperity. Consider, also, the cost of courts, of officers, of trials. Consider, furthermore, the need of depriving him of his liberty, and the danger of his escape; and, above all, consider the means and the duty, if possible, of his reform. A single crime often costs, not only life, but thousands of dollars to community, and unless we subject the criminal to the most sure and wise imprisonment, we encourage crime and multiply losses and evils to an indefinite extent. In this view, if a suitable prison is expensive, still it ought to be built, not extravagantly, but thoroughly. The cost of the octagonal building and one wing, at Charlestown, Mass., with fixtures, was one hundred thousand dollars, fifteen years ago. The new prison at Joliet, Ill., had cost, a year ago, over seven hundred thousand dollars, and estimates were then made for expending one

hundred and seventy-nine thousand dollars more upon it; and, possibly, when completed it will cost one million dollars. The new prison at Michigan City, Ind. will cost, as per estimate, from four to five hundred thousand dollars. The cost of the older prisons cannot now be ascertained. Much can be saved by the employment of the prisoners in making brick and in the construction of some portions of the edifice and walls.

19. *Convict* labor is a subject which will continually be discussed by officers of prisons and a portion of the outside public. The question is asked, whether the state should employ the convicts in its own workshops, and make the profits, or whether it will furnish shops and sell their labor at a given rate per day to contractors? The former method is the most troublesome; the latter is perhaps less remunerative. In the former, however, the state classifies and controls the convicts better for their discipline and welfare. In the latter case, contractors are apt to get an undue influence in the prison management. The former may be the best investment, but the latter yields the surest income. The contract system prevails in nearly all the prisons visited. It works well, if the prison officers are permanent, and are sustained in complete control of the shops and yards, so as to preserve the prison discipline; and provided, also, that the demands for workmen shall be kept subordinate to the objects of the prison itself. Contractors often nurse strong and skillful workmen, and crush the weak. It is money against discipline at one moment, and against humanity at another.

On the other hand, the labor of convicts, being very cheap, enables either the state or the contractor to compete with free labor, so as to drive the latter out of the market. The saddler and collars, and brick, perhaps, made at San Quentin, California, are beginning to control the San Francisco market, and to drive other men out of business. The same tendency appears with their boots and shoes and flannel shirts.

The furniture, brushes, whips, barrels and castings, made at Charlestown, Mass., have the same tendency in Boston, and it is only overruled by the greater extent of the market. The prison contractor enjoys a kind of monopoly, which largely compensates for all his risks.

In a few cases, prisons have become self-supporting by their convict labor. In other cases, the annual deficiency varies from $10,000 to $50,000.

20. The monthly income of the San Quentin prison is $2,400, and the monthly expenditure about $7,000.

All expenses of the Charlestown, Mass. Prison, in 1860, were	$80,243.11
All receipts, mostly for labor	80,747.97
Being an excess of receipts	504.86
In 1855, their ordinary disbursements were	52,611.06
Ordinary receipts	40,915.15
Deficit	11,695.91
The income of the New Hampshire state prison at Concord, for 1863, was	12,417.60
Expenses for the same year	8,451.83
Gain to the state	3,965.77

In 1865, expenses exceeded receipts, $471.68.

21. Prison statistics are now made to include all important facts concerning prisoners. For example, the Massachusetts tables give us the whole number received and the whole number discharged, ages of convicts, crimes, periods of sentence, states and countries of which they are natives, places of conviction, previous employments, expiration of sentences, life sentences, and the crimes, re-commitments, number of convicts each year and per month, and their daily rations of food. To keep such accounts and compile these statistics accurately in the larger prisons requires all the time of a clerk. The information is of more value than its cost.

22. Prison clothing. This subject is awakening some discussion. The black and white striped cloth is still worn in nearly all prisons. Its value is to prevent escape, and to expose for easy detection the man who has escaped. An effort is made in Massachusetts and California to furnish prison clothing with less distinctive marks.

23. Apartments for females are usually within the same enclosure of walls, but in a separate building, and under the care of a matron. That at Columbus, Ohio, seems to be very well conducted, and to be a model for such a department.

24. Adornment of the grounds is now a noticeable feature of some of our best prisons. The yard is laid off with neat walks, grass plats, flower beds, and occasionally a fountain of water and a few trees. It is desirable, for both officials and prisoners, to have both shade trees and flowers in these grounds.

25. Insane prisoners form a peculiar class, for whom strong rooms have to be especially provided. In some cases they are sent to asylums, and re-committed after recovery, but the guardians of the insane generally object to receiving them.

26. The subject of unjust or inconsistent imprisonment is receiving the attention of gentlemen familiar with the details of prison life. It is found by officials in their acquaintance with prisoners that men guilty of the same crimes are committed for very different periods— as one man five years for stealing and another for fifteen years for exactly the same offense. When prisoners become aware of the facts—and they always do so—they feel the injustice and become more reckless. Others are found guilty of no crime, but merely unfortunate dupes of their associates. Such cases call for a careful discrimination in the discipline, and a more careful inspection by officers of the law.

27. The architecture of a prison with all its departments for security, labor, comfort and improvement, is a subject de-manding careful study and a close observation of the careful workings of prison discipline. Incomplete and unsuitable structures spring from imperfect plans and ideas. Among the foremost in the knowledge

of this subject, so far as I was able to ascertain, were the architects of the new prison buildings at Charlestown, Mass., and of the new jail at Boston.

Respectfully submitted,
G.H. ATKINSON
Visitor for the commissioners of Oregon penitentiary.

THREE

A History of Early Oregon Education

In 1876 the U.S. centennial exhibition in Philadelphia sought exhibits from each state about its history and progress. George Atkinson submitted a concise history and outline of Oregon's educational activities and structures to State Superintendent of Education L.L. Rowland, who included it among the Educational and Scientific Reports that were forwarded to the committee planning the national event. Locally, it was published both in the *Oregonian* and in the Superintendent's Annual Report to the Legislature. As a result of a gift from his brother Charles, of Moline, Illinois, George was also able to travel to Philadelphia to visit the exhibition.

Early History of the Public School System of Oregon, with a General Outline of its Legal Aspects.

Source:
The Oregonian Archives
Multnomah County Library

BIENNIAL REPORT OF THE SECRETARY OF STATE OF THE STATE OF OREGON

TO THE LEGISLATIVE ASSEMBLY, NINTH REGULAR SESSION—1876

SALEM, OREGON: MART. V. BROWN, STATE PRINTER

CENTENNIAL: EARLY HISTORY OF THE PUBLIC SCHOOL SYSTEM OF OREGON, WITH A GENERAL OUTLINE OF ITS LEGAL ASPECTS

BY REV. G.H. ATKINSON, D.D.

At the request of Hon. L.L. Rowland, M.D., State Superintendent of Public Instruction, and Chairman on Centennial History of our Public Schools, I have sketched the following items:

The legal status of our school system from the first is doubtless a fair expression of public sentiment. In tracing the more obvious principles of the school laws, we may find a concise view of the subject. Were the laws reversed, its history would be reversed also. The organic law of Oregon, article 1st, section 3d, passed in 1844, as the basis of the provisional government, provided that schools and the means of education shall be forever encouraged. At that period and under the provisional government, which continued until March, 1849, there were no public funds to maintain schools. All were supported by voluntary tax or subscription, or with mission funds. The educational sentiment had been nourished by the mission schools of the M.E. church from their commencement in 1834, and from the A.B.C.F.M. from 1836, and those of the Catholic

Church in 1841 or 1842, and doubtless by the earlier schools at Vancouver, and perhaps other posts of the Hon. Hudson Bay Co., supported by the gentlemen of that company.

It is presumed that all these local schools, though supported by private or by mission funds, were open to all classes of children and youth, and so for the public. The earlier settlers were intelligent men and women, and eager to secure permanent institutions of learning for their children in the territory, as was shown by their readiness to aid in establishing the Oregon Institute at Salem, and the Tualatin Academy at Forest Grove, which were commenced one before and one during the provisional government.

As yet no plan had been devised to sustain a system of free schools. The pioneers had no sure title to their claims. There had been no surveys of public lands. The United States Territorial Government was not then established here. There was no appropriation of the 16th section of every township for free schools, as in all new States since the ordinance of 1787. The whole subject was inchoate, except the earnest desire felt by a large majority of the people for a definite plan of action.

The commission given Rev. G.H. Atkinson by the American Home Mission Society in 1847 to labor in Oregon, instructed him to aid in the work of education. This led him to spend several weeks before coming, in carefully examining various series of school books, which resulted in the choice of Sanders' *Series of Readers and Spellers*, Thompson's *Arithmetic*, Davies' *Algebra*, Smith's *Geography*, Wilson's *History*, Wells' *Grammars*, and the *Spencerian System of Penmanship*. An invoice of $200 was brought by him on the publishers' commission in 1848, and sold in 1848 and 1849, and an invoice of $1,700 were soon ordered, which were in 1850 or 1851 sold in bulk to Hon. L.D.C. LaTourette, of Oregon City, whose store was the first to have a school book department, and finally re-sold to Hon. S.J. McCormick, the veteran book seller of Portland. Meanwhile Hon. J.Quinn Thornton had gone with letters of credit to Washington to present the urgent claims of Oregon to recognition by the United States Government. He had succeeded in inducing Congress to pass the bill of August 14, 1848, organizing the

Territorial Government for Oregon, which included among many other important subjects the 20th section, providing that when the public lands shall be surveyed, the 16th and 36th sections in every township shall be set apart for public schools. This act was a silent force planted in Oregon, and in every new State of the future, doubling the power of the grant secured by the Hon. Nathan Dane in the ordinance of 1787, in the interest and for surer permanent endowment of the American system of public schools.

After the arrival of the Governor, General Joseph Lane, early in the summer of 1849, a public meeting was called at Oregon City, then the capital of the Territory, by a few gentlemen, among them Hon. G.L. Curry, Hon. W.W. Buck, Dr. John McLaughlin, Rev. G.H. Atkinson, to consult upon the subject of a system of free schools. After a rather warm debate it was finally voted—only a few dissenting in an audience of 40 or 50—that it is desirable to establish a system of public instruction among the first enactments of our territorial legislature. The dissenters to this resolution were gentlemen whose early abode or training in other countries led them to the opinion that every man ought to educate his own children and wards, and not tax others to do it. Mr. Smith, of Yamhill County, who was present, did himself honor by strongly defending the American principle of educating every citizen of the nation at public cost for the preservation of the republic.

Up to the date of this meeting, efforts for the object had been chiefly individual, and without mutual knowledge or consultation. Doubtless many other minds had been moved in the same direction, who never became known to the writer. After that time the friends of education were found cooperating. Gen. Lane sought suggestions from one, and perhaps more of the gentlemen present at the meeting, and incorporated them in his first message, recommending the Legislature to pass a law establishing a system of public education. That act was passed September 5th, 1849, and was one of the first acts of the first Territorial Legislature of Oregon.

Chapter first was devoted to the school fund, providing that the interest of any funds arising from the sale of school lands be applied annually for the support of public schools, according to the reports of pupils of school age in the several school districts, to be made to the County School Commissioners. This principle has continued in every school law since. The revised school law of January 31st, 1853, section 1st established a common school fund, the income only to be appropriated. Section 2. The principal of all moneys from school lands, bequests, liens, fines, forfeitures or penalties to be an irreducible school fund, etc. The revised laws of January 12th, 1854, provided: Section 1. That the fund arising from the sales of school lands, and all bequests constitute an irreducible fund, the interest of which is to be annually divided among all the districts reporting schools kept in proportion to the number of pupils in each of school age, which was 4 to 21 years. Section 2 provided that the Commissioners of every county should lay an annual tax of two mills for the support of schools, and collect it with all other taxes of the county and State. Section 3 provided that the County Treasurer set apart all moneys collected from fines or any breach of penal laws of the Territory for the support of the public schools.

While these enactments did credit to the judgment of the Oregon legislators, they did greater credit to the citizens who were willing to be taxed in order to give immediate efficiency to the public school system.

These provisions have, in substance, been preserved in the revised statutes of 1866 and 1872. The revised acts of January 31, 1855, Section 7, confirmed every school district as a body corporate with power to assess and collect taxes by their legally chosen directors and clerks for school purposes. The act of January 31, 1853, section 5, gave districts the right to assess and collect taxes to support school teaching three or nine months per year. The Constitution of Oregon upon education and school lands, (See *General Laws, 1866,* p. 116, Deady):

Section 2, on the subject of a common school fund, provided that lands granted, money and property by escheat, or forfeiture; moneys on exemption from military duty; gifts, devises, bequests—grants to Stated not stated—proceeds of 500,000 acres, by act of Congress of 4th of September, 1841; 5 per cent of net sales of public lands, on

[43]

our becoming a State, if Congress consent, all shall be set apart as a separate and irreducible fund for common schools, the interest, with other revenues from school land to be applied to the support of schools in each district, and to buy libraries and apparatus.

Sec. 3. The Legislature shall provide by law to establish a uniform and general system of common schools.

Sec. 4. The Legislature shall provide by law to distribute the income of the school fund to all counties of the State pro rata to all children from 4 to 20 years of age.

Section 5 constitutes the State Board of School Commissioners, of the Governor, Secretary of State and Secretary of the Treasury, for the sale of the school lands and the investment of the funds; provided, no part of the university funds or interest be expended until a period of ten years from the adoption of this Constitution, Sept. 18, 1857, unless Congress otherwise dispose. Congress granted 72 sections for a State University and 90,000 acres for an Agricultural College. The net proceeds of sale of estrays goes to the common school fund. (*General Laws*, page 723). Forfeitures under usury laws go to the common school fund of the county (756). Fines under the license law go to the common school fund of the county (772). Also fines for violating the Sunday law, and fines for failure to obtain license and such moneys or fines (773); also fines for selling or giving liquor to minors under 18 years (774-5); fines for billiard tables and fines under the salmon laws, go to the common schools fund (831). Attorneys, Sheriffs, Constables and Justices knowing must complain and see to the execution of the laws (773). About $500,000 worth of public school lands have been sold and part of this fund has been paying annual income for six or eight years for school purposes. About 3,000,000 of acres of Oregon school lands remain unsold.

Some of the investments of school funds, especially one or two authorized by the Legislature, have been profitless and probably failures. Generally extreme caution and care are taken by the only authorized State Board of Commissioners in making these investments.

The legal history of the School Fund reveals a steady purpose of the people to preserve and increase this princely heritage for the use of their children to the latest generation. Palsied be the hand that wastes or perverts this priceless gift.

STATE SUPERINTENDENTS

The office of Territorial Superintendent of Schools, elective triennially by the Legislature, according to the law of Sept. 5, 1849, Dr. J. McBride being first Superintendent, was abolished by the act of February 1, 1851, and revived again by constitutional amendment.

Section 1 made the Governor Superintendent of Schools five years from the adoption of the Constitution, Sept. 18, 1857, thereafter leaving the Legislature to provide for electing a State Superintendent of Schools. After an additional interregnum it has been established by vote of the people and invested with *duties* of general oversight and information; the imparting of information by speech, writings and institutes; the careful collection of all facts respecting the schools and the system; counsel with the State Board of Commissioners; the provision of blanks for teachers and Superintendents, and biennial reports to the Legislature. The State Superintendent is relieved from the special oversight of the schools lands and funds—a duty imposed by the first law. This office now bids to be permanent and of increasing importance, as the population becomes more compact and the lines of travel more convenient, and the good character of the public schools more established.

TEACHERS' CERTIFICATES

The cumbrous office of a trio of school examiners, appointed by the District Court for each county triennially, under the law of 1849, was made elective by the people by the act of January 28, 1851, and finally abolished by the act of January 12, 1854, and its duties of examining teachers and giving them certificates committed to County Superintendents, who have retained them until now, with the addition of assistant examiners, selected by each Superintendent from his corps of teachers. The history of this law shows that its first idea was correct, and that its practical realization in the present mode commends its value and secures its efficiency in raising the standard of qualifications in the corps of school teachers.

COUNTY SUPERINTENDENTS

The office of County School Commissioner has been continued in that of County Superintendent, with all its duties, only the name being changed, to the present time. When the office of Territorial Superintendent was abolished, by the act of February 7, 1851, his duty of disbursing the school moneys to the several districts was wisely committed to the County School Commissioner and thence transferred to the County Superintendent. Ideas, like lines of silver, trace their way by devious paths and, under much rubbish of form, yet keep their value untarnished.

No office has proved more important to our public school system than this. Its frequent and direct contact with the people in personal speech and by the press, enables the faithful officer to watch every feature of the school system in its practical working in every district, and to flash the light of the best experience and the warmth of earnest conviction upon every little company of co-workers, to stimulate their efforts and cheer their progress. It is just to say that the County Superintendent of Schools can be the local inspiration of the system, or the dead weight upon its vitality. It can be the radiant light of full reports for all the people, or the center of darkness.

DISTRICT DIRECTORS

The original plan of three School Directors, elected by every district, embodied in the law of September 5, 1849, seems to be the type of all public school systems, from the New England coast to the shores of the Pacific. Its essential features have been retained in all the revised and amended school laws of our State. Section 18 of the law of 1849 made them a body politic and corporate, to execute the will of the people in renting or building of schoolhouses, hiring teachers, assessing and collecting taxes, supervising the schools, directing the management of them after intelligent study of them by frequent visits, and, more than all, in choosing the books to be used. This trust is given on the sole condition of faithful use of the funds and full report of their work, and on the further condition of making the schools *free* to all the children of the district. It is the office that comes most directly from the people, and abides constantly under their notice. Its features have been slightly modified, but its substance remains, so that the directors, under the revised statutes, scarcely vary their duties performed under the first enactment. Once drilled to the work, a director ought to be able to serve well at any future time. The defect is in the drill practice according to law, and the result is awkward marching and poor field work ever after.

SCHOOL BOOKS

The law of 1872 has assigned the choice of School Books to a State Board, for the sake of uniformity. This experiment, often tried elsewhere, has not proved all that was hoped for it. Several valuable series of school books have been used in our schools, making numerous classes in small schools in the same grade and study, and much confusion therefrom.

DISTRICT TAXATION

The experiment of district taxation has succeeded only in part. In tested cases, defects have been found in some of the laws, and more in the proper action of the districts. Yet the late law has added one mill to the annual school tax, making three assessed and collected with county and State taxes. This uplift increases the school terms over the State. Complaints of the inefficiency of the system arise from neglect of working it, and from sparse settlements more than from any inherent fault that further legislation can cure. The call is for a revision of the school laws, but they have been amended repeatedly, making their operation more direct. New laws on this subject, or more of them, will not execute themselves. The best workers under the present system complain the least of it, and their fruits prove good.

SCHOOL STUDIES

The class of studies required in the public schools at first—as reading, writing, arithmetic and geography—have held their place steadily. History and algebra have been added. A high school course has been pursued in a few places with good results, as a stimulus to graded schools, and a proof of the educating power of the system. The high school is to the common or grammar school what the ripe fruit is to the green, or the yellow harvest to the green fields of summer.

SCHOOL MORALS

The law of 1849, requiring every teacher of the public schools to procure a certificate of qualifications and of good moral character, has been retained in every revised law, and enforced more strictly by its trial. It is a false charge that the public schools are any less moral than the private schools. The mental and moral standard of teachers as a whole has risen. From a wide observation and experience in the schools during the last twenty-seven years it can be affirmed that they promote good morals by virtue of the moral sentiment that pervades all the schools, small and large, in our State. If adverse facts are adduced, they are the exception, not the rule. That the demand for moral teachers has been made and enforced for a quarter century and more, by the whole State, and embodied in every law, is a standing witness for this truth and a withering rebuke to every one who charges the public schools with being godless and immoral. He who makes the charge insults the community in which he lives and proves himself recreant to its blessings.

SCHOOL DISTRICTS

The law of Sept. 5, 1849, requiring the School Commissioners to district their entire counties has been modified to apply to the settled parts. The conflicts of districts have caused the usual disturbance incident to a new and changing and sparse population. The utmost fairness toward all parties is sought by the statute, and secured generally by the County Superintendents, who have this duty in charge, coordinately with the people in the districts interested.

INFLUENCE OF OUR SCHOOLS

The self-educating power of the school district system in all the elements of self-government has shown itself in our own as well as in other States. Its effect has been to produce a better social life among all the people and to ennoble the American citizen. Its educating power on the young, besides the class-book exercises, is of untold value. He who has noted this carefully in the State will admit its force. Its power to harmonize and mould together the diverse elements of our population has no equal. For this alone it is worth its cost. Gently and surely the free school pupils become homogeneous in habits of thinking, feeling and acting. They are thus fitted to launch into life's duties and achieve their tasks. Witness the boys and girls of our free schools in all the walks of business. Test them in private or public callings. They are the peers of any who emerge from other schools and other discipline.

HOPEFUL FUTURE

In this brief review only the most salient points of the system could be touched. But a system so environed in the laws of the people; so full of their ripest judgment and noblest desires, sustained by their free will offerings year after year, should command our profoundest thought and highest admiration. Its future, springing from the present, may bear fruit richer and more abundant than its friends now think. Its stability rests not on the caprices of a few, but on its providential history and its almost perfect adaptation to the wants of a great and free people.

The log school house of the early days gives way to the neat, white, well-furnished school house of the present growing settlements. The progress in some places has become an example to others. The citizens of Portland, in 1849, raised $2,000 by subscription for a school building. The three large public school buildings which now adorn the city and accommodate twenty-eight teachers in all the departments of a well-graded system, attest the intelligent liberality of the citizens and the efficiency of the school directors, superintendents and teachers. The past assures the future for this city.

ONE DISTRICT IN A CITY

The citizens of Oregon City, in 1850 and 1851, gave over $4,000 to establish the Clackamas County Female Seminary, which afterwards, by purchase, became the city graded public school, and which, during the quarter century, has given knowledge to hundreds, and perhaps thousands, of pupils. The rule of making one public school district of the entire city, which has been adopted in these two places, has proved the best means of improving the schools.

IMPROVEMENT OF THE LOCAL SCHOOL

The habit of sending their children from the country to the city schools, adopted by the richer farmers, on the principle that every man must look out for his own, is perhaps slowly yielding to the purpose to spend the money in providing better country schools. In carrying out this plan the best results will accrue to the greatest number of people and raise all the schools of the State to an equality in character. It is proper to notice the efforts of the citizens of Portland to make their public school a model. They have given liberally of their time and of their money during a quarter of a century to perfect their own schools. Men of wealth and high social and professional standing have consented to serve as directors, and to employ every means to make the system a success. They have proved that it is an enterprise that rewards faithful care and repays well for the investment.

Some schemes do not bear culture or handling, but our public school system will bear to be worked, as you work a garden, until every square inch bears a fruitful plant instead of a weed or a thorn. Its success in our city, from the first growth upward, commends it to every town or city, which stands in doubt, and to every settlement that would put the best magnet to draw a choice population. With all the advantages in sparsely settled districts—and we know they exist—the advantage of a good school, which everyone can have three, or six, or nine months, is more than mills, stores and roads can bring. No investment of a district pays so well to all the interests of a family as a first-class public school. It is a central light, attractive, quickening, guiding, even controlling the mental and moral forces of the young, and shaping very much their plans and habits, thus enriching a people by its power, more than the richest bonanza of silver and gold.

Biennial Report of the Secretary of State of the State of Oregon to the Legislative Assembly, ninth regular session, 1876. Oregon Historical Society.

FOUR

Reports of the Multnomah County Superintendent of Schools

George Atkinson's lifelong commitment was for education for all. The ways in which he expressed that belief were many and varied.

He was the first person to bring textbooks in quantity for use in the schools of Oregon. While sailing on the *Samoset* from Boston to Honolulu he taught sailors to read. During his first year in Oregon he led in forming Tualatin Academy in Forest Grove, later to become Pacific University. He served as the secretary of that institution's Board of Trustees for the rest of his life. In 1849 he prepared, and lobbied for, the legislation submitted to the first Territorial Legislature that led to the establishment of a system of common schools. He worked hard to recruit school teachers from the East, and to establish institutions for teacher preparation in both Oregon and Washington.

Atkinson's most intensive involvement in education was during his nine years as pastor of the Congregational Church in Portland. Six of those years (1864-8 and 1870-2) were also spent as the elected Superintendent of Schools for Multnomah County, Oregon. This was a salaried position, but not considered full time.

Thirty-one districts had been drawn for the county, though only about half had enough residents to justify establishing a school. Each of the districts having a school had a three member school board. Although the Superintendent made many visits to schools, a regular visitation schedule was not realistic.

He chose to report on his work as superintendent in the columns of the *Oregonian*, the editor and publisher of which was Harvey W. Scott, Pacific University's first graduate, and a member of Atkinson's church in Portland. The reports made him able to inform and educate readers across the county about the work, needs, goals, and vision of a large, complex, rapidly growing educational enterprise. A significant benefit for Atkinson was the growth of his reputation for intelligence, integrity, and dedication.

Nineteen reports have been found. Taken as a whole, they give a comprehensive, fascinating portrait of an energetic administrator involved with all dimensions of the school enterprise, supporting, challenging, chastising and praising the various districts under his care.

Reports of the Multnomah County Superintendent of Schools July 1864 through June 1868 July 1870 through June 1872

Source:
The Oregonian Archives
Multnomah County Library

COMMON SCHOOLS IN MULTNOMAH COUNTY

T he undersigned has visited most of the districts and found ten public schools in operation in as many districts, and two private subscription schools in other districts. Four schools in four districts—three public and one private—have recently closed. Of six or eight other districts he has yet no account.

Seven of the ten districts have comfortable, and some of them very neat, school-houses, which are a credit both to the district and the county. Three have rude, temporary structures. A disposition is manifested by some, at least, to make the children's *school-house* convenient and attractive; yet improvement can still be made in this department, even in the foremost districts. Some school-houses need shade trees, of which others have a full supply; some need curtains to keep the hot afternoon sun from the heads of feverish and weary lads; some need to be ceiled before winter; all need outline charts or maps. One had no black-board until supplied by the teacher. In several, the seats and desks require remodeling. But with all these suggestions, we notice pleasing evidence of interest and attention to the subject on the part of the people. Often the school-house surpasses the farmer's house. It is a wise rule to let the former keep pace with the latter. There is no finer ornament for a settlement than a neat, painted school-house among the trees, enclosed in an ample yard, with its number in legible figures over the door.

The ten schools visited number only from six to twenty-six pupils each, while the average is from five to twenty-two. Districts suffer because families move from their claims to town for the sake of schools, and because the wealthier class, in some cases, send their children away to what are called high schools. This practice takes from $100 to $1,000 or $1,500 annually away, which might be expended at home with more profit to all parties. For instance: a girl or boy has no need to go to an academy until he has completed the Mental and Practical Arithmetic, the four Geographies, the Common Grammar, the Common School History, and until he has become a good reader and a good penman. *The walls of an academy give him no advantage in these studies, unless it be in outline maps and charts.* Usually he learns faster in the district school, under a good teacher, with his fewer pupils.

He comes to his daily task fresher and in better health, from the genial duties of home, than he can from any boarding house or stranger family. His vigor of body and mind are better preserved and his morals are under better care at home. If he attends the academy, it amounts only to a district school for him, because he must pursue the same studies. He often annoys and impedes those teachers by his poor reading, writing, spelling, arithmetic, geography and grammar lessons, for he is expected to know these things before entering the academy. Soon his expenses burden parents and his term is shortened, so that he returns home more deficient in the primary and fundamental studies than he would have been by diligent application in the district school. If such pupils take higher studies, as philosophy, chemistry, algebra, botany, geology, geometry, rhetoric, logic, or music, drawing, painting, French, Latin and Greek, they will only acquire a smattering, and will stumble continually, because these higher studies are interwoven with and dependent upon the common studies.

Academies cannot remedy these evils. They must take such pupils as come. The only remedy is with parents and district schools. If these latter are kept on the shortest legal allowance of three months in a year, under an ordinary teacher, the high schools will be kept low, and lasting injury will be done to the mental habits, if not to the physical and moral health of the youth, who are sent away to half learn what they can wholly and more easily learn in the district school.

This injury can be and it is done at four or five times the cost of the opposite benefit.

On the other hand, parents, who are wealthy enough to send their children away, can use the same money to hire good teachers and keep them longer in their own districts, and what is better, have their children at home. If neighborhood bickerings arise, a little forbearance and generosity will usually unite the discordant elements. *Let every district resolve to make its school a first class school. Let every voter attend the school meeting with the sole purpose and vote and pay tax enough to put the house in good order and to hire the teacher for six or nine months.*

The incidental benefits would be to make such districts popular, to attract more families, to transform scattered settlements into thriving and compact neighborhoods, to introduce the blacksmith, wagon-maker and other artisans and laborers, to raise the price of land, to open and improve more farms, and to increase taxpayers and lighten taxes. It is a sign of disease in the system when the blood determines to one part, whether the head or the limbs. It is a mark of ill-health in the body-politic, when the families—its life blood—"all rush to town." A good district school is one of the best correctives of such abnormal tendencies.

G.H. ATKINSON,
Super't. of Public Schools, Multnomah Co.

Aug. 25, 1864

I n a recent communication I called attention to the commendable interest which several of our districts had shown in their organization, in their support of good schools, three, six, and, in some cases, nine months in a year; and in the suitable location and convenient structure of a majority of the school houses.

It is due to the district committees to say that they have evidently sought to employ competent and faithful teachers, and to make the schools worthy of the patronage of all the families in their districts. With the limited funds, which some committees have at command, they cannot of course do all that is desirable for the highest efficiency of their schools.

In some cases, there are divisions of sentiment in the district, which seriously cripple the action of both the trustees and the teachers of schools. In others there is a most desirable co-operation and harmony, and such districts reap the greatest advantages. In every

[58]

case the regularly chosen committee, *with the school law before them*, ought to exercise *their authority and do their whole duty for the good of the school*, without fear or partiality, and they will at least be appreciated.

It is hoped that time, experience, and observation and great teachers, will produce favorable changes and improvements in districts, now troubled with divided counsels. There is need of united, firm, and patient action on part of all, who love the cause of popular education; and, more than all, a *purpose unchanged*, that they will *have a free school* in their own districts; that they will organize and report regularly, and draw their share of the public money, and that they will visit and watch over their own school, become acquainted with its excellencies and its defects, and seek to become its *intelligent guardians*.

Fellow citizens of Multnomah County, you can know very little about your schools or your teachers unless you visit them. You must not depend upon your school committees alone. You must visit your own schools. The teachers will be glad to see you at any time. The children will be glad to see you. The eyes of your little ones will sparkle if they see you, father or mother, or uncle or aunt, older brother or sister coming into their school.

They will study better and behave better for your visit. The sight of your face, for five or ten minutes even, will do more good in the school than you imagine. The older children will take courage and even pride to do their best, especially if they may expect to see you. I have often noticed that the promising scholars are those whose parents attend most to these schools, and who often visit them. The committee will not be envious of your attention to these matters. Possibly they may never meet you in the school or know that you were in.

Yours in behalf of popular education,
G.H. ATKINSON, Supt. Com. Schools

Nov. 22, 1864

MULTNOMAH COUNTY FREE SCHOOL—THE PRIMARY DEPARTMENT

In previous articles, some praise has been given to our citizens for the many good school houses in the country, and for their effort to get able and faithful teachers. We need now to look a little at the *plan* of the school itself, for there should be a plan in every school, as truly as a plan of the house.

Indeed the plan of the school ought to give form to the building in which it is kept.

The idea of the school should *lead* and not *follow* the fixtures for it. We do indeed have some attempt at this in the two or three low benches to suit the short legs of the little ones, but even these fail to fit. They have in many cases no backs to rest the weary child. Too often his feet cannot touch the floor and they hang in pain over the edge of the seat. If he lies down he is out of order and must get up. If he slips on to the floor for rest, he is worse off, for a switch will perhaps startle him. His seat too is often inclined out, so that he slides off. In a word, the building committee do not study well the wants of the little ones. At home they have nice little chairs, and stools, and lounges. They rest often by change of position. Their muscles are soft, requiring each rest. The result in school is to make them tired and uneasy. A child will sit as still as a grown person, but he cannot so long. Nature keeps him on the move, though it be but a short move.

In his early school days we must not resist this law, but guide it. Would you have the Primary Department quiet you must have low seats inclining in, like a child's chair at home. You must have a desk for the little boy's books as well as for the larger boys. He can rest on that also. Why should he hold his book up all the time, while others can lay theirs down? His small primer is as heavy for him as the larger books for the larger boy. But you often see the little boys and girls on the front seat, without a desk with a high perpendicular back. Lying down and turning every way to be comfortable, they fail to be so, and they care for nothing as much as to go home.

The little ones are often too cold. They suffer sooner than older ones. They are nearer the floor and cold currents of air sweep over them continuously. They get chilled when the teacher thinks it warm enough. Stoves are set up high and they cannot get their feet up to warm them. At other times, I have seen little children kept in seats upon which the sun blazed in, keeping them in a fever. They actually wear thinner shoes or boots than older scholars and even thinner clothing, while too often they have less care to keep out of the rain and the mud. They sit all day with wet feet, or a wet jacket. School directors and school teachers must attend first and most wisely and constantly to the comfort of the primary pupils. In my next I will plead that they may have proper teachers and the right teaching.

G.H. ATKINSON,
Superintendent of Common Schools

January 7, 1865

THE PRIMARY DEPARTMENT

I n my last article care for the physical condition of the small children in our schools was urged upon directors and teachers. We ought to care most for the young and tender plant. As age develops strength less care is needed.

What is true of the body, is true of the mind. The little child's mind is in a tender state. It is as strong as a man's for his age, but, like his body, wants growth, and thus the proper care and culture in order to grow. The minds of some bright little boys and girls are stinted by wrong habits of teaching, as I have seen their bodies stinted by wrong habits of work in the shop and factory, and even, though not often, on the farm.

There is a natural way for every child to learn at school, as at home. What he learns at home and in the shop is by imitating and by trying to do certain work. The trial educates and trains him, while it encourages him to make new trials. How many self-educated farmers, carpenters, blacksmiths, gunsmiths, printers, merchants, lawyers, doctors and ministers we have in America and especially in our new State, and they generally do their work well. It is a marvel to some to find a man who cannot read or write doing a large and intricate and successful business. But we have had such cases in Oregon. We say that the man has no education; but this is a mistake. He has learned some things well, and he has learned how to use the knowledge of men. He sees quickly, studies deeply, reasons correctly and acts promptly respecting matters in which he is interested; two things have been true of such a man: he has felt an interest in knowing some things, and secondly, he has succeeded.

These two things are elements in every child. The first day of school you can see interest in every child, however small. His curiosity is all awake. The boy has much to tell pa and ma when he gets home at night. This curious interest of the child is the golden thread which the teacher may take, and which he *must take in his hand* to guide the child's mind from one subject to another, and from one truth to another. The first days in the primary department might be spent in pointing out the objects in the school-room.

The teacher might ask the little boy or girl what the stove is for? What the house is for? What the black-board? What the slates? What the chart? What the primer? What a letter is? What a figure is for? At every step questions and answers should keep alive the child's interest and he should feel that he succeeds. Soon he will learn the sounds of letters, or a verse of scripture or of poetry. He will see that he can fold his hands as others do, and know the letters and words and figures. His mind will begin to grow, or rather it will not stop growing. It will develop easily and naturally in new directions. If the teacher keeps a faithful hold of the child's interest by such means, he or she will be able to lead on the pupil, step by step, to new truths with increasing success.

It is at this point that children are stinted. Their curiosity is not kept alive, or they do not succeed in getting the idea which they need to get. The task then becomes hard, even if it be in the alphabet, or in words of two or three letters. True it is, that our modern school books contrive to arouse children by pictures and stories, and they help the teacher; but the teacher, after all, is more than the book. He must point out the way, give a cheering word, and make *every child* feel that *he* is doing something.

One little boy can make a good figure or letter, or draw the outline of a horse or cat, or the lines of a man. Another can read distinctly. Another spells well. A fourth is good for his quietness. A fifth sings well, and a sixth is a smart speaker. Each differs in mind from his companion as much as in looks. Two cannot be made exactly alike mentally. It is of no use for the teacher to expect the same things of every child. Uniformity in learning the letters, or to read or spell, or to give the sounds of the letters, or in studying Geography or Arithmetic, does not appear in the smallest collections of children, much less does it in large primary departments. The teacher must look for variety of talent and aptness in the little ones. They are scions of different families, and they are to be our future laborers, artisans, traders and professional men.

Cowper's parents tried to make a lawyer of him, but he could be nothing but a poet. Some girls cannot help being good musicians. The music is in them, and they sing even when they are very small. Others can never sing or play with ease and success though you give them the best instructors. Yet the singing child may stumble over the simplest rules of arithmetic, while the unmusical child will find arithmetic and grammar a pastime. The teacher failing to find the same powers in both, must not call the one a dunce, and the other a bright scholar. The teacher must not have a chart marked for reading, spelling, writing, geography and arithmetic and grade all the pupils as they meet the bill, putting zero against the names of two, five or eight, who have no faculty for anything in the bill, but who have a faculty for something not in the bill.

I have seen smart boys and girls put down as nobodies because they could not do just what the teacher required as well as others, or even at all. Such children soon feel hurt and discouraged, and they give up all effort. Parents feel sad, and sometimes ashamed of their little ones. The fact is, these dunces are smarter to do some things than the brighter scholars are. They are little heroes to do what they have an aptness for, and it is the teachers' as well as the parents' duty to find and bring out every child's peculiar faculty, so that he may himself see it, and feel encouraged. Then he will go on to learn what will help him to know what he wants to know.

The fact is, that some of the best minds are stinted in primary instruction and they never outgrow it. More care is needed to start the young plant well than to make it grow well afterwards.

G.H. ATKINSON
Superintendent

January 19, 1865

PRIMARY DEPARTMENT

T he work to be done in this department, we admit, is not easy. It is a task to find the nature of each mind and heart, and then deal rightly with each one. It requires wisdom, skill and patience. It demands some experience, with a habit of close observation. No such task is put upon any person in the community, as upon a teacher, and no teacher has so responsible a place as the one who conducts the primary department. If he takes a wrong step he breaks a tender spirit, as the nurseryman who treads down his choicest fruit trees.

The maturest and most skillful teachers ought to be put into the primary school room, and then all the fixtures should be made to suit the little one's demand. Much freedom should be allowed to train them. The lesson should be simple and so varied, that weariness and sameness shall be avoided. Much effort should be made to bring out every child in something; in reading, spelling, writing, the sounds of the letters, counting, singing, making figures, drawing, sewing, even, and knitting; anything that the child can do. One thing will help another. Soon the teacher can awaken dormant powers and bring every one forward to a fair standing.
We know that the advancement of scholars is checked for want of thorough study in the primary department. Pupils take higher

studies, who have not mastered the lower ones, and hence they are always superficial and imperfect. This is due to defects in the start. The child has not had the care, which his mind demands, and he suffers. No sure remedy exists in the upper departments. It must be found in the primary school. But it cannot be found here, if this is left to be a chance development. If it does not seem important to teachers and directors how the little ones get along, then the annual loss of mental development will fall upon a large per cent of pupils. But if we take good care of the primary department, the others will succeed with comparatively little difficulty.

This leads to the final remarks, that the best rooms—as to size and location and comfort—the best play-grounds, and the best teachers should be provided for the primary departments of our schools.

It is not right to crowd a room with little children, and expect any teacher to care of them and train every one successfully. There must be room enough for all the classes and for all the changes and movements which the primary Department requires. There must be classes enough to meet the advancement of the pupils, and time enough allowed to learn the condition of every child's mind and to afford every one help.

Hence the labor of the primary departments ought to be well divided between two or three teachers.

The tendency is to impose too much upon those who conduct this department. In large schools like the public school in this city, the tendency is to lay too heavy burdens upon those who teach the little ones. This occurs just now incidentally on account of the rapid increase in the number of pupils, and measures are believed to be in progress to increase the number of school-houses in the city. But in all our schools there are liable to be the greatest defects in the instruction of small children, and too low an estimation of their wants in the selection of teachers.

G.H. ATKINSON,
Supt. Common Schools.

January 27, 1865

COMMON SCHOOLS OF MULTNOMAH COUNTY— PERMANENT TEACHERS

P ersons familiar with the operation of schools have noticed that a change of teachers produces a change in the course of studies. Very often the new teacher puts the pupil back to the beginning of every book which he is studying. The Grammar classes begin the Grammar again; the Geography, Arithmetic, Reading and Spelling classes do the same. If teachers are changed every six months, this putting back occurs as often. If the school is kept only three months, the new teacher begins where the old one did, and advances but little farther. Some children are annoyed and discouraged by this process; others like it, because it gives them a very easy time. Parents know not why their children make so little progress from term to term; yet teachers, knowing little or nothing of their new pupils, can do no better. For instance, if a teacher should call up a boy or girl of twelve years, and on inquiry, found that he had ciphered to fractions, and conclude to let the child begin at fractions, but after trial find that the child did not know how to divide or multiply readily, he would naturally suppose him deficient in addition or subtraction, and numeration and rotation. His only remedy of course would be to have the boy or the girl begin the book. If a child proposes to parse a simple sentence, and yet fails to give the parts of speech correctly, the new teacher concludes at once that he needs to be drilled in the elements of grammar, and so puts him back. The teacher cannot know in what, or to what extent a child is deficient. His plan of review must therefore be general, but his term closes before he has done much more than review what his predecessor has done, and what his successor will do.

Hence teachers, hired for a single term or two terms, are comparatively of but little use to a school. In this time they become fairly acquainted with the minds and standing, or advancement, of their pupils, and thus well prepared to carry them forward, to direct their view of needed points, or rules or sections, and to assist them in what they are deficient.

[66]

To illustrate the subject, let the school at East Portland be continued a year under the efficient instruction of Mr. Garlick, the present teacher, and all the pupils will be well advanced in their several studies, and they will be thorough. But if the people let Mr. Garlick go, and hire a new teacher—say after three months vacation—their children, a year from this time, will not be much in advance of their present standing, or of that which they will attain during the present quarter. The same remarks are true of the school in District no. 2—that which includes Brooklyn. If the Directors can possibly secure the continued service of the present excellent teacher, Mr.McLaren, it will be of great advantage to their children.

One reason why our city grade school and our subscription schools and academies are superior, is in the fact that the teachers seldom change, or are changed. The teachers know their pupils. The first and second terms give them the opportunity to find the mental culture of every child, and after that they can direct the studies, or afford the help which every child needs. Unless the teacher has this knowledge he cannot adapt himself to the pupil.

Parents may and they do complain that the teachers do very little good, while they themselves are at fault, because they will not give them time to produce desirable results. If you hire a man to till your farm, and tell him that he must do it in three months, and bring you the proceeds, he will very naturally object to the requirement and say that crops cannot be raised in three months. But how much more unreasonable it would be for you to reply: Sir, I have only money enough to hire you for three months. If you have a mind to work for that time on my terms it is well; otherwise I will find a man who will. There's the land, sir. It is part unbroken prairie, part hazel brush and part thick woods. It is unfenced, sir, but that's my farm, and if you have a mind to take it and bring me the crop in three months, you can have the job.

Equally absurd is it to require a teacher to put a wild school into good, productive order, and gather the mental harvest in three months.

But it is objected that we cannot afford a nine or ten months school per annum. Yet you expend one, two and even five thousand dollars upon your wild land, and hardly make a show of a farm at that. Besides if a district like East Portland will tax itself to keep a school ten months in every year, and to add another room for the increasing number of pupils, the population will increase, the lots and farms will rise in value far above their cost. A graded school, conducted by permanent teachers, is the best investment which any district can make for itself.

Another advantage in having permanent teachers is, that teaching thus becomes a profession, honorable as it is useful. If candidates for this service understand that they will be wanted permanently in a school, they will prepare themselves for it, and we shall have a less and less number who want to teach a few months to get a little money in order to go into some other business.

It is to be hoped that the district directors in our county will, so far as possible, employ their old teachers, and hire them for a longer time. It is also to be hoped that the people will vote to tax themselves in every district, as one of the best means to promote the improvement of their children, and also to advance their own pecuniary interests.

G.H. ATKINSON
Supt. Of Schools

March 17, 1865

SCHOOL STATISTICS (*Oregonian*)

R ev. Mr. Atkinson has left with us the facts for the following compilation of statistics in reference to the schools of Multnomah County. They relate to an important branch of our progress, and will be read with interest. The schools of our county have, under the management of the present incumbent of the Superintendent's office, fared well, and appear to be prospering finely.

There are twenty-seven School Districts in the county, of which fourteen have school houses, the total value of which, estimated with grounds, is placed at $20,000. The average number of quarters of school in each District is found to be one and a half, or a little more than four months. The average number of scholars attending has been twenty-five in each District. Eighteen female and sixteen male teachers have been employed in Public Schools in the past year, at a monthly salary of $40 for the latter, and $28.74 for the former. The number of High Schools or Academies in the county are seven, with an average attendance of one hundred scholars. The pay of teachers, in each, is averaged at $75 per month. The whole number of voters in the county, according to the District reports is given at 1,009, which is, properly, including only those estimated as residents, taking part in the School Meetings of the various Districts, we presume. The returns show 1,982 persons over four and under twenty years of age, 981 of whom are males, and 1,001 females. The taxes levied and collected for the past year amount to $1,373.04. Teachers have received from the School Fund $2,018.76. Teachers have received from other sources of taxes and subscription, $3,093.76. Incidental expenses have been $1,115.04.

Sanders' series of readers and spellers are used in 20 districts, Parker & Watson's in 7; Monteith's and McNally's Geographies in 20; Davies' series of Arithmetics in 10; Thompson's in 16; Clark's Grammars in 11; Bullion's Pieno's and others in 10; Willard's U.S. History in 7; Spencer's Copy-Book in 7; Colburn's Mental Arithmetic in 3; Thompson & Davis' in 3. A few other varieties of text-books are scattered among the schools, multiplying classes, confusing pupils, and hindering teachers. The Superintendent urges a thorough statistical return of the text books used in the whole State, so that any future attempts to establish a uniform series upon the different subjects of study may be wisely made, and if possible, so as to save expenses to the families, who desire and receive the benefits of our Public Schools, while, also, the best books are chosen.

July 19, 1866

OUR FREE SCHOOLS

M ost of our schools outside of Portland are in operation during the late spring and early summer months. Those are the most convenient seasons to spare older children, and the best for smaller ones to go to and from schools. I find eleven schools in progress, eight or ten others have either closed their terms or have been stopped by the high water. The city schools with their ten teachers amount to more than all the others in the county. They may be fairly set down as ten schools numbering seventy pupils each equal to twenty-five or thirty outside schools. Enrolled in the twenty schools outside the city there are, according to a pretty careful census, about 536 pupils, and within the city, 722 pupils—giving about five twelfths to the former seven twelfths to the latter. Of 2,333 children between the ages of 4 and 20 years in the county, only about 1,232, or one half are enrolled in the school registers. Of this deficiency, 850 are in Portland. The Academies and private schools have nearly 350 of these, leaving 500 unprovided. Two hundred and fifty in the outside districts fail to attend school, or about one-third of the whole number. The proportion of boys and girls is very nearly equal.

The School Houses remain much as usual. Some are well built, with good ventilation, light and heat, and comfortable seats. We can still commend those in Districts 1, 2, 3, 4, 15, 17 and 21. Districts number 14 and 26 are now erecting good houses. Some districts may have erected good houses within a year or two, which I have not visited; but the houses in 8 and 10 need better seats and desks. No. 18 ought to build a good house. They have a central and fine location. No. 21 needs one or two additional rooms to meet the wants of their increasing population, and especially to grade their school. The site is very fine. The proprietor of East Portland has given a block, which furnishes ample room for a building with all the Departments of a good school. It would add as much to the desirableness and value of that village as the present school has done.

[70]

District no. 10 has done honor to itself and to the cause of education by the erection of a beautiful school house on Harrison and 5th sts. The site has, however, been found unequal to the wants. The plan is according to the earlier, instead of the later ones for graded schools. It would be very desirable to have in this city a school building like that for the Denman Grammar School on Bush Street, San Francisco. To illustrate its importance, take the school in our new building just named. In the Grammar Department, 115 pupils were enrolled. They assemble in one large room, under the care of Mr. Warren, who, indeed, kept them in admirable order; yet classes were frequently going out to another room, under the care of Miss Lewis, to recite. These classes were in the same book and grade as those who remained and recited to Mr. W. For instance, there were in the Third Reader two classes—one of 26 pupils who recited to Miss L., and one of 28 pupils who recited to Mr. Warren.

These classes might have been together had there been a room of the proper size. They were of about the same standing in Geography and Arithmetic. These fifty-four pupils might have been under the same teacher, until prepared to enter another and higher grade. It is so in the Denman School and in others in San Francisco and Chicago, and other eastern cities.

There were thirty-five in the Fourth Reader who read to Mr. Warren, and thirty-six in the same who read to Miss Tower. These were of about the same grade in other studies, or they could have been, and thus have occupied another room until fitted for a higher grade, under one teacher, had a suitable room been found. Thus two grades of the Grammar Department might be formed. All the disturbance of passing to and from the rooms, and all the loss of time would be saved. The pupils would finish a prescribed course, be examined, and if qualified, would pass to the next room, and so on, until all the grades had been completed. Taking Wells' graded system, which is now the American standard, as our guide, we should soon have the four grades of the Grammar Department. The present large room of the new building might be divided by sliding doors at little expense, and thus give us two departments. Possibly the two small recitation rooms might be large enough for the third and fourth grades as our population now is, yet they are too small and confined for such permanent use.

We may illustrate the same subject by the Primary School in the same building. Miss Stevens had 237 pupils enrolled who assembled in one room. The average attendance was 150, who were closely packed. It was impossible to keep them quiet by "Rests", "Singing", "Recesses", or any appliances with their lessons. Miss Kelly took class after class to her recitation room, but this necessarily kept up some confusion. There were thirty-seven learning ABC, who with a few more advanced pupils might have been happily taught and exercised in a room by themselves under one teacher. These two ladies had seven classes in the primer, comprising about one hundred pupils. These would have filled two rooms, or one of the ABC classes, and one a little more advanced.

There were two classes in the First Reader, comprising twenty-five pupils. These, with some retained at home because of the crowd, might fill a third room and be the third grade.

The two classes in the second reader, comprising 27 pupils, might occupy a fourth room and comprise a fourth grade, each under a separate teacher. Thus in that school we might have eight grades—four primary and four grammar, in as many rooms, under as many teachers—giving about fifty to each. The studies and exercises would be prescribed for each room. The pupils would be retained in one room until be examination they were found to be prepared for the next, the time for the primaries being six months, and for the grammar scholars one year.

The Central school needs a similar grading also to be extended to the higher department.

It is obvious that we cannot apply this system to outside schools, which have only twenty-five to fifty pupils. It could, however, be commenced with marked success in East Portland. Our children would be thus properly distributed, more fitly and thoroughly instructed, and be made to see their own steps forward, and they would be stimulated to make progress. The only power of real advancement in our schools is by such a system of grading, and the school building must be adapted to the system.

GEORGE H. ATKINSON,
County School Superintendent

August 10, 1866

CHANGE OF TEACHERS IN OUR FREE SCHOOLS

C hange of teachers has a two-fold view, as relates to our schools. We are not to look at the subject in its relations to the private pecuniary interests of teachers or their friends, except as they have an individual interest in the common welfare. No class, sect, society or Church has a right of monopoly or dictation in our public schools, and no monopoly can be justly held in the list of teachers employed. Neither one, two, or three societies can justly combine interest in this matter and exclude a fourth, fifth or sixth class. In the choice of a committee, the public seek intelligent and faithful men to represent them. In like manner, the committee, in the choice of teachers and their continuance in the schools, are expected to have reference to their fitness for their work, not for their family relations nor social standing. It is true in the case of equal fitness, some preference ought to be given to the most needy, because of that need, and because such persons, by the stimulus of necessity, may be expected to improve most rapidly, and thus the school will, in the end, be the gainer.

Among the reasons for changing teachers we may mention their indolence or unfaithfulness in obvious duties, or immorality, or ignorance and unwillingness to improve themselves. For if a teacher is ignorant on some points, and yet if he has a desire to improve, and if he make the effort, he or she can become intelligent on any subject to be taught in our schools. Defective control of the school may be remedied by the support of the committee, who are required by law to assist and sustain a teacher's authority.

When one of the first four reasons exists and there is not a disposition to improve, the teacher should be removed from the school and so reported, at least to the Superintendent, so as not to be liable to be transferred to another school. Such a person is unfit to be a teacher anywhere. His or her place should be supplied by a new candidate for the profession, and he should not be allowed to displace some other one, but should be dropped from the list of professional teachers.

It is obviously proper to transfer teachers from one department, or school, to another, because of their superior fitness for the position; but this has many abating circumstances, which should render it infrequent rather than a habit and a purpose. The path of improvement of schools does not lie so much in the transferring or advancing teachers to new places, as in greater efforts to improve the schools or departments in their charge. The teacher of a primary school can become eminently fitted and skilled for that department, and thus do more for the cause of thorough instruction in that office, than by any change; although the same teacher may fit himself for another department. A faithful primary teacher deserves, and he or she will receive, as much consideration as a sub-principal or even principal. High position is not so much to be desired as faithfulness to one's position, whatever it may be. We cannot advocate frequent changes from what are called lower to higher departments. The fact is, one department is as high as another in its importance, and bearing on the future. If an apprentice is poorly taught he will be a bad journeyman. If a boy or girl in the primary school be imperfectly taught, he will always be unfitted for the grammar school.

It is an injury to parents, secondly, to change the instructors of their children. They wish to know and have confidence in a teacher, which they cannot do if he comes only for three or six months. A change is a subject of great anxiety to them, even if they proposed it, or have become so habituated to it as to expect it. The more prudent and watchful of the educational welfare of their children parents are, the more anxiously they await the result of these changes. It puts them in a state of suspense, which is always painful. Persons who have no children, or whose children have passed their school days, may not feel much solicitude on this point. Some, from curiosity, may delight in frequent changes. But, as they occur, the tendency increases, until it comes to be expected that every new term or year will bring a new teacher into the schoolroom. Thus, confidence in the value of a free school system is diminished, and the parent feels less and less encouragement and disposition to help the school, or to attend school meetings, or to raise and pay taxes for its support or improvement. While on the other hand, the faithful teacher, from term to term, gains upon the regard, esteem and confidence of the real patrons of the school, and they consider him or her an integral part of their society, and not a mere exotic. We admit that many patrons expect and propose changes, but it is because they have formed such habits, though much against their interest as heads of families and guardians of the training of youth.

It is an injury, thirdly, to teachers and their profession to change them frequently from place to place.

For their own efficiency and improvement they need to know every pupil and every parent and guardian. The teacher must know whence the pupils come, and what has been their home training, what are their parents' wishes, hopes and habits, and what is the child's knowledge; why so little, or so imperfect, and what his habits? I often hear children attempting to read in the Fourth Reader, who ought to be in the Second, and on inquiry, I find that they came with the Fourth Reader; that the former teacher had put them into it, or that their parents desired it, and thus the teacher allows them to stumble on during his or her term. When another comes it will be the same. A permanent teacher, if careful and conscientious, would correct this fault, and would do justice to himself in his own teaching.

He must know every pupil's progress in order to classify them properly. It often happens that pupils will go in a class for several weeks, because they claim to be in it, before the teacher becomes fully aware of their real status, and in his ignorance of them, his teaching was unadapted and apparently unskillful. A machinist must know perfectly every screw, rod and pipe and their place in their engine, or he will fail to work it successfully. The teacher's idea of or acquaintance with his school must be hardly less minute and intimate in order to a complete organization and progress. If he changes often he loses interest in any one school or class of pupils, or he will not allow himself to become much interested in them. He cannot lay plans for their improvement, or improve himself for their sakes. The stimulus to do it is removed by his removal elsewhere. He cannot do himself that justice which his self-respect and his profession demand. Witness a class of teachers, rotating from district to district or from room to room with no certain house or resting place, but with a certainty that they will be pushed along in a few weeks to another place! How it tends to destroy confidence in themselves, and also in their profession, and compels them to leave it in disgust so soon as they can find another means of support. How it makes the teacher's office a mere means to get a little money, and lowers it for the reception of persons very poorly qualified for its duties. The lawyer, the physician and the minister keep their position for a term of years. The principal of the academy and the professor in the college hold their situations often for life, or at their own choice, and thus their offices have a value which secures fitness and confidence.

Some teachers, knowing the tendency to change, strive to arrest the evil by extraordinary toil and sacrifice, which is not requited; and some endeavor to do it by exhibitions which take much time and money, but which please certain parents and put forward those very forward children who ought to be restrained. But all these means fail in the end, and react to the injury of the teacher. Frequent changes keep salaries low, and tend to make them lower. It is a bid for new candidates. It destroys confidence in free schools, so that the citizens will neither vote for nor pay taxes for them, as they do for that which they value.

In view of these facts we hold that the most careful selections should be made for the teachers, and then they should not only be assured of their places but urged to keep them, and fit themselves more and more for the profession. There should be one question put to them—Do you design to teach for a series of terms or years? And an affirmative answer ought to be an element in the engagement for the service.

I desire earnestly to call the attention of school committees and friends of public schools in our county to these suggestions.

G.H. ATKINSON
Superintendent Schools Multnomah Co.

January 24, 1867

SCHOOL BOOKS

T he failure of our last Legislature to appoint a State Board of Education still leaves the choice of school books entirely to the District Committees. Sec. 8, Art. 8, of the law, under the head of "School Districts", declares that the committee shall "secure as nearly as possible a uniform series of school books for their districts." This law makes the local committee of every district a board to examine and require a uniform series only in the schools under their care, and *thus constitutes as many Boards as there are Districts in the State*; say, in one county, 10; in another, 20, and in another, 50. These District Committees never meet and consult so as to secure uniform books throughout a county, and much less through the State. They have no bond of union in this matter, but they, for the most part, leave the subject to the market which furnishes books for the schools. Those offered for sale are purchased. Hence authors of school books, or enterprising publishers, or teachers, or some interested agent, can introduce and thrust upon the market, and thus upon the schools, any series of books which either one of these parties may prefer. The result is from two or three to a dozen series of text books upon every branch of study taught in our schools. American zeal in the cause of education has stimulated the preparation and multiplication of school books to an enormous extent. It is a safe and profitable business. The demand is steady and increasing, and in no more danger of declining than the demand for groceries. Authors not only increase in number, and also strive to perfect their books, and thus command the market; but they are forced by the competition to issue new editions of the same books, with only slight changes from former editions. The number of new readers, grammars, arithmetics and histories annually increases, and we not only find the shelves of our book-stores loaded with varieties of books on the same subject, but we find in every family, piles of books, little worn, yet thrown aside, because the teacher or the Committee have required new ones to be used. Our book sellers being obliged to keep on hand a stock of all kinds used, accumulate large amounts of dead stock, which must be at least paid for by a large per cent on the books sold. The people ultimately must bear the loss, both in buying the new books at higher rates, and in throwing away the old ones. The publisher also puts a premium on the new books in order to pay for the old ones that have become dead stock on his shelves. This is one of the reasons why prices of school books have advanced so much of late. To illustrate the subject, I have been permitted by the three principal book sellers in this city to examine their catalogs and collate the varieties which they are compelled to keep, much to their own inconvenience and loss. Under the head of anatomy and physiology I find text books by four different authors on their shelves; on astronomy, text books by twelve authors, on book keeping, by four; on chemistry, by eight; on composition and rhetoric, by eight; on English dictionaries, by one; on drawing, by six; on elocution, by nineteen; on French, by five; on geography, by three; on geology and mineralogy, by four; on German, by seven; on grammar, by eleven; on Greek, by seven; on history, by nine; on Latin, by six; on mathematics, by eight; on natural philosophy, by thirteen; on penmanship, by four; on readers and spellers, by six; on teachers' registers, by three. Yet these are not half the number of authors on the different subjects, which books are kept elsewhere, and which are liable to be introduced here. Still, for the use of the schools in Oregon, these could be reduced to a single author or two on each topic, and thus save thousands of dollars to the parents, and much confusion of classes in our schools, and the greater loss of time of teachers and pupils.

I find that the sale of school books in the three houses above mentioned, is $30,000 per annum. There is at least the sale of $20,000 per annum within the State. Probably 15 to 20 per cent of this sum is wasted on needless varieties of books.

The difference between the text books by different authors is not so great that the school would suffer much by adopting any one series and rejecting the others. Every author strives to make the best book, and they all make good ones.

It is important in a school to have as few classes as possible. Let the time be given to a few subjects, and let them be pursued thoroughly. But I have found in a school of thirty-five pupils twelve classes in arithmetic, eighteen in reading, three or four in geography, and as many in grammar. I find that even one series of books provides far too many classes, in small schools. The second and third geography classes might, in many cases, be united together, and also the second and third reader classes, and the whole time spent upon the two, given to one class with more profit. But instead of this, two or three series of books make the classes still more numerous. Frequent changes from place to place increase these difficulties to both schools and families, which would all be obviated by using one set of books.

We have no complete remedy for these evils until the law shall be changed and a State Board appointed, who shall decide what books shall be used in our public schools, for a term of years. Meantime, the District Clerks and County Superintendents, who are by law required to ascertain the books used in their several districts and counties, and furnish the list to the Governor, who is Ex-officio State Superintendent, from whom it can be known what varieties are most used in the State, can also ascertain what are most generally preferred by the teachers and friends of schools. The State Teacher's Institute, which convenes in Portland early in August, might assist in the future choice by making this a subject of examination, and perhaps of discussion. Our chief confusion will arise from the variety of readers, grammars, and arithmetics. In geographies we are almost a unit, but we are exposed to division on this subject.

Those State journals, desirous to promote the welfare of our schools in this matter, are requested to call attention to these suggestions.

G.H. ATKINSON,
Sup't. Schools Multnomah Co. and chairman Teachers' Association

Dec. 10, 1867

TEACHERS' INSTITUTE

T he Multnomah County Teachers Institute will meet as adjourned at the Central School Building, Portland, Dec. 28th, at 10 o'clock A.M. It is hoped that teachers and friends of education will be present and take part in the exercise. A good degree of interest has been manifested during the season in all our schools, some districts having shone enterprise in raising funds to prolong their terms. No. 5, Mt. Tabor District, setting a good example, agreed to keep their excellent teacher, Mr. Pershin, a year at a salary of $800. No. 2 recalled their excellent teacher, Mr. Kittridge, and they seem determined to secure his services for an indefinite time. This is wise. If employers and teachers have confidence in each other, it gives great success to the labors of the school room. No. 7, though the smallest in area, with few pupils and a log school house, has done nobly in keeping Mr. Pratt, at an increased salary, and he has done honor to his profession by his faithfulness and zeal. His set of object charts, bought by himself for the good of the school, not only adorn the walls, but furnish much valuable information that would hardly be otherwise acquired by the majority of the pupils. We trust that Mr. Pratt will bring them to the Institute and give some illustrations of their use and value.

No. 4 have not only done well to employ Mr. Riley for two terms, but to engage him for another summer. The school showed much improvement in discipline and thoroughness.

No. 8 found in Mr. Brown a faithful instructor, but having as yet few pupils and no school house, and only a single term, little could be done this year. It is to be hoped that the addition of another section to the district will result in the erection of a comfortable school house on the Base Line Road, and that the district will be an honorable continuation of East Portland and Mt. Tabor. The finally harmonious division of old No. 8, into three districts, proves best for all.

No. 20 had a successful school term under the care of Miss S. Barker. Their enterprise is preparing to erect a school house on the river road, central to the families, it is to be hoped will be carried out in season for the summer term.

No. 16, once a part of No. 8, will need to exert itself early to have a school house and to stand fairly in the long line of Columbia River Districts. A little energy on the part of its prosperous farmers will give it the position. The locality is inviting to more settlers.

No. 17 has maintained its reputation this season, by employing for more than two terms, so steady and earnest a worker as Mr. Paddock. No. 30 has done well to recall him to teach during their winter term. No. 3 has received Mr. Riler for the winter, having previously tried two teachers for a short time. Often a little mutual forbearance will give success to a school, while a little hastiness would break up.

No. 18 has received a large addition, extending now to the Columbia, and they seem disposed to prolong the school terms. It is a favorable sign to recall a former teacher, Miss Brown. It would be still more encouraging to have a new and commodious school house at or near the junction of the Telegraph and Columbia River Roads. It would add more to the value and desirableness of the farms than it would cost. Besides its necessity for the school, it would be a gratifying sight to the eye of the many strangers who pass, and local benefit and honor to the people themselves.

No. 9 has been enlarged and harmonized. We were sorry to hear that Mr. Gullet, whose penmanship resembled engraving, remained but one term. The school seemed to be in the way of permanent prosperity under his care. We hope Mr. Hunter will have success there.

No. 25 needs to *secure* and *retain* a good teacher. The frequent changes of teachers gives an unstable character to the school, which manifests itself in the irregular attendance of the pupils, and also in their habits of study and recitation. That district has provided a great school house. We hope they will employ a teacher for six or nine months. It will amply reward parents to do so, as it will be far better than to send their children from to board and attend school.

The school house in no. 19 is one of the most favorable spots on Sauvie's Island. If the building is repaired, reseated, painted and enlarged, it will be an ornament to the neighborhood and a great advantage to the school. Money enough is drawn by this district to support a good school two terms annually. A little liberality on the part of the rich farmers there can support a third term, and thus furnish their children about as thorough instruction as they could get in our crowded city schools, and at the same time keep them under the influence and restraint of home. Will the good citizens there think of this matter?

No. 11 has lost so many pupils by the removal of families that school is sustained with great difficulty. The families on the slough across the mouth of the Willamette should be united to No. 11 or No. 25. Will they choose which? Their children should draw funds for the benefit of some district.

No. 22 chose to employ a teacher two terms, allowing a long interval, instead of having one separate term per year. In both cases the vacations treble the terms, and afford little opportunity for children to progress. Yet 24 weeks of study are better than the same separated by twice as many weeks of vacation.

No. 14 has a good school house, in a good location. Removals from the district weaken the school, yet with united efforts to sustain a good teacher, parents would be saved the inconvenience and some extra expense of sending their children to the city schools.

No. 27 employs a teacher two terms for a small number of pupils. Soon the growth of the city in that direction, will perhaps unite more supporters as well as more families to maintain the school.

No. 10 had a more flourishing school than usual the past season, and wisely employed the same teacher, Miss Scott, during nearly two terms.

No. 6, it is to be hoped, will be united and prosperous under their present agreement with Mr. Wilmot. Divisions injure pupils as well as teachers.

No. 12 is just renewing an old organization, and erecting a school house in a convenient locality.

No. 21—"East Portland", finds the value of their permanent school. It needs to be graded and another room furnished for the large and interesting class of advanced pupils, now under the care of Mr. Sellwood.

No. 31, with commendable earnestness, employ new teachers, as the former ones for any cause, retire. This evinces a purpose to maintain a good school, which will doubtless be more and more crowded with success.

"Portland", employs eleven teachers in its Public Schools and from ten to fifteen in its private and corporate schools for about 1,800 pupils, or one teacher to 75 pupils if all attended. It evinces wisdom in continuing the services of a well known and successful corps of instructors. The crowded and overflowing rooms will, we hope, soon be relieved by the exodus of pupils to the new and commodious building in the North part of the city. The time should not be far distant in which a more thoroughly graded system shall be established. The chief work in this respect is needed in the lower department. Deficiency in elementary instruction increases with every advanced grade, while excellence in the primary department will shine more and more as the pupil goes onward and upward. The course of instruction in Miss Batchelder's school illustrates the value of thoroughness in the primary teaching and training.

One section of the county (the South-west part) fails to revive its school organization. It is a local and a public loss. The present effort to form a new district on the macadamized road deserves the approval of all interested citizens. The law requires the assent of a majority in the district affected by the change. Three years ago it was suggested to the districts outside the city to maintain their schools for longer periods, and to employ teachers of more experience, instead of sending their children to the city schools and letting their own schools dwindle and die. Some districts have done so with evident profit to themselves and their children. What wise parent is willing to expose his children to the constant and powerful temptations of the city, if he can avoid it? What good economist wishes to incur the increased set of costs of books, clothing, board, and other nameless expenses, if he can secure as good instruction for his sons and daughters near home at less cost? Besides, if Directors in the country will employ first class teachers at first-rate salaries, they will soon be more than repaid in the community that will gather around their schools, to enjoy the benefits.

This topic will be up for discussion at the Teachers' Institute. The policy of congregating in homes from the country is injurious to both. It compels the city to provide for the instruction of children who do not belong to it, while it deprives the country of their help.

The value of a good teacher, one who makes this work his profession, is beginning to be felt not only by the teachers themselves, but by employers and by pupils. The demand is slowly creating the supply. To raise the standard of examination in this country according to the legal schedule of topics – the Institute will be requested to appoint two or three teachers to assist the Superintendent at quarterly sessions to examine teachers for the county. Those who pass such a board with a certificate will rank, no doubt, all others in public esteem and secure the best positions and the best rewards.

G.H. ATKINSON
Superintendent of Schools, Multnomah Co.

Feb. 7, 1868

ELOCUTIONARY EXERCISES IN OUR PUBLIC SCHOOLS

I t is common for teachers to devote two or three hours per week to exercises in declamation and composition. In some of the more permanent schools, companies of pupils are detained a few minutes on previous evenings, to rehearse or submit their compositions for review. Some aid is given by teachers and others in the selection of pieces to declaim, or of topics for composition. Generally, however, pupils make their own selections, the result of which is a variety, and often a strange mixture, revealing their own tastes and habits of thought. Some, however, stumble at the beginning, unable to make any selections. On declamation day we are treated with bits of speeches from great men, scraps of poetry, here and there a comic piece; not infrequently a trifling story, occasionally a touching narrative, or a poem full of pathos, like Barbara Fritchie, or eloquent passages from some of the old masters of the art.

As one observes these facts, and recalls his own school days, he will remember the abiding and powerful influence upon his own mind of the pieces learned by him, or spoken by other students. His own taste was excited and cultivated, his style of writing took its form, his habits of thought were directed, his curiosity was aroused, while the themes, the spirit, and the very names of the authors seemed to enter in and become a part of his own being then and ever after. When there was some stirring rehearsal of such speeches as Otis', Henry's, Curran's, Burke's, Wirt's, Webster's, Clay's or Calhoun's; or passages from Chalmers, Story, Phillips or Headly, he felt the pulsations of a new mental life; his ideals were adopted unconsciously and his aim was evermore in that direction. On the other hand, a poor, trifling piece, or a bit of comedy made an impression like itself. The pupil was estimated by his piece. The comic lives in memory only as a comic. The penny-a-line poetry lifts its author no higher. He who was satisfied to repeat a section from Mother Goose's Melodies, stamped them upon his own mind, to be forever ringing there to the exclusion of worthier subjects, besides making the same impress of himself upon others.

Similar facts are true regarding what pupils read, but how much more respecting what they commit to memory and often repeat, and thus make a part of their own mental treasures.

In a word, he who fills his mind with rubbish will find only rubbish there in the future, and it will attract its own kind.

Elocutionary exercises probably make a deeper impression and lead to more settled judgments and habits than any other class of school exercises. They ought to be the subject of corresponding care and attention. Teacher and parent should see that a worthy and ennobling piece is selected and well learned, not simply for the speaking day, but for its effect upon the mental habits of the pupil. Nothing low, vulgar, or trivial ought to be allowed. Even comic articles should have but small if any space. The mind abuses itself, if it is filled with grotesque ideas, or the antics of the buffoon. There is but a step from the sublime to the ridiculous. A false clip will mar the most beautiful statue, and a blot will deface the finest painting. One of the most powerful of living preachers deforms his productions and degrades himself by his inveterate facility of uttering witticisms.

Teachers do much to guide the future thoughts and studies of their pupils, and in no way more distinctly than by these united public efforts. They have many facilities to give a wise and happy direction in this department. Books are abundant on the subject. Reading books abound with choice extracts from the productions of the ablest minds in the world. It is easy to lead our children and youth into communion with those whose writings are imperishable monuments of excellence.

G.H. Atkinson,
Superintendent Schools, Multnomah County

June 17, 1868

MAP OF THE SCHOOL DISTRICTS OF MULTNOMAH COUNTY

S chool clerks are often unable to tell what families live in their districts. They may, through mistake, report too many or too few people, and for the same reason they are liable to error in the assessment and collection of taxes. In order to prevent error and let the people know their own friends, the County Commissioners authorized the County Surveyor to make a new map, according to notes furnished from the records by the Superintendent of Schools. The map has been completed and colored in good style. One copy of it will be found hanging with other county maps in the office of the County Clerk, and one copy will be found in the office of the Superintendent of Schools.[i] In order to secure the utmost accuracy, all the records for ten years past have been reviewed and compared, and a new record made of every district in the order of their numbers, with references in footnotes to the original and to explanatory records.

The maps, made by Mr. Pennoyer, during his official term in 1860, have been final authority to that date in doubtful cases. Conflicting or incomplete boundaries have been defined according to the best evidence of the petitioners, and the official act of the Superintendent at that time in office. In one or two cases the lines did not return to the starting point but ran on indefinitely and in courses that could give no limit to a district. These errors have been corrected.

SUPERINTENDENT OF THE SCHOOLS

Several school districts continue their terms six months, a few nine months, and one or two outside of Portland have continued the whole year, employing the best teachers. This is wise, if the expense can be paid by the income of the current year, or by tax or

---

[i] Despite concerted effort by the editor, no copy of the map has been found.

subscription; but if the Directors must draw upon the next year's appropriation to pay for the present salary of the teacher, it is not wise to prolong the term so much. Six months of school every year are more valuable to pupils than nine months one year, and only three months the next. Yet it is believed that parents are finding it cheaper, and in all respects better, to educate their children in the common subjects within their own district, and under their own eye, by employing good teachers, than to send a few off to the boarding schools; and it is better for the Academy that the pupils come more mature and better prepared. Our schools have suffered by the haste to put children forward before they have understood the elementary studies. The most thorough teaching in the primary department gives the best results in the higher ones. This fact appears in graded schools. The present arrangement in the North Portland, and to some extent in the Central School, by which only two classes occupy a room, so that while one is reciting the other is learning their lessons, thus alternating through the day, affords ample time for every lesson, enables the teacher to attend to the progress of every pupil, and gives promise of steady and thorough advancement. Such division cannot be made in small schools with all grades of scholars, but that can be the aim of directors and teachers as their pupils increase in number.

TEACHERS

Teaching is a profession. Like all other professions, it will be chosen by those who have a desire for it. When a person acquires the knowledge and exhibits the wisdom and skill needed to govern and teach a school, that person should be employed and well paid for the service. A man who wants a good wagon or a good plow, or a good house, is willing to pay for the skill and the labor of the mechanic; and he who wants a good lawyer or physician, is willing to pay for the use of their knowledge and skill. In like manner he ought to be willing to pay for the services of those who teach his children. The law of demand and supply ought to come into full play in this matter.

Let the teachers who receive number one certificates from Normal Institutes, or Boards of Examiners, or who bring other assurance of their fitness for office, agree upon a tariff, or fix the minimum of their prices for the term, or per year, and they will secure better salaries. Let one well-tried teacher do it and he will be in greater demand. There are some who cannot be spared from the school room. Intelligent employers know this to be so. They soon become weary of poor teachers. On the other hand, let districts learn that it is as truly a wise economy to have first-class teachers as for a trader to have first-class goods. Let them make provision for such teachers, and in due time they will have them.

It has been the aim of the undersigned during his official term to stimulate every district in the county to improve its own school by employing good teachers for longer terms; by improving school houses when needful, by reducing the number and variety of books and thus of classes, and by giving a thorough drill in the common studies.

It has also been his aim to encourage and call attention to those teachers who seem to devote themselves to this work as a profession, and who love the work. It has not been done invidiously, but from a sense of duty to them and to the friends of education. If there have been any omissions or errors in this matter, or if any statement respecting any district has been at all inaccurate, it has been unintentional. In giving up the care of the public schools of the county to my successor elect, it is with the earnest hope that they have increased prosperity under his supervision.

G.H. ATKINSON
Sup't. Pub. Schools Multnomah Co.

March 24, 1871

SCHOOL MEETINGS

PRACTICAL SUGGESTIONS TO BE CONSIDERED AT THE APPROACHING ANNUAL MEETINGS

T he law requires that "organized districts shall hold annual meetings on the first Monday of April and shall elect one Director every year, for each district, who shall qualify, and shall hold his office for three years; and also a District Clerk, who shall qualify, and give bond to the Directors for such sum as they may require, as an additional pledge for the faithful performance of his duties, and who shall hold office for one year, or until his successor is elected and qualified." Directors can authorize clerks to call meetings, but it is not often done.

The chief school meeting of the year is the annual meeting on the first Monday in April. At that time the reports of the previous year are made, and plans proposed for the new year. It devolves of course upon the Board of Directors to present the facts respecting the schools and the property of the district, and make recommendations, if they have any, under the general law that "Directors shall perform such other duties, not provided for in this act, as the wants of their districts may from time to time demand."

The people have a right to expect of school directors a vigilant attention to the interests of the public schools. Men should be elected who will give that attention. Clerks also should be chosen who will faithfully serve in that office. They keep the records, collect the taxes, make the annual reports to the County Superintendents, draw the funds and disburse them, as audited and ordered by the directors, act as attorneys for their several districts, and act as Secretaries of all meetings. The law aims evidently to make the system efficient. The annual meeting is the place to show whether it is so conducted, and to provide that it may be continued efficient.

Time should be taken, especially by the district officers, to prepare for this meeting on the first Monday in April. Time should be taken on that day for hearing and deliberating upon the reports presented and measures proposed. Our public schools vitally affect our social and civil conditions as a people. The Monday evening usually given to the school meeting in Portland is hardly enough for the full discussion and wise action upon the subjects proposed. Would it not be better to have an afternoon session and an adjourned meeting for the evening? A year ago it was proposed to buy and prepare a block for a new public school in the western part of the city. The subject was briefly discussed and decided in the negative, and it has proved to the loss of the city. Whether more consideration would have produced an opposite decision cannot be told, but it is certain that important questions require time and all the light that can be thrown upon them. The tax proposed was reduced in amount much to our injury, as money has been borrowed and interest paid to keep our present school in operation until other funds come in. The same thing will have to be repeated, especially if we mean to provide schools for the eight hundred children now in Portland, who have no provision for their instruction in either the existing public or private schools. And here it is proper to remark that the carefully matured plans of directors deserve to be well considered, and they ought not to be hastily set aside.

But it may be objected that our deficiency of funds this past year was due to excessive expenses during the previous year, that the annual report of the Treasurer showed unusual payments, even without vouchers. It has been reported on the street that the claims were not audited, and that money was drawn without legal orders, and thus several hundred dollars were misspent and the treasury depleted. Whether this was so or not demands an inquiry, and report by those who hold the documents. But if directors deem it necessary to spend a little more than common to furnish schools with maps, charts and apparatus, or to furnish themselves with information by books or by visits of one or more to other cities to learn the better methods of conducting their own schools, or to perfect the plan of a school building, or if they occasionally hire a carriage, instead of walking two or three miles to visit their own schools (being men of dignity and gravity), why should it be thought strange, or spoken against, and not rather a sign of more enlarged views of school interests? Certainly such action is worthy to be reported fully at the annual meetings, that the people may imbibe the spirit and give it their sanction.

There are certainly grave questions to be decided respecting grade schools and suitable buildings for them. It is wise to profit by the experience of other cities that have the best public schools, rather than to build what we think will do, and soon find, as we have in Portland, our buildings defective, and practically a loss. Better for the Board to spend a little money for information than to act blindly. Better also for every district to raise a little more tax and provide a suitable building or buildings for the not distant future, than to come to that period with buildings wholly unsuited to the wants of the district. Had the East Portland District three years ago put up a larger frame for a two story building, as advised by some friends, and finished one room, they would now be prepared to extend their grades and meet the demands of their growing city at small expense. Instead of this, they have two small buildings on hand which can accommodate only about 90 of their 265 pupils. Let the Board be authorized now to erect a two story center building, with high ceilings, making wings of the present buildings, and the defects of provision for pupils will be partially removed. If Districts Nos. 2, 4 and 5 provide for grade schools, as it is hoped they will, the experience of other districts should teach them to make liberal provision for buildings.

Such questions, of course, bear upon that of annual district taxes for schools, to add to the funds distributed, and prolong the schools from one to two, and from two to three quarters each. Twelve districts voted taxes last year. The people seem more willing year by year, to do this. They find that good schools can be provided and continued at home cheaper than to send their children abroad. They know that the country is a better place for their children than the city, and that home is better for them than a boarding house, and far more economical.

It is easy to see that a good grade school continued six or nine months in every district that is large enough, gives worth, attractiveness and dignity to that district, and *adds far more to the value of property than its cost*. Besides such thoughtful and enterprising plans, presented and adopted at the annual school meeting, will react upon directors and clerks and other officials to make them more efficient and faithful to their trusts, more careful in securing and disbursing school funds, and will impress a public sentiment of the value and dignity of our public school system, which it has received and retained in other States of the Union, and which will not allow its character or its friends to be sacrificed to the prejudices of its foes or the greed of the avaricious.

G.H. ATKINSON
Supt. Public Schools Multnomah County

March 29, 1871

TEACHERS

T he school law requires that "teachers, *before making applications* to teach in any district organized, or perpetuated under this act, shall secure from the County Superintendent of Common Schools a certificate of qualification and character, and they shall produce the same to the Directors on making application. If any person shall violate this section they shall be liable to a fine of twenty-five dollars, to be recovered by law, for every such offense, payable to the county school fund." The school law further declares that "if any district shall employ a teacher who has not obtained a certificate as required by this act, and laid the same before the Directors for their inspection before commencing school, such district shall forfeit its proportion of the county school fund for the year." This requirement is again enforced upon Directors with a penalty for violation.

The law further requires that the County School Superintendent, *under penalty* for its neglect or violation, "shall strictly examine all persons who apply to him for certificates with the intention of teaching in his county in the following branches, viz.: Orthography, reading, writing, arithmetic, English grammar, geography, modern history and mental algebra, and if they possess a good moral character and are loyal to the United States Government, he shall give them a certificate. And if the applicant pass an examination so satisfactory to the Superintendent as to justify him to set the figure one (1) opposite all the branches named in the foregoing certificate, the certificate shall be good during the term of office of the Superintendent issuing the same, but if the Superintendent rate the applicant number two (2) or three (3), the applicant shall obtain a certificate for every quarter's school they teach under district organization, and such Superintendent may, when he deem it advisable, set apart a certain day or days in any quarter for teachers' certificates, giving due notice thereof, and an applicant failing to be examined at such a time shall pay to the Superintendent a fee of two dollars and fifty cents for such certificate."

The law further requires that the teachers shall maintain order in the school, so conduct as to command the respect of pupils, commence school at half past eight o'clock, A.M. and close at four o'clock P.M. of each day, giving one hour for recreation at noon, unless otherwise ordered by the directors, labor incessantly during school hours to advance the scholars in their studies, to create in their minds a desire for knowledge, principle, morality, politeness, cleanliness and the preservation of physical health, to keep a register of daily attendance, and hand a copy of the same to the District Clerk quarterly, and give a public examination on the last day of each quarter's school, and invite the County Superintendent to be present.

It will be seen from this law that the people aim to have well qualified and faithful teachers, and to guard themselves against incompetent ones, or mere hirelings, who seek the office as a means of temporary support, without any love for teaching or desire to do good to the pupils, or honor to the profession. If fully applied, this law would sift out the latter class of teachers. It discriminates as carefully respecting the character and qualifications of candidates as any corporate Board of Trustees of an Academy or Superintendent of a select school would do, except that the grade of scholarship may not be quite so high. It aims to put all our children and youth under such mental and moral training as the most prudent and watchful parents would desire. Its design, if carried out, would thereby reflect dignity upon the teachers' profession, as well as become one guarantee for the intelligence and virtue of the rising generation.

But to enforce such a law respecting teachers requires help from the districts. If you ask teachers to be *fitted* and *devoted* to such a work, you must hold out proper inducements. It is not enough to declaim against them for lack of qualifications, if you will not encourage them to be prepared and faithful. Accountants, merely good penmen and arithmeticians, honest withal, command from one hundred to one hundred and twenty five dollars per month, for the year; and bank clerks receive from eighteen hundred to three thousand dollars per annum. Sheriff's clerks, and other county officials, get salaries large enough to be sought, and their terms of employment and pay are rendered sure for one or more years. They have a motive to fit themselves for their mere business occupations. But a teacher deals with the mind in its most tender and susceptible periods. He must have many qualifications of mind and heart, must be familiar with many studies, must be intelligent in respect to current and general affairs, must have prudence, discernment, good judgment and skill to understand how to deal with pupils, and often with parents, also; he must win favor by success of some kind, and all this he must do in a few weeks or months at most. Judged by any rule applied to other persons, his office is a difficult one to fill. His task is a hard one. All eyes are upon him. All lips speak his praise or dispraise; all hands are ready to retain or eject him. His tenure of office is controlled by the popular breath of the district. At longest, his engagement is a short one, and he is made to feel that his life is but a pilgrimage from district to district and from village to village. If by any fortune, like marriage, he is anchored awhile, he is soon made to feel the uplift of unseen tides, warning him that his bark may soon drift, if it do not sail for other ports. If he strive to make his calling a profession, he know that it cannot have even the definiteness and certainty of the 'itinerant's' life. If he buys a lot and builds, the probability is that another will occupy his dwelling. If he plants and cultivates, it is with the prospect that others will eat the fruit. Others can fix themselves for a term of years, or for life, but he only for a term of months. Others can form plans, but his plans are subject to the caprice of a feverish, and not always wise and just community.

The usual application, for a common school teacher, is for one who will perform all the duties, for a term of eleven or twelve weeks, "for seventy-five or a hundred dollars and board." Seldom is an offer made, or a promise given, for a second or third term. You ask a teacher to qualify himself to do a greater work than an accountant's, or clerk's or sheriff's, for one-third, or one-fifth, or one-tenth, or one-twentieth of their pay, and you agree to employ him only one-half, or one-third or one-fourth of the time. You complain of the lack of fitness, and skill, and experience of school teachers, but forget that those best prepared for the office escape from it as soon as they can get a more settled employment.

The law aims to raise the grade of teachers as well as of pupils, but the policy of the people in many districts is to lower them both. Those in cities and villages usually have better and more permanent situations than those in the country, but theirs is an uncertain hold of their places.

What is the remedy?

First, evidently to give material encouragement to the teacher's work. Pay the gentleman or lady whom you employ to teach your children, according as you value the minds and hearts , the intelligence and virtue, of those children, and not simply as you pay those who dig, and plough, and chop, and reap, or who spin, and sew, and cook well. Let them know that you prize the work by your demands upon and pay to the workman. Tutors in palaces get honors and rewards according to the dignity of the princes whom they instruct. Every school teacher is an appointed tutor over those who may yet become princes and princesses in the empire of thought, and the realm of morals, and who may wield the scepter of world-wide beneficence and of permanent power.

Who ever enters the humblest school room, and does not think of its possibilities? Who looks upon one of the world's heroes like Adams, Webster and Peabody, and, on tracing their biography to its early direction in the village school, does not bestow grateful eulogium upon the faithful master or mistress who guided and impressed that young life?

Second, employ the same teachers, if possible, term after term, and year after year, and make them feel sure of their places, and thus encourage them to prepare themselves better for their work, and to be more faithful.

Third, provide the best buildings and grounds, and furnish the best helps for teaching, such as charts, books, blackboards, platforms and good seats.

Fourth, visit the school, become intelligent respecting its modes, its excellencies and defects, encourage its discipline and sustain its reputation, not only by good words, but by sending your children regularly.

Fifth, give teachers a day or two every quarter to attend County Institutes, and require them to do it, and to show their earnestness to improve in their art. Such methods will speedily be felt as a powerful stimulus among teachers, and will not only honor their work, but redound to the welfare of their pupils and thus to that of the district.

Saturday, April 1st is the first day appointed for the examination of teachers in this county. It will be conducted in writing. Schedules of questions will be furnished to each candidate, and slips of paper for the answers. It will be at the Central School building, as the desks and blackboards furnish more conveniences than my private office. The room will be open at 9 o'clock A.M., and the bell will be rung. An adjourned meeting of the County Teachers Institute will be held at the same place at 10 o'clock A.M. All teachers are especially invited to become members and workers in the Institute. The second examination day will be Saturday, July 1st, the third will be October 7th, the fourth, December 30th. The County Institute will probably adjourn from time to time, so as to include those days.

G.H. ATKINSON
School Superintendent, Multnomah Co.

April 5, 1871

SCHOOL GROUNDS

The present school law provides that School Directors "when authorized by a majority vote of the district, shall purchase, lease or build school houses, and buy or lease land for school purposes."

The lands specified evidently mean sites for school houses—not fields or farms.

The practical question is, how much ground ought to be laid off for the school building, outbuildings, and play grounds? In large cities, in which land is very costly, almost all the ground is covered by the whole building, in which rooms are prepared for physical exercise, and apartments assigned for fuel and other needed uses. One objection to this is, that the air and light within any building cannot be so pure and good for children as that without. In new cities of moderate size, like Portland, it is comparatively easy and economical to secure an entire block for the grounds of a single school. This policy of our late Boards of Directors has proved wise. It has given children ample room for play, the best light and air without and within the building, and has kept the schools as free as possible from contact with the houses and grounds of neighboring families, which has also proved to be a mutual benefit. The evil of the opposite policy is seen and felt in the half block occupied by the Harrison street school. The value and comfort of that school and of the houses there, are alike diminished.

It is to be hoped that the city will authorize the directors to pursue the liberal policy of purchasing full blocks of lots for all of our future public schools. A block, with the streets on all sides, gives an open area of 115,200 square feet or 2.2640 acres. In this proportion the schools in the country, which are much smaller than in the city, need a full acre, and even two acres would not be amiss. The object is to let children have room enough for their health and their sports without annoying neighbors or being annoyed.

School sites ought to be well chosen for views, for air currents and sunlight. A free circulation and a bright sun, will quickly carry off malarious vapors, prevent contagion, and render rooms comfortable on the most sultry day; while a fine prospect of river, forest and mountain will impress itself indelibly upon a child's mind, render him more cheerful and happy, improve his taste, refine his manners, and aid in various ways in mental and moral culture. The high and beautiful site of the Bush street, or Denman School, of San Francisco, overlooking the city, the harbor, the magnificent bay, the hills and mountains beyond, adds very much to the value and attractiveness of that school. But while children need the sun, they also need shade trees. It requires ten years for our transplanted maple to afford much shade, and fifteen for the elm. As the older forests are cut away, or liable to be, we cannot be too early in surrounding our school grounds with trees that in time will afford graceful shade in a hot summer noon. Our present municipal law has provided for this in the city, but it is apt to be rejected in the country districts. No. 18 did well two years ago to enclose their school ground and set it with shade trees, upon completing their cheerful looking school house.

As much as possible, grass plots should be laid out and guarded within school grounds. This is a difficult matter, but the plays of children seem to have no rule but the utmost freedom, but it may be possible, in large grounds, to save some spots in the corners, and along the fences and walks, for grass.

Our wet winters make it needful to have some well-graveled plots, as well as good plank walks, to the entrances, and around the buildings. Small school yards are planked in some places, which give pupils opportunity for exercise in calisthenics, military drills, swings, ball and marble playing; and which contributes to their cleanliness, and that of the rooms.

School grounds are a part of the teacher's domain as much as school rooms. Two teachers, in our large schools, a gentleman and a lady, should always oversee the pupils, during recess and intermission, on the play grounds, or in any basement, or other room appropriated to recreation. The boys, under the care of a gentleman, should have their section; and the girls, under the care of a lady, should have theirs. In no other way can quarrels, or bad words, or vexatious and oppressive conduct of older, and stronger pupils, over the younger, weaker, and more timid ones, or immoral tendencies be checked or repressed, and the best manners and habits be cultivated. The most common evils of our schools, and the chief complaints, arise from the rude, wild, improper and some reckless conduct of a few pupils during recess and intermission. Good order in the playground will secure it in the recitation room. Whether high fences should separate the two sections, depends somewhat on the plan of the house, and the separation of sexes into rooms by themselves. But teachers, for their own sake, as well as that of the pupils, ought to be present with them in their recreations. With such oversight, they will secure higher character for their schools, and command for them greater respect and confidence.

G.H. ATKINSON,
Sup't Schools Multnomah County

April 29, 1871

SCHOOL HOUSES

T he object of a building should govern its construction. The clearer and more comprehensive the idea or aim, the more distinct will be the outline, and the more simple and harmonious all the parts. A dwelling for a family must differ from a store, or a church, and a school room should be unlike a hothouse, a furnace room, or an ice cellar. A prison even ought not to be underground, or destitute of good light and air, in order to gain the ends of punishment, discipline, or reform; but rather to be built so that light, air and comfort, as well as confinement and toil, may serve these ends, and thus impress the benevolence of justice, as well as its power. The brightness of a school room ought to be adapted to the wants of the human eye, not flaring, not deeply shaded, and its temperature ought not to be oppressive or chilly.

The Boston School Report for 1864 properly says: "If the light can be admitted only on one side of a school room, the pupils should be seated with their backs toward it. If the light is admitted on the opposite sides, the seating should be so arranged that the blank walls may be in front and rear." Very often school houses are so placed as to receive the full midday rays of the sun. The tax upon the eye's power to exclude such needless brilliancy, tends to weaken the strong, and to destroy the weak. The rooms for some of the primary departments of our city schools have this defect.

The temperature of a school room ought to conform evenly to that of the body in its normal condition. Upon this subject Mr. Wells remarks: "We are so constituted that a certain degree of heat is essential to health and comfort. The proper temperature of a school room, according to the testimony of a large number of the best physicians and educators, is about 68 degrees Fahrenheit. When the thermometer in a room rises above 70 degrees, measures should immediately be taken to reduce the temperature; and when it sinks below 65 degrees, measures should be taken to raise the temperature. If at any time the thermometer sinks below 60 degrees the pupils cannot be confined in their seats without an exposure of health."

Good ventilation is also essential to a school room. Mr. Wells says: "The healthy action of both mind and body requires a constant supply of fresh air for the lungs. A pure atmosphere is composed of about 80 % of nitrogen, and 20% of oxygen. The life-giving principle is oxygen. Air that has once passed through the lungs is deprived of a large portion of its oxygen, and charged with a poisonous gas. If it is retained in the lungs a few seconds, it will not even support ordinary combustion. Besides the impurities, sent out from the lungs, the insensible perspiration from all the pupils in a room contribute very considerably to increase the pernicious quality of the atmosphere. To those who value the health of their children, it needs no argument to prove that this devitalized, poisonous mix should be constantly removed from the school room and pure, life-giving air be introduced in its stead."

Dr. Reid, "from an extreme variety of experiments, made on hundreds of different constitutions," recommends at least ten cubic feet per minute as a suitable supply for each individual. No physiologist estimates the amount required by each individual at less than five feet per minute; and yet not one school in a hundred receives even this supply. The North American Review says: "That ventilators should be open near the floor of the apartment to be ventilated, in order to carry off the stratum of air in contact with the floor, which is always the coldest, and usually the foulest, in the room."

Mr. Wells adds that, "in constructing school buildings, ventilating registers should generally be placed both at the top and bottom of rooms." With this idea the report of the New York Board of Education agrees.

The size and shape of a school room should be governed by the number of pupils committed to the care of one teacher.

The average number admitted into one room in San Francisco is fifty.

The Superintendent and Architect of the Boston Schools in 1864 submitted the following outline and plan of a model primary school room:

"Fifty-six being the number to be accommodated, the arrangement of the desks for this number is the next things to be done. The best mode of disposing of them seems to be to make seven rows with eight in a row. Arranged in this way, they will occupy a space in the form of a rectangle, of which the longest side will be parallel with the teacher's platform. Each desk is one foot and a half long. The center aisle should be two feet wide, and each of the others sixteen inches. A chair and desk together require a little more than two feet from front to back. Fifty-six desks and chairs, with the above dimensions and arrangements, would occupy a rectangle twenty-two feet by fifteen. In the rear and on the sides of the space appropriated to seating, there should be a space not less than three feet wide. The teacher's platform should be at least five feet wide, and the area between the scholar's desks and the platform should be at least as wide. These measures will requires a room twenty-eight feet square in the clear. The height should be twelve feet in the clear. This size gives one hundred and sixty-eight cubic feet of air to each child, which would be sufficient to last thirty-nine minutes without a fresh supply. This plan makes provision for black boards in the rear and in front of the pupils, and for light on both sides."

The 26 class rooms of the 23d St. Grammar School, in the eighteenth ward of New York City, average about 19x22 feet, which will seat one thousand five hundred scholars, or fifty-seven each. The two assembly rooms, 44x70 feet, will seat nine hundred scholars. The second and third stories are fourteen feet in heights and the fourth seventeen feet, which allows about 100 cubic feet of air to each pupil, or enough for ten minutes. See annual report of 1864, of the New York Board of Education.

A building with a central entrance and hall, evidently allows the best and most convenient divisions into school rooms, clothes rooms, stair-ways and areas. The plan of the double cross and wings, tho it increases the cost, yet like the Washington Square primary school in Boston, affords good egress to the yards, and better light and air to all the rooms.

The plan of the school house on 23d street in New York City is one of remarkable completeness and economy. The idea is that of a thoroughly graded school. It has all the advantages of large reception rooms, one of which can be turned into four classrooms by sliding doors, leaving a smaller reception room 30x45 feet, besides numerous adjacent class rooms. Its outline and divisions help to protect and confirm the school grades, while every architect knows that a few feet added to the size of a building increases its capacity far above the proportionable increase in cost.

It is safe to calculate the size of school rooms at the rate of twenty-eight feet square, and twelve or fourteen feet to the ceilings, for fifty-six pupils. In cities the plan seems to be adopted to have primary schools entirely separate from grammar schools. It is also an increasing custom to have the grammar schools for boys and girls separate from each other and on different blocks and streets.

Such separation removes one of the most common objections to the public schools and adds much to their efficiency and value.

It is evident that our city has the finest opportunity to profit by the experience of other cities in the purchase of school grounds and the erection of school buildings.

Mr. Failing justly remarked at the last school meeting that "the erection of the Central schoolhouse had proved to be the best investment which Portland had ever made;" and we may add that the city owes to Mr. Failing a debt of gratitude for his laborious efforts, freely made, to establish our public schools. Gratitude is due also to many other gentlemen, who have for years, quietly and freely, but effectually, done similar service.

Duty now calls us to extend and perfect the system. An investment for public schools, that has been found wise and remunerative for the last ten years, *by inviting hither and adding many families* to our permanent population will, if increased, prove equally, and perhaps doubly, valuable during the next ten years.

What is true of Portland will be true of East Portland, if the citizens there will make wise provisions for graded public schools. And what is true of the cities, will be true of the village centers in the country, if the citizens pursue the same policy. A good free school draws and binds to itself the families that comprise the real strength, intellectual and moral, of every community.

G.H. ATKINSON
Sup't. Schools Multnomah Co.

Sept. 29, 1871

THE PUBLIC SCHOOLS OF THE CITY

I t may be important, especially to recent citizens, to know that our free schools offer increased advantages of education. The Directors have enlarged the Harrison Street building; reslated the blackboards in several rooms; provided more comfortable seats, especially for the little children, and added one or two to the corps of teachers, besides filling the vacancies with well accredited instructors. A visit to all the rooms shows that teachers and pupils are refreshed by the long vacation and ready for vigorous work. It is a pleasing fact to note the steady, upward progress of the different classes. Pupils that, not long ago, were among the tenth grade primaries, are now in the fourth and even third grades of the grammar department.

It attests the value of our Public Schools, in keeping, as far as possible, the same teachers, who, while working together harmoniously, and knowing well their pupils, advance every class as far and as fast as they are prepared to go. This stimulates pupils and encourages parents.

Division of labor by the graded system helps both teacher and scholar. Yet our ten grades can be worked even more efficiently. No room should, in fact, have more than one grade. This is the plan in St. Louis, and in other large cities in which the Public Schools have so justly attained, and maintain, preeminence. The grade in each room is, for greater convenience and profit, formed into two divisions or classes, of about twenty pupils each. While one class is reciting a lesson the other is preparing a lesson. The first division will, of course, be the more advanced pupils of that grade. Thus the grades are practically doubled, and the steps of progress are made easier and surer. These two classes alternate between study and recitation every day without confusion, or loss of time. Their work is simple and plain to themselves as well as to their teachers. In fact a casual visitor can tell where every class is. The studies will be better pursued and illustrated, and also remembered. The room itself will help the mind to recall the subjects, as the workman's shop, the printer's case, and the merchant's shelf helps one to find his tools, the other his types, and the other his goods. Our public schools have two grades to a room, and in one case parts of three grades. This is a great improvement upon the jumble of mingling all classes in one or two rooms, but our desideratum is *a single grade of two divisions to each room.*

But it is obvious that our school buildings are not well constructed for this object; some rooms are too large, while others are too small for the purpose. The entrances are in the wrong places. The light, ventilation, seating and blackboard arrangements should be adapted to such a system of grading. In fact every school building should conform to the improved school idea, as our later built residences conform to the improved idea of the family home. Every architect makes and follows the plan of his employer, and it is very unfortunate if any man attempts to build without a distinct plan.

It is plain that graded schools require central halls in every story but the attic. Grade rooms are easily and economically arranged on both sides of such halls, the lower grades below, and thus rising to the upper story, which should be a single room for the assembling of the whole school, for general purpose, or for musical instruction, like the upper room in the Bush street school of San Francisco.

For the convenience of departments, sliding doors, as in some of the St. Louis school buildings, should be placed between some of the rooms. A few such simple outlines in the plans of our future school edifices would greatly facilitate the comfort and success of our schools.

The North school building needs just such a hall through the center, above and below—if its size will admit of the change. Our Central building is too small for the change. It should be moved into a corner of the block for primary departments and a center building worthy of admirable location, the city's growth and the school interest, should be erected on that site. Our High School should be in this central location for the obvious convenience of pupils from all parts of our widely expanding city. At present it cannot well be removed from the North building, though that will soon be so crowded as to need all the room.

For the welfare of all lower classes, it is imperatively necessary that pupils prepared for the High school and so designated by their teachers, should enter it at once. Their delay confuses teachers and pupils in the Grammar departments. Distance is an objection made by the girls in the south part of the city, and this is to be regretted, but this evil is not so great as that of confusing the succeeding classes—for that confusion will increase more and more. Good plank sidewalks on Sixth, Seventh and Eighth streets render it much easier to reach the North school from Caruthers' Addition than it was to reach the Central school formerly from the same points.

Our High school teachers have been long tried and most successful educators, and although their time is still divided among too many grades and classes, yet they are doing vigorous work in their department.

In every review we ought to remember the little ones, who are forming their first idea of school. They need special and kindest care and culture. Like tender plants they can be easily crushed in spirit and power of growth, or they can be nurtured to a beautiful mental and moral development. It depends very much upon the spirit of the teachers which result shall be achieved. Their station and office is more important, if possible, than that of teachers in the intermediate or grammar grades. They need many helps, such as comfortable seats and rooms—which some have—good charts and outline maps, and the constant aid and sympathy of Directors and friends, that their pupils may be well fitted for and happy to go into higher grades.

As a whole, there is much to cheer and encourage in the respect of our public schools in the city and county. If the people will take broad views of the subject and furnish Directors with funds enough to erect or improve buildings and pay current and justly increasing expenses for more teachers and furniture, our public schools will more and more attract families and enrich and ennoble the whole community.

G.H. ATKINSON
School Supt. Multnomah County

March 23, 1872

REPORT OF THE PUBLIC SCHOOLS
OF MULTNOMAH COUNTY FOR 1871-2

T hirty-one districts have been laid off in this county, twenty-five of which have been organized. Twenty-three have reported schools the past year, and received their orders for school money. Two failed to report, and thus forfeited their right to funds. Four districts of other counties reported pupils in this county, and drew their pro rata of funds.

The following summary of the reports will give an outline of the condition of the districts:

Number of voters reported	2,407
Number of children between the age of 4 and 20 yrs.	3,730
Number of males " "	1,923
Number of females " "	1,807
Number of terms of school taught	124
Number of pupils enrolled	2,155
Average attendance	1,360
Number of teachers employed	65
Number of male teachers	33
Number of female teachers	32
Amount paid teachers during the year	$20,889.49
Average paid teachers per term during the year	$168.54
Amount paid teachers from county fund	$14,402.08
Amount of incidental expenses	$4,454.33
Amount of district taxes levied	$22,301.73
Amount of district taxes collected	$20,381.73
Amount of cost of new buildings, lots and repairs	$15,137.11
Whole amount paid for school purposes	$40,692.00

Value of public school buildings	$46,300.00
Value—approximate—of school lots	$53,700.00
Value of public school property	$100,000.00

District No. 1, Portland, reports 2,452 children of school age —a gain of 82; of whom 1,126 are enrolled in public schools, and 815 in private and corporate schools, leaving 511 who do not attend any school.

Great credit is due this city for the liberal provisions made by voluntary taxation to support and improve the public schools the past year.

District No. 2, Brooklyn, reports a gain of 20 pupils; No. 3, "Dufur," reports a gain of 6, No. 4, "Powell's Valley", reports a loss of 3; No. 5, "Mt. Tabor," reports a gain of 12. A majority of the districts report about the same number as last year. No. 21, East Portland, reports a gain of 49, and No. 31, "Holladay's Addition," reports a gain of 54.

In several districts confusion still exists from the great variety of school books. This evil can be corrected by a State Board of Education, authorized to prescribe text books.

In thirteen districts of the county, schools were continued two terms each. The schools of East Portland continued three terms each. Those of Portland had four terms each, equal to eighty terms for the twenty rooms or teachers.

The public schools of the city have for the most part improved in character, in order, in the methods of teaching and in the habits of the pupils about the school buildings. Improvements of this kind have appeared in some other schools, while some have made little or no advance. This is due in part, perhaps, to a lack of interest in the patrons, in employing and sustaining teachers, and in providing proper school rooms and furniture. It is hard for little children to sit all day upon high benches, with their feet dangling, unable to touch the floor. It is hard for teachers to illustrate subjects without blackboards or wall cards, outline Geographical maps or charts. It is hard also to instruct pupils, who come irregularly. Directors can do much to aid teachers and improve the scholar by the monthly visits and care which the law requires.

Our schools have less public money per pupil this year than last, owing to the fact that $2,227.41 of the two mill tax had not been collected on the first Monday of March, the legal day of distribution to the several districts. Orders have been issued for $12,012.39 coin and $769.82 currency; a sum in coin of $1,268.47 less than the amount distributed in 1871. These sums afford $3.68 coin per pupil for the current year, against $4.28 coin per pupil drawn in 1871.

It was expected that the interest of the irreducible fund would relieve our school treasury, but the portion assigned to this county has not yet been received, and the sum is declared to be small, about $1,157.36 coin, or 31 cents per pupil.

The law needs to be changed so that taxes collected and funds accumulating after the annual distribution in March may be distributed to the district on the first Monday in September, instead of lying in the treasury ten or eleven months.

It will be seen from this report that local taxes will be needed to keep the schools up to their present condition. It is hoped that funds will be raised and efforts made to improve them in quality and to extend their terms.

We are inviting immigration, and one of the most effective motives with the intelligent, industrious and skilled classes, whom we most desire to secure as settlers, is the prospect of good schools for their children. The policy of improving our schools and school system is the policy that will enrich ourselves. The best families go where their children can have the best advantages.

The American system of free, graded English schools, including Primary, Grammar and High School Departments, as conducted in many of our eastern and western cities like Boston, Worcester, Chicago, Milwaukee, Winona, Sterling, Moline, Rock Island, Omaha, Sacramento, San Francisco, Portland and hundreds of other places, forms not only one of the brightest ornaments of American society, but one of the most conspicuous and attractive objects of intelligent immigrants from different States and other lands.

A higher consideration than this is the confessed power of such schools to enrich and discipline the mind, and, to some degree, to mold the character of our youth. It is surely the most effective means to render our heterogeneous population homogeneous in language, in proper freedom and habits of thought, and thus in fitness for their privileges and duties as citizens of the Republic. While we vote taxes and subscribe money freely in material investments, let us not forget that our richest possessions derive and retain their value more from the mental and moral character of the people than from their own abundance. Gold and silver, houses and lands, manufactures and merchandise, are almost worthless in an ignorant, debased and irresponsible community.

The lesson of history is that the better we make our schools, and the more completely they reach and train the masses, the safer and happier shall we be, and more assured will be our future prosperity.

G.H. ATKINSON
Supt. Public Schools of Multnomah Co.

FIVE

Occasional Writings on the Railroad

George Atkinson's family was significantly involved in railroads. His father, William, was a founding director of the Vermont Central. Older brother Charles, of Moline, Illinois, played a key role in beginning the Chicago and Rock Island. The town of Atkinson, Illinois, thirty miles east of Moline, is named for him. Even George's son married into a railroading family when he wed Clara Chamberlain. Her father, Horatio Nelson Chamberlain, had laid out two rail lines. One, the Massawippi Railroad, connected Newport, Vermont with Sherbrooke, Quebec. The other, the Connecticut and Passumpsic Rivers Railroad, connected Newport, Vermont with Wells River, Vermont.

George was convinced that railroads would be the key to the growth and economic development of the Pacific Northwest.

The first transcontinental railroad, the Union Pacific/Central Pacific, extended across the midline of the U.S. from Omaha, Nebraska to Sacramento, California. It had been completed in 1866, with the driving of the "Golden Spike" near Promontory Point, Utah. Congressional legislation that authorized it also gave initial support to the concept of parallel transcontinental railroads across the northern and southern tiers of states.

By 1873 the Northern Pacific Railroad (NPRR) was well under way, with lines completed from Duluth, Minnesota to Bismarck, North Dakota and from Kalama to Olympia, in Washington. Everything came to a halt, though, when a massive national financial crisis was triggered by the sudden collapse of the financial empire of Jay Cooke, lead financier of the NPRR.

Later in the decade, as the economy began to grow again, there was strong interest in completion of the railroad (as well as substantial opposition). George submitted several articles to the *Oregonian*. Four of them appear here.

An additional railroad article is also found here, following the earlier four. It, too, was published in the *Oregonian*. George had secured a seat on the first passenger train to travel east from Portland through the Columbia Gorge. When the train arrived at its destination, Dayton, Washington, he telegraphed the story to Portland.

The Northern Pacific Railroad

Source:
The Oregonian Archives
Multnomah County Library

April 4, 1876

EFFECT OF THE NORTHERN PACIFIC RAILROAD AND ITS BRANCH TO PUYALLUP COAL MINES UPON THE MANUFACTURING INTERESTS OF THE NORTHWEST

T he first effect of the Central Pacific railroad was to produce excessive speculations in San Francisco lots, and in California lands.

Its second effect was to overrun California with Eastern goods, sold mostly by sample, among country merchants, thus tending to dry up the city trade and depress city property.

The third effect was to arouse the capitalists and business men of San Francisco to protect themselves at once by establishing and encouraging all kinds of manufactories, and thus give employment and the means of living to all the people, to shut out Eastern goods by competition, and furnish a home market for their own productions, while sending an increasing margin of manufactured as well as farm and mine products for the markets of the world.

The fourth effect was to bring in a large supply of all kinds of skilled laborers, while increasing greatly the employment of the unskilled— the women and girls, the boys and the Chinese in all manner of trades; also the importation of all varieties of the most improved machinery. Under this fourth head, too, is the great increase in importation of raw materials, such as coal, iron, hides, jute, cotton, lumber, and some classes of provisions.

The fifth effect has been to stimulate by a surer market at home a larger variety of agricultural productions, thus raising the price of farm lands to the former speculation prices, and increasing immigration over one hundred per cent, and carrying city property steadily and strongly above the rates in 1868-9, those years of special excitement in such property.

The sixth effect has been to make San Francisco one of the great manufacturing centers of the world, able to compete with many classes of goods in any market, while excluding others from their own. The editor of the *Journal of Commerce* says that San Francisco produced in 1874 nearly $300 worth of manufactured goods per capita, and over $2,000 for every artisan employed. Three years ago, in 1871, the manufactures of the city equaled $52,603,475 in value, besides the value of gold and silver refined. The exhibit for 1874 was $67,333,930 —a little over $2,600 for every artisan employed. The exhibit for 1875—the panic years—was $63,000,000.

The eighth effect has been to overcome every natural hindrance to the growth of the business of San Francisco and vicinity, by the use of capital to supply the raw materials for goods of the motive powers. Their great want is iron, coal, and water. By every means and at any cost they propose to get these things cheap, and thus compete forever with the world.

Reasoning from these facts, the building of the Northern Pacific Railroad ought to produce like effects at its termini—Portland and Tacoma. The success of the first is proof that a second and a third continental road will bring about similar results. The fact that manufactures can be built up on the sand hills of San Francisco and the State made rich and populous by connecting that spot with all the interior and the East by the iron track, and with all parts of Western America and Eastern Asia and Polynesia by steamer lines, is proof also that a like result can be attained for Oregon and Washington and for the cities which enjoy such facilities of commerce. The experience of San Francisco may be ours in the way of sudden speculations in lots and land, in the influx of goods as well as population. We may not have the same capital, but what there is will be compelled to be invested so as to employ labor and be productive. The town or city that refuses to use its means and employ its people, preferring to raise and export the raw materials, and buy goods, will decline relatively if not absolutely. It is to be hoped that our pupilage of a quarter of a century in buying furniture, clothing, hardware, implements, glassware, crockery, groceries and many kinds of provisions from other people's labor, and paying them in gold and silver, wheat, lumber and wool, leaving us out of funds and out of work much of the time, draining our soil and exhausting our resources, and enriching only those merchants who make the exchanges and those bankers who loan the money, will be a lesson that we shall not continue to learn for the next twenty-five years. Oregon and Washington have exported over $28,000,000 of gold since 1848.

The manufacturers of San Francisco have proven that almost every variety of goods can be made at a profit even there, although they have to buy water, wood, lumber, coal and iron. They find that in the future these materials must be at rates common in the East and in England, in order to hope for success. Their extending commerce with the countries that furnish the raw materials is their mode of supply, yet they must contend at a disadvantage with any of those countries that furnish the raw materials and manufacture them also.

Oregon and Washington have this opportunity if they choose to use it. They have the lumber for the finest furniture, as the factories show, and also for all manner of farming implements. They have the iron and the coal in abundance. It has been found that they export to San Francisco increasing quantities of these articles. The Seattle coal displaces for steam and domestic purposes that of other mines. The Puyallup coal, as tested, proves superior to that from Nanaimo for gas, for coke and for steam. For the forge and steel welding it equals the Cumberland. The anthracite veins thus far found give promise to be a smelting coal, so much needed in place of the Lehigh. No doubt iron will be found in the same vicinity.

On Guemes Island, in Puget Sound, a copper and an iron ore have been found, but the tests of quality and quantity have not yet been fully made. The iron ore bed of Oswego has enough in sight to last a half score of years, Its quality ranks highest in the market. Oregon and Washington furnish the lumber for the markets of the Pacific, and possibly it may be sent to Atlantic and European ports.

The wool product of Oregon in the last fifteen years was 18,000,000 of pounds. That of Washington Territory was 3,000. The total wool product of the Pacific States and Territories was, from 1855 to 1875, inclusive, as per record of the San Francisco Journal of Commerce, 321,570,223 pounds, California having produced of the amount 274,224,433 pounds and exported to the East 249,668,890 pounds, for which she received $53,818,442. They cannot compete in its manufactories with the Eastern factories. In this Oregon and Washington have the advantage. Our facilities for the supply of wood can be superior to that of Eastern manufacturers. Our water powers and means of supporting operatives are superior to theirs.

These facts have been tested by the small manufactories in operation. With a railroad connection eastward, the supply of skilled labor and the best machinery can be easily obtained. Our unemployed men and women, boys and girls, will furnish a ready supply of help. In the sharp competitions of labor our manufacturers have the same opportunities as those of California. As it is now, we send off the wool at twenty-five cents a pound and buy it back in clothing at $5 to $15 per pound, paying the bonus to the eastern laborer and capitalist.

We export hides to the amount of a few thousand dollars, and import leather, boots and shoes to the amount of more than a million dollars annually. We send away hides, paying freights and tanners, while the best hemlock forests go to decay near Astoria. Our fields will raise the choicest flax, but we buy over $300,000 worth of poor jute bags that perish quickly and waste a large per cent of their cost of grain, while we are paying for them with six or seven cargoes of the choicest of our wheat.

Our grain and lumber are shipped to foreign ports in foreign vessels, compelling us to pay one-half their value, for the freights, or which is the same, lose half of the price. While our ship timber is cut down for cord wood, or burnt off to clear the land. We exhaust the soils, and destroy their natural resources for the sake of a mere pittance, instead of putting labor and skill upon that which will return lumber and riches, and develop the industry, economy, intelligence and virtue of the youth of the land.

Since the overland railroad has been in operation, the Californians have been reversing this suicidal process and have now got well on in the high road of sure prosperity. They make all people pay tribute to their skill and enterprise. Their contact with the Eastern manufacturer daily by train and telegraph stimulates them to an intense and steady activity not known in the days of mere gold mining and speculation. If we get into that contact by the completion of the Northern Pacific R.R. we shall either wake up and go to work or be run over. Plodding and guessing, and 'waiting for something to turn up' will not do by the side of the men who see the finest furniture in a maple, an ash, a cedar or an alder; or by the side of the men who see a grand ship in one of those tall firs, or by the side of him who sees the linen factories of Dundee and Belfast springing up near these waving fields of flax.

In the manufacturing centers of the East and of England the great want is material to work upon and good food and home comforts for the workers. These are the costly things. The sight of forests like ours, of waterfalls so high and constant, of iron mines and coal mines so near at hand and so exhaustless, of wheat fields and orchards so luxuriant, of an ocean so vast for commerce, and of rivers and bays so convenient, means to such men the most varied and most extensive plans and enterprises. Cheap lands invite immigration; climates favorable for work invite those whose life is given to toil. Regions little infected with malaria will be sought by those worn with the heat and miasma of eastern and southern climes. Such are the prospects opened by the railroad to the northwest coast.

To illustrate more definitely these business prospects, the following items taken from the San Francisco Journal of Commerce of January 12, 1876 are appended:

[120]

THE COAL DEMAND AND SUPPLY

Imports (in tons) and receipts at San Francisco for the past two years are as follows:

Australian	(1874)	130,281	(1875)	138,164
English	"	31,981	"	65,634
Eastern	"	28,843	"	30,126
Vancouver Island	"	47,982	"	62,339
TOTAL FOREIGN	"	242,087	"	297,043
Bellingham Bay	"	17,949	"	10,440
Coos Bay	"	48,451	"	29,078
Seattle	"	7,840	"	59,327
Port Townsend	"	....	"	36
TOTAL PAC. COAST	"	73,920	"	98,881
TOTAL	"	316,007	"	395,924
Mount Diablo	"	205,256	"	142,808
Rocky Mountain	"	363	"	53

RECEIPTS OF COAL (IN TONS) FOR 16 YEARS, 1860 TO 1875, INCLUSIVE

Cumberland, 107,603; Anthracite, 448,053; English, 413,100; Australian, 869,534; Chile, 75,523; Vancouver Island, 307,880; Coos Bay, 252,932; Bellingham Bay, 196,817; Russia, 440; Seattle, 102,695; Rocky Mountain, 4,270; Mount Diablo, 1,591,914.

The increasing production of Pacific Coast coal diminishes the prices and imports of foreign coal. The value of the coal deposits of the Pacific Coast is just now known. The increase of Australian for 1875 was 8,883 tons. Prices $8.50 to $9.00—$2 less than at the beginning of the year. Imports of English and Scotch increased 50,653 tons during the year. Imports of Eastern increased 1,283. Cumberland held its own. Lehigh got scarce and rose to $37 per ton; new supplies have reduced it to $22. Receipts from all Pacific Coast, except Seattle, have declined: Bellingham Bay, 7,000 tons; Coos Bay, 17,000; Mount Diablo, 62,448 tons. The owners expect to ship 100,000 tons of Seattle coal this year. The Renton supplies its shareholders at $8 per ton. Australian and English quoted, to arrive at $8.50 to $9; Scotch splint, $10 to $10.50; Pittston egg, $18; Cumb., $14 in bulk, $15 in casks; Lehigh, $22; Pacific Coast, $10; Coos Bay, $6.25; Mt. Diablo, $8.50; Nanaimo, $10; Wellington, $10 to $10.50; Seattle, to $10.50.

In January, 1874, the editor of the San Francisco *Journal of Commerce* remarked:

Among the drawbacks to manufactures in San Francisco is the lack of certain descriptions of material. Dear coal and dear iron have long stood in the way of the manufacturer and do so still, the cost of the former ranging from $8.50 to $17 per ton, averaging $12, and the price of the latter at the present time being $16 per ton for jobbing lots. The dearness of good coal is not so much felt as (?) by and by. The foundries in 1874 used 9,256 tons, of which 4,250 tons, used for smelting, was Lehigh, and 4,296 tons was Mt. Diablo, used for steam. Most of the imported coal is used by glass and steamship companies and for domestic purposes. But as we advance in the manufacture of articles from iron and steel, we shall require cheap and good smelting and steam coal. With cheap iron ore the way to produce iron for pig and railroad, for home use and for exportation the way is opened unto us, as also the manufacture not only of millions of dollars worth of hardware, which we yearly use, but also the manufacture of supplies for every nation bordering on the Pacific. Coal and iron—the two main factors of industrial progress now-a-days, we possess in sufficient abundance. Of wool we produced 40,000,000 pounds last year, It is increasing at the rate of 33% per annum. In a dozen years we shall largely produce flax, cotton and the sugar beet. The acclimatization of the blue gum promises abundant supply of hardwood lumber, while the leather of California is among the best in the world.

The question of cheap water supply is of particular interest to the manufacturers, as some of them pay over $1,000 a year for this article, but most of the establishments south of Market and east of First Streets have solved the question for themselves, procuring all the water they require from artesian wells.

The labor employed in the manufactories of the city represents, with those dependent on it for support and the trades people patronized, at least one-third of the whole population. The total number of hands employed last year was 24,496, of which 10,813 were Chinese. Of the rest, 6,713 were white men, 2,697 white women and girls, and 1,483 white boys. The wages amounted to $11,251,943, or about $500 per annum. The average white man employed had about $700 per annum. Skilled artisans got from $3 to $5 per day.

With such an outlook before them, we may surely follow the California pioneer manufacturers on the Pacific. Their success may be in part ours. Their failures may admonish us. Their materials can be exchanged for ours, and jointly the industries along the coast may use the resources so bountifully provided in promoting the welfare of all the people.

G.H. ATKINSON

January 8, 1878

A FACT ABOUT OVERLAND RAILROADS

The C.P.R.R. have spent fifteen millions of dollars—more or less—to head off Col. T. Scott's Texas P.R.R. and control its rates, and direct its traffic to San Francisco. They have gained the point. Their Southern P.R.R. is in fact the continuation of the Texas and Southern P.R.R. San Diego was its objective point in Col. Scott's plan. That city can be now only a side station. Gov. Stanford & Co. have bagged the game. San Francisco is the real terminus. The business of Arizona must pay tribute to that city. All traffic, freight and passengers across the continent on that route must conform to the rates of the C.P. and U.P.R.R. Col. Scott is understood to yield, and to unite now with Mr. Huntington to get the Texas P.R.R. bill through Congress.

The Southern members of Congress are a unit for the measure. If they do not ask too large a money subsidy their bill will pass. The second railroad will soon be completed across the continent. The Texas Pacific railroad will own the eastern end, and the Central Pacific will own and operate the western end, and dictate rates. The Union Pacific railroad own and operate the eastern end of the present overland road and the C.P.R.R. own and operate the western end. They control the U.P.R.R., so that the latter cannot extend their own road to the Pacific ocean at any point. The C.P. Co. do and will control the Texas R.R. so that they cannot extend their railroad to the Pacific ocean at any point. Side or branch railroads, say to Dakota, the Black Hills, Montana and Colorado and Utah and Idaho along and against the Union Pacific railroad route will be allowed to them to buy or build and control.

Side or branch railroads along and against the route of the Texas Pacific will be allowed to that railroad company to buy or build and control. Roads to Arkansas, Indian Territory, New Mexico, Colorado, south Utah on the north and the provinces of Mexico on the south must and will pay tribute and be more or less controlled by Col. Scott's road. A branch road to western Mexico must and will be built by the C.P.R.R. This latter company is pressing eastward so as to control Arizona and get a large per cent of all branch roads north and south.

It already owns and controls nearly the entire system of branch railroads in California. It owns or controls all in Nevada. It proposes a branch railroad to the Columbia River at or near The Dalles, along that comparatively level route east of the Cascade Mountains. It wants timber, and it will thus have a sure and abundant timber supply. It will tap the upper Columbia basin, as the Northern Utah narrow gauge railroad will tap Montana, and will divert the trade of both regions to their route and to San Francisco on the west, and to their eastern terminus. The plan is to leave the Willamette Valley to its ocean route, which will soon be in control of the C.P.R.R.

The only competing line to this almost completed scheme is the N.P.R.R. The only rival to the grand consolidation plan of these

C.P.R.R. magnates is the N.P.R.R. company. If they can divide the counsels of the people of Oregon and Washington, and Montana and Idaho, they will have the whole northwestern Pacific, as they have the whole southwestern Pacific under permanent tribute in themselves. San Francisco will be the sole metropolis on the entire Pacific coast. There will be no large city on the Columbia or on Puget Sound. Our goods will be imported under taxes and commissions paid to outside companies.

It is a business operation worthy of the C.P.R.R. Co. They work for money, not for glory. They show wise forecast. They work with energy and skill and unchanging purpose. We admire and honor their pluck. We commend their wisdom. Seeing their opportunity, they would be unwise not to use it. Knowing the present crisis, they do not rest, and they will not rest until they have closed the gap and shut out the N.P.R.R. from the coast and compelled it to own and hold only the eastern end of the northern overland railroad, while they hold or prevent the western end. This is the effect if not the aim of the Mitchell bill.

G.H. ATKINSON

March 8, 1878

THE RAILROAD SITUATION
THE N.P.R.R. CONNECTION BETWEEN THE MISSOURI AND COLUMBIA RIVERS

It was the plan of the government to aid three transcontinental railroads. Congress granted a large sum and sent surveyors to explore the three best routes for the northern, the central and southern proposed roads, and to make preliminary surveys and profile outlines of the gradients of the same—to collect all possible facts about these several regions, their climate and their resources. Able scientific men were employed in this initial work; one of them was Gov. I.I. Stevens who, as general in the Union army, lost his life in the war.

In about two years their reports were received and published by the government, which was a further pledge to the people of its purpose.

The Central road received very large government subsidies—partly as a war measure and partly in view of the supposed difficulties and the unknown facilities and helps along this route. The southern road was arrested by the civil strife. Since that is over government can aid it now. As a stronger bond of the union and peace, it will add force to the original argument for its construction.

Doubtless it will be built on the Texas Pacific or on the Southern Pacific, or as a union of the two.

To the North Pacific railroad was granted a large land subsidy. It began to build on a grand scale at both ends of the route. Confident of means to finish the road, and in full faith that the government would trust and aid their plans, its builders loaned their money and their credit. The sudden and widespread bankruptcy in 1873 involved them. In 1875 all their property, with 550 miles of finished road and the land earned and their 'corporate life' passed into the hands of their creditors, the bondholders, who became the new board of stockholders. The lost years caused by this bankruptcy and the honest transfer of all assets to the creditors, took most of the time granted by Congress to finish the whole road. To do it and get more funds they must have more time, and they have asked Congress to extend their time. The Senate, last Congress, by a large majority, voted the extension. The house, by a majority of 30, would have done the same but Speaker Randall ruled it to be a new grant or subsidy—which, by the rules, required discussion, and carried it too far down the list to be reached during the electoral commission excitement (ed.: the reference is to the disputed 1876 presidential election).

THE SOLE GROUND OF OPPOSITION

Meanwhile the opposition to subsidies documented as reported by the C.P.R.R. and the U.P.R.R—has put in peril both the Southern and the Northern roads.

CONFIDENCE BETRAYED

The people along both lines are liable to be defrauded. Pioneers moved along the routes of both at the risk of Indian wars—which they have had—and invested all their means to make farms and houses in the wilderness. During the Nez Perce War last summer in Whitman and Stevens counties and in northern Idaho the people fled to the towns for safety, leaving houses, gardens, wheat fields, stock, butter in the churn and flour in the sack, utensils, beds, trunks of clothing, all they had on earth, the savings of years, and the hope of the future. Some lost all. (Line missing) . . . until their capture, removed all danger, and let most of those families return to their homes. Over 3,000 more settlers moved into that region of natural wheat fields last autumn. They may this year be followed by as many more.

THEY RELY ON THE N.P.R.R. CO. TO TRANPORT THEIR GRAIN TO MARKET

After the middle of August the Snake River is too low for navigation. Their grain must lie over at a loss, or they must raise stock to get money for the comfort of their families and to pay taxes. They represent the long waiting pioneers in Montana and Dakota.

The N.P.R.R. pledges to connect the Missouri and the Columbia—the two great highways of commerce—at their first step, and then finish the roads to both oceans. It pledges to sell its lands to be thus earned, at $2.50 per acre. It protects the settlers in all their rights and hopes. It inspires their confidence. If it is defeated, those settlers must suffer more than any others. They must also remain in peril of new Indian outbreaks, which the road built would prevent. If Congress is misled to load the new bill so as to destroy it, those settlers, with all those in this northwest, will be defrauded of their just expectations and their rights.

THE OLYMPIA AND TENINO RAILROAD

T his enterprise was thought impossible two years ago. When the plan was completed and the county bonds pledged for the iron and rolling stock, and when the citizens had graded most of the road bed, many said it would not be finished, and more distrusted its value as an investment to the city and the county. A few men, five years ago, saw that Olympia and Thurston County could not afford to do without it.

The N.P.R.R. had located its terminus at Tacoma. In order to keep a fair portion of the business, which had centered at Olympia, and in order to grow with the sure growth of Washington—which must soon be a sovereign state—this enterprise was a *sine qua non*. They felt that it must be pushed on and made tributary to their own welfare, and thus to that of the public. It is the old story, which all sections must learn, that every trunk line railroad must have branch lines, as much as a tree must have branches in all directions. The vital sap of the trunk and branch is the business, which flows to and from every settlement, village and city. The only question is that of economy of transit. Time and power are the chief factors in the problem. It is the wagon against the railroad car. It is here a trip of two to six days, hauling a load of grain to market from Tenino or the Chehalis valley, and a load of goods back over rough, dusty or muddy roads, at a cost to the farmer of $2 a day at the least, instead of hiring the railroad to do the job in one day or two at one fourth the cost. In the former case you wear out your teams, wagons and harnesses on the road and spend money every day. In the latter your team is at work on the farm, opening new fields and cultivating the old ones better, while you board and lodge at home. The iron horse does your marketing cheaper and quicker than you can do it, and the $5 you save per week you can add to the value of your acres and the increase of your comforts.

This branch road was opened August 1st, when the first passenger train went through to Tenino. About 50 men, in small gangs, are leveling up, lining and ballasting the track. A powerful engine, named the E.N. Ouimette, for the gentleman who has been among the foremost in the enterprise, does the construction and train work, making two trips per day between Olympia and Tenino. Side tracks and turntables are to be made and cars completed immediately. The engineers have shown skill in the selection of the route and the construction of the track. When completed the road will be smooth, of easy grade, capable of a large freight and a quick transit business.

THE USE OF OUR NATIVE WOODS

The passenger car was built at Tumwater and furnished with the native ash and curly maple, shellacked and varnished, showing a neatness, beauty and durability far superior to every style of graining or painting. Too much cannot be said in favor of the use of our native woods in house finishing and furnishing. Their cheapness now commands their use. Their rich and ever-varying contrasts in texture of growth and coloring furnish a constant and pleasant picture in the hall—the parlor, the dining room, the library and the chamber, as well as in the public offices, steamboats and railroad cars. Examples of them can be seen in the finishing in part and furnishing of the Palace Hotel in San Francisco; in the custom house at Portland, mostly done in Oregon ash; and in the fine and tasteful furniture made by O.F.M. Co. for the O.B.N. Co.'s magnificent steamer *Wide West*. It is to be hoped that the O.S.N. Co. will finish wholly as well as furnish one of their new steamers with our native woods. Oil and shellac and varnish will give all the protection which painting and graining now do. The public taste is changing from dark mahogany and black walnut to the lighter colored ash, maple, cedar, spruce, oak, poplar or cotton wood and alder. It is a pity that farmers along the Cowlitz, Toutle, White, Chehalis, Willamette, and Columbia rivers have been burning off those trees to clear the land for grain, hay and vegetables. Soon every tree thus wasted would bring more money than the acre on which it grows. Such lumber sells now in market at an average of $30 per M.

A system of narrow gauge railroads running into our numerous valleys will bring those products of the forest, with those of the fields and orchard and pasture, into the manufacturing centres and marts of trade. The Seattle and White River railroad is one pioneer in this business. The Olympia and Tenino railroad—to be extended, we trust, into the Chehalis valley—will be another.

Yesterday, August 8th, Messrs. McMicken, Glover and Treadway, a committee appointed by the county commissioners to inspect and report upon the road-bed, construction and rolling stock, made their first official visit along the whole line, with a large excursion party from Olympia. Ex-Governor Gibbs being present on official business with the company added much to the pleasure of the occasion. The present officers of the company are Hon. J.P. Judson, President; Gen. P.I. McKinney, superintendent; Mr. Mason, Engineer.

When finished, the road can be run with three or four men. Trips will be made twice a day between Olympia and Tenino, connecting with the N.P.R.R. trains south and north; fare $1 and freight $1 ton from Olympia to Tenino, 15 miles.

EFFECT OF THE ROAD

It has given more confidence to property holders and business men in Olympia. People can come and go easily to all points. Freight and fares from Portland avoid the circuit via Tacoma, which will bring, it is said, more purchasers from Portland. The completion of this and other narrow gauge railroads into the valleys of Oregon and Washington, connecting them easily at all seasons with the navigable rivers and bays, and thus with the ocean will give more proof of the economy of this system for interior commerce. The energy and enthusiasm of the promoters deserves success. As a question of law, the late Judge McFadden, while in Congress secured an enabling act so well drawn and carefully guarded that the county bonds rest on a sure basis. If the managers put rates low enough to do all the present carrying business of the people, and increase it, as they can do annually, the investment will pay the banker and secure funds for an extended line.

G.H. ATKINSON

The First Train

Source:
The Oregonian Archives
Multnomah County Library

It will not surprise the reader to learn that George's interest in railroads
extended beyond the theoretical to the concrete, so it was fitting that
he was an enthusiastic passenger on the first passenger train headed
east from Portland through the Columbia Gorge and on to Walla Walla
and Dayton, Washington, November 21-2, 1882. Writing as he rode, his
telegraphed report to the Oregonian appeared on the day after he arrived
in Dayton. — Editor

REFLECTIONS OCCASIONED BY THE RAILROAD RIDE
UP THE COLUMBIA

BY REV. G.H. ATKINSON

(Oregonian, Nov. 23, 1882, p. 3)

DAYTON, W.T., Nov. 21, 1882

The O.R. & N. Co. had laid the plan and arranged all the
details. The river steamer R.B. Thompson waited at the dock
to welcome passengers. Clerks at the offices had tickets on sale all
day. The large wharf boat lay quietly at the Albina incline as it had
lain at other landings above. The train was ready with coaches and
Pullman cars. At 4:15 the transfer steamer glided gracefully down to
the wharf boat, guided as usual by the skillful hand of Capt. Troup.
A hundred or more passengers quietly passed into the various cars.
At the minute fixed, 4:35 P.M., the car bell rang and the train moved
out. Scores of spectators on the boats and along the line gazed at
the first through train to Montana, signal of the first through train
to New York, less than twelve months hence. Children cheered and
friends waved adieu and safe trip. At the first station, at the Depot
of the O & C. R.R., Willamette Valley passengers on the afternoon
train, destined for the upper Columbia valley, came aboard, having
had little delay. At 4:50 o'clock the train moved eastward, and at
6:50 we were at Bonneville, 42 miles from Portland. A half hour

for supper at the crowded restaurant of Mrs. Lee, gave a chance to those who had to wait for the second tables. Three hours later we were at The Dalles, 45 miles further, or 87 miles from Portland, thus saving 21 miles by the direct R.R. route to the Cascades. At 4:45 A.M. the train arrived at Umatilla, 99 miles from The Dalles, and 186 miles from Portland. At 6:30 we were called to breakfast at Wallula Junction, 26 miles from Umatilla and 214 from Portland. After thirty minutes for transferring to the N.P.R.R. we were en route to Walla Walla, 30 miles east and 240 from Portland, arriving at 8:30, dropping Pullmans and many passengers and receiving more, we were off at 8:45 for Prescott, 10 miles, near the junction of the Texas Ferry R.R. Here at 9:35 passengers separate for their respective destinations, either the Snake River and Palouse region, or Dayton and its numerous tributary valleys. At 10:15 AM with mixed train we leave Prescott and arrive at Dayton at 11:00, twenty miles more, or 282 miles from Portland, the end of the branch road.

INCIDENTS

The misty rain at Portland ceased at the Cascades, and further on the moon shone through the clouds. At The Dalles, the lighted hotels received a few passengers, but the throngs of past months had disappeared. It was pleasant for Mrs. Gov. Moody to leave part of her family at Salem at 1 P.M., and meet her older sons at her house in The Dalles at 10:30 P.M., riding in Pullman cars for the first time.

Above Hood River the light shone clear from the window of Mrs. Warner's hospitable home across the Columbia, but the sadness came to the heart, that one who had for many years looked out of that window, upon the grand river, would look out no more and greet friends and welcome them no more to her earthly home. Her work is done. She is welcome to the "mansion prepared".

THE SEASON

Mild weather and clouded skies indicate rain or snow. The mountain crests are already white. Light frosts have trimmed the deciduous trees and induced the plowed lands to finer tilth. Fall sown wheat in a few fields, already spreads a thick green carpet in the contrast with the sere, dry, brown of the bunch grass plains. Plows are in motion on the hills and the whole region is fast coming under the hand of the diligent cultivator.

The enterprise of Dr. D.S. Baker in building a railroad from Wallula to Walla Walla marked a new era in the upper Columbia basin. The mines had ceased to furnish business for the O.S.N. Co. and stock shipped down and goods shipped up, even at high rates, were insufficient factors to support a costly line of transportation. Its business was becoming dull part of the year and its future of uncertain outlook. A few farms were tilled along the streams, but wheat would not bear the tax of freight wagons 30 to 50 acres for through shipment, neither could it be brought to the river steamers in amounts large enough and so promptly as to win ships to our ports. It was a drug on the farm and at the mills.

Dr. Baker saw the absolute necessity of railroad transportation, at least from the interior valley to the boats on the Columbia river. He devised the plan for the Walla Walla valley first and laid it before the business men of that community. Some thought well of it. Others sneered at it as a wild scheme. Few helped and fewer sympathized when he undertook the work alone and with no experience at such things.

Having built and equipped the road as well as possible, mostly at his own cost, the light began to break. Freight and passengers sought the line. Plows broke wider areas of land. Agricultural implements came in larger quantities. Warehouses were built and filled. Steamers were piled high with merchandise. Thrift succeeded on the farms, and towns and villages grew. Prices were high, but crops were large. The upper Columbia was opened. A new empire was begun. Dr. Baker has been rewarded by dollars. He deserves the reward of honor among the people.

On a grander scale, the O.R. & N. and the N.P.R.R. have taken up and extended that initial enterprise of the O.S.N. and Dr. Baker. With combined wealth and energy, they proposed to do for the entire valley what Dr. Baker did partially for one valley. They push out railroad lines to all settlements with goods from the wholesalers, and in return receive the cereals, fruits, wood and stock of the farmers, within sight of their homes, and convey these products to central markets for foreign commerce. They have greatly lowered freights on necessities. They seem to work on the plan that it is wise railroad enterprise to create and extend business by giving the men who produce and who exchange products the chance to make profits. This is business. It pays them and secures their future. It pays the people and invites immigration.

OUTLOOK

With such opportunities of investment of cash and of labor, and such saving of time by quick and reliable transportation, the vast and varied resources of Oregon, Washington, Idaho and Montana bid fair to be rapidly developed.

Illustrations

Much of Atkinson's 'Report on Prisons' discusses the physical structure and inmate program at Charlestown, Massachusetts.

West Union school in Washington County, Oregon, circa 1900.

School classroom, late nineteenth century.

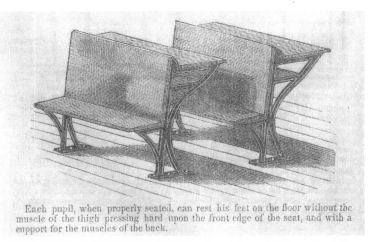

Each pupil, when properly seated, can rest his feet on the floor without the muscle of the thigh pressing hard upon the front edge of the seat, and with a support for the muscles of the back.

School furniture, mid-nineteenth century.

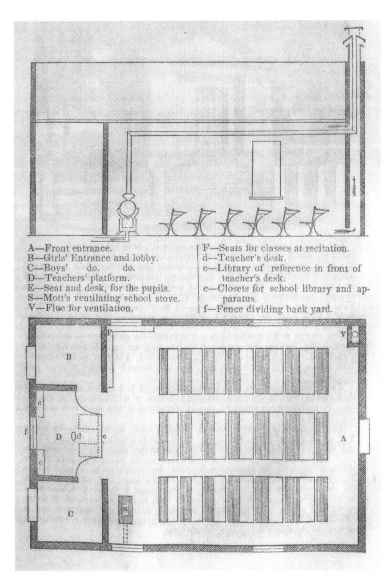

A—Front entrance.
B—Girls' Entrance and lobby.
C—Boys'   do.   do.
D—Teachers' platform.
E—Seat and desk, for the pupils.
S—Mott's ventilating school stove.
V—Flue for ventilation.

F—Seats for classes at recitation.
d—Teacher's desk.
e—Library of reference in front of
    teacher's desk.
c—Closets for school library and ap-
    paratus.
f—Fence dividing back yard.

Source: Barnard, Henry. *Practical Illustrations of the Principles of School Architecture.* Hartford: Case, Tiffany and Company, 1851. p. 45.

School classroom design, mid-nineteenth century.

TEACHER'S REPORT,

OF THE

Public School in District No. _5 3_____, County of _Washington_

Abstract of Monthly Summaries taken from the School Register for the School Term or Year commencing

April 23 188_3_ . *and ending* _July 18_, 188_3_

NAME OF MONTH.	1 Number of days taught	2 Whole No. of days' attendance	3 Whole No. of days' absence	4 Whole No. of days' tardiness	5 Whole No. of pupils enrolled on Register	6 Whole No. of pupils enrolled or Register	7 Total No. belonging	8 Average No. belonging	9 Per cent. of daily attendance	10 No. of new pupils entered Boys. Girls.
April	6	41	12	4	4	5	9	8	_	1
	28	93	62	18	4	5	9	7	5	
	24	84	43	8	4	5	9	6	4	
	7	38	12	4	2	5	9	5	4	
Total	68	215	129	84						

NOTICE.—Teachers will carefully read the instructions on the opposite page of this blank, and follow them strictly. County Superintendents must accept none but complete and correct reports.

[envelope fold with vertical text]

Public School

TEACHER'S REPORT

District No. _5 3_

County of _Washington_

STATE OF OREGON

I certify that the within report is a true statement of the condition of the Public School therein mentioned.

_____
Teacher.

FILED.

This ___ day of _____
188_3_

_____
County Superintendent.

Student enrollment and attendance forms were sent on to county superintendents. This attendance record is from Cornelius Public School, 1883.

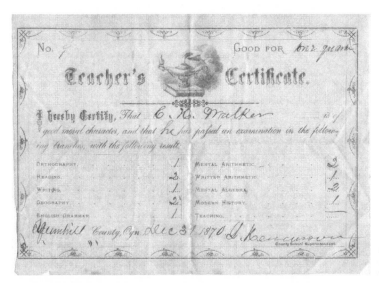

Source: Teacher's certificate from Yamhill County, Oregon. 1870. Cyrus Walker Papers, Pacific University Archives. (Used with permission)

Teaching certificates were required in order for local districts to receive state funding. This certificate is from Yamhill County.

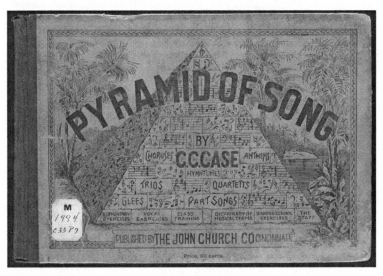

Source: Case, Charles Clinton. Pyramid of Song. Photograph of cover. Cincinnati: John Church Co., 1889. Library of Congress, Music Division. Web.

An instructional singing book from the 1880s meant for students of all ages.

REPORT OF THE PUBLIC SCHOOLS OF MULTNOMAH COUNTY FOR 1871-72.

Thirty-one districts have been laid off in this county, twenty five of which have been organized. Twenty-three have reported schools the last year, and received their orders for school money. Two failed to report, and thus forfeited their right to funds. Four districts of other counties reported pupils in this county, and drew their pro rata of funds.

The following summary of the reports will give an outline of the condition of the districts:

Number of voters reported.............................2,407
Number children between the age of 4 and 20 yrs..3,730
Number of males   "   "   "   "   ...1,923
Number females   "   "   "   "   ...1,807
Number of terms of school taught.................... 124
Number of pupils enrolled............................ 2,155
Average attendance....................................1,360
Number of teachers employed........................... 65
Number of male teachers employed...................... 33
Number of female "   "   32
Amount paid teachers during the year.. ....$20,889 49
Average paid teachers per term during the yr.   168 54
Amount paid teachers from county fund........ 14,402 08
Amount of incidental expenses.................... 4,454 33
Amount of district taxes levied.................... 22,301 73
Amount of district taxes collected................ 20,381 73
Amount of cost of new buildings, lots and re-
    pairs.. 15,137 11
Whole amount paid for school purposes......... 40,602 00
Value of public school buildings................... 46,300 00
Value—approximate—of school lots.............. 53,700 00
Value of public school property..................100,000 00

District No. 1, Portland, reports 2,452 children of school age—a gain of 82; of whom 1,126 are enrolled in the public schools, and 815 in private and corporate schools, leaving 511 who do not attend any school.

Great credit is due this city for the liberal provisions made by voluntary taxation to support and improve the public schools the past year.

The lesson of history is that the better we make our schools, and the more completely they reach and train the masses, the safer and happier shall we be, and the more assured will be our future prosperity.   G. H. ATKINSON,
Sup't. Public Schools of Multnomah Co.

Source: *Morning Oregonian.* Portland, OR: 23 Mar 1872. p. 3.

Atkinson's "Report of the Public Schools of Multnomah County for 1871-72" as it appeared in the Oregonian on March 23, 1872.

WILLIAM MILNOR ROBERTS*
CIVIL ENGINEER ; UNITED STATES ENGINEER OHIO
AND MONONGAHELA RIVERS.

Source: Smith, Percy F. *Notable Men of Pittsburgh and Vicinity*. Pittsburgh: Pittsburgh Printing Company, 1901. p. 28.

W. Milnor Roberts, a civil engineer who was engaged in building canals, bridges and railroads in many states. Roberts directed the engineering study that fixed the route of the Northern Pacific Railroad through the mountainous areas of Montana and Idaho.

Source: *Morning Oregonian*. Portland, OR: 20 Sep 1873. p. 1.

In 1873 the Northern Pacific Railroad was well under way. However, progress halted when a massive national financial crisis was triggered by the sudden collapse of the financial empire of Jay Cooke, lead financier of the NPRR.

EASTERN NEWS.

(BY TELEGRAPH TO THE OREGONIAN.)

The Suspension of Jay Cooke & Co.—Its Influence on the Exchange.

NEW YORK, Sept. 18.—The day in financial circles has been one of unusual excitement growing out of the suspension of Jay Cooke & Co. Failures which have heretofore occurred were mere local affairs and produced little excitement compared with the one of to-day. The connection of Jay Cooke & Co., with the Government in effecting loans during the war and in funding operations since has given the firm a national reputation, which, of course, only intensified the excitement consequent upon their suspension. The money market was unfavorably affected by the failures of to-day and a general distrust was enforced thereby. The *Express* says the Government to-day in refusing to sell gold took the first step toward stopping a spread of the panic and calls upon Secretary Richardson to let loose a portion of the currency balance. The Government's are weak and unsettled in tone. At the close State bonds were quiet. The effect of the suspension was decided on the Stock Exchange where a heavy decline in values took place, with a feverish, unsettled market. During the afternoon there were constant rumors of failures but at the close of business the only additional ones were Robinson & Snydam and Richard Schell.

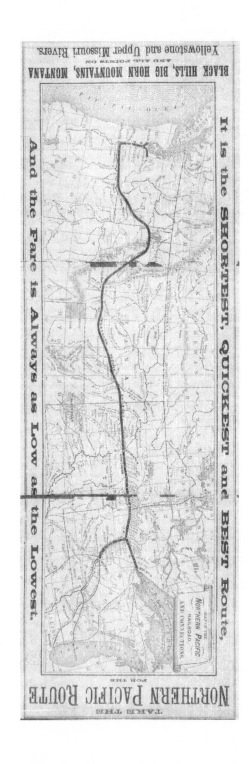

Source: Northern Pacific Railroad Company, 1879. *It is the shortest, quickest and best route : and the fare is always as low as the lowest.* Rand, McNally & Co., Printers. Beinecke Rare Book & Manuscript Library, Yale University.

Projected route of Northern Pacific Railroad in 1879 advertisement. At this time the eastern end of the line had been completed as far as Bismarck, North Dakota and the western end completed from Kalama, Washington as far as Olympia and Tacoma, Washington.

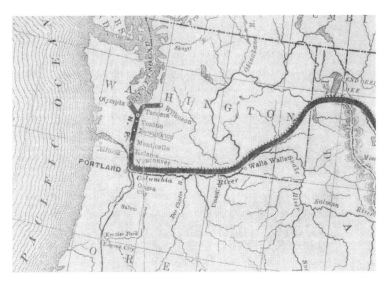

Detail from 1879 Northern Pacific Railroad advertisement.

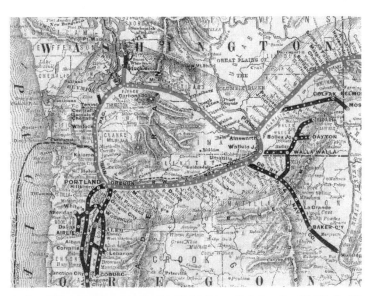

Detail from 1887 Northern Pacific Railroad route map.

Source: Davidson, I.G. *Oregon and the Pacific Northwest. Glimpses of pretty spots along the valley of the Columbia River ... Scenery along the line of the Northern Pacific Railroad, showing the new trans-continental route in process of construction.* G.H. Himes, printer. Beinecke Rare Book & Manuscript Library, Yale University.

This 1879 view of Portland was used in a Northern Pacific Railroad viewbook, showing scenery along their rail lines.

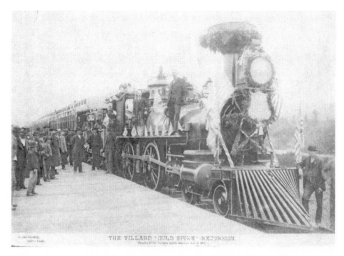

Source: F. Jay Haynes. Villard 'Gold Spike' excursion. Photograph. 1883. Washington State Historical Society. (Used with permission)

Northern Pacific Railroad locomotive during the opening of their first New York to Portland run in 1883.

CAPT. J. C. AINSWORTH

Source: Wright, E.W. *Lewis & Dryden's marine history of the Pacific Northwest ...* Portland: Lewis & Dryden, 1895. p. 31.

Capt. J.C. Ainsworth, President of the Oregon Steam Navigation Co. and officer in numerous banks, played an important part in river and railroad transportation in the Columbia River Valley.

Source: WCPA 10-1. Oregon Digital. Wasco County Pioneer Association/Columbia Gorge Discovery Center. (Used with permission)

The Oregon Steam Navigation Company's Lower Columbia River Steamboat "S.G. Reed", 1878.

Entrance of the Columbia River
Ship Tonquin crossing the bar. 25th March, 1811

Source: Franchère, Gabriel. *Narrative of a Voyage to the Northwest Coast of America in the years 1811, 1812, 1813, and 1814 ...* New York: Redfield, 1854. p. 88. Web. Project Gutenberg.

Fear of wreckage on the Columbia River bar hampered full development of the harbors along the lower river. George Atkinson stated that the deployment of river pilots in the Astoria area had greatly reduced the risk of wreckage, leading to greater commercial development along the river, and lower insurance rates.

Source: Kiehl, H. Ambrose. Northern Pacific Railroad loading area for the ferry TACOMA, November 8, 1900. University of Washington Libraries, Special Collections, UW 36698. (Used with permission)

Ferry loading structure in Kalama, Washington. The ferry Tacoma transported Northern Pacific Railroad trains across the Columbia River between Goble, Oregon and Kalama, Washington from 1884 to 1908.

John Mitchell represented Oregon in the United States Senate during two separate terms. He was accused by George Atkinson and others (including editor Harvey Scott of the Oregonian) of using his role as chair of the Senate Railroad Committee to sabotage completion of the Northern Pacific Railroad, in order to facilitate a connection with the Union Pacific Railroad through Salt Lake City.

Tabitha Brown, a founder of Pacific University and "Mother of Oregon". Her school for orphans of the Oregon Trail grew into Tualatin Academy and Pacific University.

Harvey Clarke, a graduate of Oberlin College, was the pastor of the Forest Grove Congregational Church at its founding in 1845. His gift of land was a critical step in beginning Tualatin Academy and Pacific University.

Source: Jackson, E.A. Old College Hall and Academy Hall c. 1864-65. Pacific University Archives. (Used with permission)

Oldest known photograph of the Pacific University campus, dating from 1864 or 1865.

Source: Pacific University 1866-67 freshman class.. Pacific University Archives. (Used with permission)

Pacific University freshman class of 1866-7. The son of George and Nancy Atkinson (also named George) is in the front row, second from the right.

Source: Shuster & Davidson. Portrait of Agero Nosei, c. 1870s; Shuster & Davidson. Portrait of Kin Saito, c. 1870s; Portrait of Hatsutaro Tamura, c. 1875. Pacific University Archives. (Used with permission)

Agero Nosei [Nose Sakae] (top left), Kin Saito [Sato Momotaro] (bottom left), and Hatsutaro Tamura [Tamura Hatsutaro] (above), Japanese students who graduated from Pacific University in 1876.

IMPERIAL PORTRAIT.

Source: Abell, Frank G. Class of 1878. Pacific University Archives. (Used with permission)

Group photo of the Pacific University Class of 1878. Front row—from left—Mrs. Mary A. (Creswell) [sic] Eagen, Miss Elvia H. Fearnside, Mrs. Laura M. (Hoxter) Whalley; 2nd row—from left—Deacon DeWitt Clinton Latourette, Milton W. Smith, Samuel R. Stott, Horace Sumner Lyman; 3rd row—from left—Mrs. Mary F. (Lyman) McCoy, [Mrs.] Ella Scott Latourette (Mrs. D. C.), Miss Mary Stacey Eaton. DeWitt Clinton Latourette, Milton W. Smith, and Samuel R. Stott all became lawyers. DeWitt Clinton Latourette married Ella Scott (sister of Pacific alumnus Harvey Scott) and they lived in Oregon City.

A side view of Old College Hall in its original location in the foreground and Academy Hall in the background.

An early photo of Old College Hall, Academy Hall, and Herrick Hall on the Pacific University campus.

Sidney Harper Marsh (above), first president of Pacific University. Served 1853-1879.

Jacob Ellis (top right), third president of Pacific University. Served 1883-1891.

Henry Failing (bottom right), a prominent Portland business leader and three term mayor, served Pacific University as both trustee and treasurer.

George Atkinson (1819-89), missionary, educator, "public spirit".

The Northwest Coast
A Booklet about the Railroad

Evidently encouraged by the reception of Atkinson's earlier articles, Editor Harvey Scott of the *Oregonian* invited Atkinson to expound further on the subject. Over a period of two years George penned a series of lengthier commentaries on issues bearing on the northern transcontinental rail project. They are studded with information about engineering, geology, agriculture, politics, meteorology, insurance, ocean shipping, and the history of both the Northern Pacific and Central Pacific/Union Pacific Railroads.

The first appeared on Apr. 4, 1876 and the last on Aug. 13, 1878. Several of them were soon republished as a booklet, "The Northwest Coast," the full text of which appears here. Sponsored by the Portland Board of Trade, it went through at least two printings, and, according to one source, was also translated into German and circulated among potential investors in Europe.

Two sections of the work are of special interest:

1. Atkinson offers an extensive, detailed criticism (185-192) of the political maneuverings of Oregon Senator John Mitchell. Mitchell, chair of the Senate Committee on Railroads, was blocking action on a bill to extend the time allotted to the Northern Pacific Railroad for its completion. Mitchell, who was trying to add to the project a line running from Umatilla, Oregon to Ogden, Utah, is described as serving the interests of a competitor, the Union Pacific Railroad.

2. Atkinson, who worked on the family farm in Vermont as a young man and majored in Chemistry at Dartmouth, adds a projection of the agricultural potential of the region, focusing especially on

eastern Oregon and Washington. Geology, climate, crops and soil composition are discussed. His effort is to show that the new railroad, enhanced by branch lines, would bring growth and prosperity to regions that were then seen as little more than deserts.

The Northwest Coast

Source:
Oregon Historical Society

THE NORTHWEST COAST

T he Northwest Coast, including Oregon, Washington and Idaho. A series of articles upon the Northern Pacific Railroad in its relations to the basins of the Columbia and of Puget Sound— endorsed by the Portland Board of Trade. First published in the *Oregonian*, and in pamphlet form in 1878.

The statistical facts, collated with other arguments, carry their own force of reason to the thoughtful citizens of this section, and to the broad-minded statesmen of every section of our country. The hope is cherished that they will give some aid to secure the needed Congressional Legislation, and thus confer a common benefit upon this prospective empire of the Pacific Northwest, and upon our country.

THE NORTHWEST COAST – LAND GRANTS – VALUE OF LAND INCREASED

Railroads give actual value to lands. Even where fares and freights equal the old coach and wagon rates, the time saved is money to the farmer and the merchant. A trip of six days for a man and a team would be required to take a ton of wheat (33 bushels) 100 miles, at a cost of not less than $12, or $2 a day, which is equal to 36 cents per bushel. The car will put that wheat into market in half a day, and leave man and team at home to work. Six days of work on, say, six acres are worth $12, which sum is added to the value of the land, or to other land. This sum is equal to $2 per acre per years, or the interest of $20 per acre. If the land was worth $5 per acre without the railroad, it is worth $25 with it, counting merely the time saved. But if the railroad rate is one-half or one-third the wagon rate, as is usually the case, it will save enough to add a hundred per cent more to the original value of the land. The Willamette farmlands, near the railroad, within a hundred miles of Portland, have risen steadily in about those proportions. The lands in the interior valleys of California have risen to a much higher value since their railroads came, although the rates of transportation are reported to be very high.

But the lands east of the mountains, far from river or railroad, have very little value, except for stock ranges. The finest wheat lands must remain untilled. Coal fields must remain undeveloped. Even minerals cannot be mined, except the precious metals in rich deposits, without railroads.

Mineral and coal regions, to a large extent, are valueless until cheap transportation is afforded. The coal of Wyoming, the copper and the coarser silver ores of Utah and Nevada, waited for the railroad car to give them value.

The original Union Pacific Railroad land grant was 12,077,981 91-100 acres. The sales to Dec. 31, 1875 were 1,193, 942 91-100 acres, for $5,336,044.02, at the average price of $4.47 per acre. An equal value, surely, was given to the same number of acres on the even sections retained by the government. The total value of the original land grant, at the minimum rates of $2.50 per acre, was $30,194,952.

The coal, iron, copper, silver, marble, lead, cinnabar, etc., long hid in the rugged mountains, but now brought into use, will far more than compensate for any poor lands.

The original number of acres of the land grant to the Central Pacific Railroad and the California & Oregon Railroad was 13, 222,400. If valued at $2.50 an acre, it makes the amount of the grant $33,056,000. It is fair to say that these two roads are giving almost the entire estimated value of $63,250,950 to these lands, and an equal sum to Government lands lying adjacent to them.

Millions of acres, lying outside the limits of these railroad grants, now have a market value impossible before the road was built. The Illinois Central Railroad added several hundred per cent to the real worth of the belt of land, sixty miles wide, along its track, enriching the people as well as the railroad corporation.

The route of the Northern Pacific Railroad is through a good belt of country. Its capacities for pasturage, for the cereal, for vegetables and fruits, have been proved. Soil and climate invite settlers. But these products cannot be transported to the markets of the world. It is useless to raise any for export. The lands lie idle, as they have done for a thousand years. The lumber of the mountains falls and decays, or is burned up. The coal beds are untouched. The minerals cannot be brought to use. The lands must remain unsold and unsurveyed for want of buyers. Complete the road from the Columbia to the Missouri, and this strip, 80 miles wide and 2,000 long, of 160,000 square miles, or 102,400,000 acres, will acquire a real worth, at one dollar per acre, of $102,400,000. At two dollars per acre it will be worth $204,800,000. At the Government price for even sections, $2.50 per acre, the whole amount will be worth $256,000,000, of which the Government will receive half, or $128,000,000, and the builders of the road the other half. That new value will be created by the road, and will become steadily available, to the Government and people. Without the road it cannot exist; without the road it never will exist.

FREIGHTS SAVED—Roads built on the basis of these land grants save certain sums in the cost of Government freights over these routes, which may be fairly added to the land values created by them. Senator Stewart, of Nevada, said that "the cost of the overland service, for the whole period, from the acquisition of our Pacific Coast possessions to the completion of the Pacific Railroad, was $8,000,000 per annum, and constantly increasing." The editor of the *Pacific Tourist* adds: "Since the building of that road, say for seven years—1869 to 1876—the cash paid to railroad companies, for one-half charge of transportation per year, was about $1,200,000 per annum, or the sum of $8,400,000 for the whole time." In 1876 it would have been over $14,000,000. The average for seven years, at $10,000,000 per year, would amount to more than $70,000,000. Thus, the total saving in seven years, to the United States Government, was $61,600,000. This is equal to the creation, or earning of $61,600,000 for the Government.

It is an item worthy of notice, that the Government paid the interest on the Pacific Railroad bonds during these seven years, an average of $3,897,129 per year, or a total of $27,279,906. Deducting this sum from $61,600,000, there was a net profit, over all expenses, to the United States of $34,420, 094. It is fair to estimate these savings as so much value added to the belt of country traversed by the road.

The writer quoted remarks that "these figures do not include vast amounts of incidental items, which would have been of incalculable trouble, or immense expense to the United States, such as the indemnities constantly being paid, by the United States, for the destruction of life and private property by Indians; also depredations of Indians on property in Government service; increased mail facilities and decreased mail expenses; prevention of Indian wars; the rapid sale of Government lands, and the energetic development of the mining interest of all the Territories."

Honorable Henry Wilson, in a speech before the Senate, Thirty-seventh Congress, boldly said: "I give no grudging vote in giving away either money or land. I would sink $100,000,000 to build the road, and do it cheerfully, and I think I had done a great thing for my country." (p.303)

The average transfer of through passengers, on the Pacific Railroad, per year, for four years, was 72, 183, and of way passengers, 318,182. The average transfer of freight, for 1872 and 1875, was over three billions of pounds per year.

This power of transportation is a definite commercial value, created by the railroad. It is a commodity produced where none existed before, as real as the product of new grain fields, or new manufacturing. The only question is, whether such wealth producers are needed, or are in excess. When the New York Central Railroad was first proposed, farmers objected to the project as an injury to the freight business by wagons, and, in fact, to the business of raising horses. The one answer to all such objections is that two, and perhaps three, broad belts of the Continent, within our National limits, can be traversed by new railroads, and their resources developed by them, and in no other way can this ever be done.

[145]

A MILITARY NECESSITY—The Northern Pacific Railroad is truly a military necessity, in its sections, as the Union Pacific or Central Pacific Railroads were in their section.

It will annually save millions of dollars to the Government in freights alone.

It will quell Indian outbreaks so quickly and effectually, that they will be less and less likely to occur. Such outbreaks do not now happen, as formerly, in Nebraska, Wyoming, Utah and Nevada. Had the Northern Pacific Railroad been completed, the Black Hills War would have been speedily closed, and with less sacrifice of life. The present war with Chief Joseph's band of Nez Perces could have been nipped in the bud if the Northern Pacific Railroad had been built.

A NATIONAL NECESSITY—The one Pacific Railroad is now developing a central tier of states across the Continent. More than any other agency, it lifted Nevada to this position. Utah would be the next State, but for the antagonism of Mormonism. Wyoming hastens to join the rank. Nebraska was ushered into the list while yet the Pacific Railroad was making its way through her prairies.

SOUND STATESMANSHIP DEMANDS THE NORTHERN PACIFIC RAILROAD—The following items show the business of Utah in 1875: The value of imports was, in that year, $9,150,851; the value of farm products, $7,861,772; miscellaneous, $860, 851; mineral products (mostly silver bullion), $6,145,211); manufactures, $2,805,000; making (exclusive of flour), $1,603, 985; $17,310,000. The valuation of assessable property, according to the Auditor's report on 1875, was $23,289,189.

On this property, the aggregate taxes, assessed in 1875, were $58.222.95. To the Pacific Railroad a large portion of this business and wealth is due.

The assessed value of property in California in 1864-5, when the Central Pacific Railroad was begun, was $180,484,949.85. The assessed value five years later, in 1869, when the overland railroad was done was $237,483,175.07. A gain of $56,998,225.22, or about 32 per cent, or 6.4 per cent per year. The assessed value in 1874-

5, five years later, was $611,495,197, a gain of $374,012,021.93, or about 150 per cent, in five years, or 31.6 per cent per year.

These values are as well sustained as any values are sustained in any other part of the country. Their vast increase is largely—mostly due to the Pacific Railroad.

It is not certain that the Northern Pacific Railroad will produce similar results as quickly; but the resources of the northern route are as vast, as varied, and more permanent; and they will ultimately be grandly developed.

Dakota, Montana, Idaho, Washington and Oregon wait for this road. It will stimulate all their energies. It will establish vigorous settlements. It will open new regions. It will unfold the hidden treasures of the soil, the mines, the forests, the river, the lakes and the ocean. It will hasten the immigrations, by giving confidence to the people that their labors and enterprise shall be rewarded.

INCREASE OF POPULATION—In 1860, the population of the Pacific slope, was 619,000. In 1870, it has doubled. In 1876, it had again increased 40 per cent.

It is safe to calculate upon six per cent increase annually on the completion of this road. Grant the present population of Oregon, Washington and Idaho to be 200,000—ten years at 6 per cent will add 158,874, or a total of 358,874. The increase may be double that amount, giving over a million of people to these three States, as they will then be, in twenty years.

It is the part of good statesmanship, to provide for the future welfare of our country, it would seem a present duty to establish this tier of States on our northern border from the lakes to the Pacific. In order to do this every hand and every voice ought to help on the building of this road.

The lands granted, if sold at $2.50 per acre minimum, will give that sum in value by the construction of this overland road. Thus the value of the grant being fairly earned, and in no sense a gift.

The Government and the people alike make a large profit by the subsidy. The builders do the same. It is like laying out a town site, and giving half the lots to settlers, who will build houses, and on them thus double or quadruple the value of the remaining lots.

A VALUABLE INVESTMENT—Land subsidies for transcontinental railroads are good investments for the people. They make one acre worth two, three and four, or a dozen acres of the same quality, which have no railroad facilities. The cry against such subsidies is absurd and misleading. To prevent such grants is to defraud the people. Its encouragement sets the wheels of industry in motion, employs laborers, feeds the hungry, opens new avenues for business, and adds to the National wealth.

The arguments which apply to the Northern Pacific Railroad apply with equal force to the Southern Pacific Railroad, or Texas Pacific Railroad.

Wilderness regions along that belt of highway will become rich States by thus opening the highway of commerce.

Similar reasons urge the building of cross-roads, like the P., D., & S.L. road, and the S & W.W.R.R., which will be of far more worth than any built in the Eastern States. If this increased value is given to regions traversed by railroads, which does not exist without them, it is fair and wise to give the builders a share in the wealth which they create.

The iron, the coal, the manufactories, the skilled and the unskilled labor of the country wait to be employed on such National enterprises.

ITS SOCIAL AND MORAL POWER—In the problem of a Nation's life easy intercommunication is found to be an essential factor. Already our nation feels the vital force of the Union and Central Pacific. The heterogeneous population that presses into new regions, especially into those rich in the precious metals, and in mineral and agricultural resources as the electric chain, needs that constant connection with the whole body politic.

Interlace the Continent with railroads and you ensure the unity of the people, by the power of community of interest which must and will be quickly felt. No power acts with such force now to harmonize the North and the South, the East and the West. This force is needed along the Northern and Southern belts from the Atlantic to the Pacific.

ITS ECONOMY OF FORCE AS A PROBLEM OF ENGINEERING— It is a fixed principle of engineering that it is as easy to draw seven loaded cars and a level track, seventy feet, as it is to raise them one foot. The wear and tear of machinery of the track, combined with the strain of force required to draw such a load show the equivalent to be as seventy feet in length to one in height. On hearing this principle stated by an engineer, as it was new to me and the revelation of important results, I stated it to General Tilton, a well-known engineer of high standing, for explanation and verification. With the carefulness of a mathematician, he answered that it was nearly correct as the elements of the problem involved could be stated; that it was often discussed and affirmed by E.F. Johnson, Esq., consulting engineer of the Northern Pacific Railroad, the teacher of us all.

It is a working rule, which we can safely follow, he said. Moreover, when weights increase the equivalents increase. For example, fourteen loaded cars can be drawn one hundred and forty feet on a level track as easy and with as little wear and tear and strain as they can be lifted one foot, but the law of equivalents is not exactly the same for the higher numbers.

Do you mean, General, that it is as easy and economical to run a freight train of seven loaded cars around a mountain seventy miles as to lift it one mile high over that mountain? Yes, he replied. Is it as easy and as economical to draw a loaded train of 14 cars 140 miles on a level around a mountain as to lift them one mile high over it? Yes, he said, that is a practical fact. How would it be with 21 loaded cars? The General replied that the same law operates, yet the tests and figures have not been made to show how much it may be modified.

General, how do the two Pacific Railroad routes, via the Northern Pacific Railroad and the Union and Central Pacific Railroad, compare as to gradients? Those of the Northern Pacific Railroad are far the lowest and easiest. For example, they (the Central Pacific Railroad) climb the Nevadas over 7,000 feet, descend into the valley of the Humboldt about 3,000, ascend again about 2,000 at Promontory Point, and 1,000 more at Coopers'; and they reach 8,200 above the sea at Sherman. The Northern Pacific Railroad runs through valleys from 1,000 to 3,000 feet, and at no point rises higher than 5,000 feet above sea level. It is the valley route across the Continent. This is the substance of a conversation with General Tilton, at Tacoma, four years ago, which is reported from memory, as I trust, accurately.

In conversation with Edwin F. Johnson, Esq., in Chicago, in October, 1868, who was then understood to be the engineer-in-chief of the Northern Pacific Railroad, he said that he began more than 30 years before, in Connecticut, and followed his business as an engineer through New York, Ohio, Michigan and farther West, constantly studying the face of the Continent and the laws of its climate, and that he found the isothermal line constantly veering Northward, and the surface of the country more level and better adapted for agriculture and a population. He added that the proposed route for the Northern Pacific Railroad, so far as the preliminary survey had been made, showed easy gradients compared with the Central route, and that the actual distance, by measure, to ocean waters, on Puget Sound, was about three hundred miles less then to ocean water at San Francisco, and that two hundred miles more were saved by easier gradients, making 500 miles gained by this route over the other of land travel, while the ocean route from Puget Sound to China, being on the arc of a great circle, is about 400 miles shorter than the route from San Francisco.

Having given this intelligent, inquisitive and venerable engineer many facts respecting the mildness of our North Pacific Coast climate, confirming his tentative observations and carefully formed theories—which testimony seemed very grateful to him—our interview of half an hour closed. It left the conviction in my own mind that every step in the progress of such a vast enterprise must be taken under the guidance, and subject to the most rigid and accurate tests of engineering skill, and, when so made, its success will be assured with mathematical certainty.

On the subject of routes, W. Milnor Roberts. United States civil engineer and engineer-in-chief of the Northern Pacific Railroad in his special report of a reconnaissance of the route for the Northern Pacific Railroad, between Lake Superior and Puget Sound, in 1870, via the Columbia River, makes the following statements:

An examination of the profile of the Union Pacific and Central Pacific lines, between Omaha and Sacramento, a distance of 1775 miles, shows that there are four main summits: Sherman Summit, on the Black Hills, about 550 miles from Omaha, 8,235 feet above the sea; one on the Rocky Mountains, at Aspen Summit, about 935 miles from Omaha, 7,463 feet; one at Humboldt Mountain, about 1,245 miles from Omaha, 6,076; and another on the Sierra Nevada (only 105 miles from the western terminus of Sacramento), 7,062; whilst from a point West of Cheyenne to Wasatch, a continuous length of 450 miles, every portion of the road is more than 6,000 feet above the sea; being about 1,000 feet, on this long distance, higher than the highest summit on the Northern Pacific Railroad route, whilst, for the corresponding distance on the Northern Pacific route, the average elevation is under 3,000 feet, or 3,000 feet less than on the Union and Central line. The highest summit on the Northern Pacific line is about three thousand feet lower than the Sherman Summit, on the Union Pacific.

On the Union Pacific road the profile also shows that for nine hundred continuous miles, from Sidney westward, the road has an average height of over 5,000 feet, and the lowest spot on that distance is more than 4,000 feet above the sea; whereas on the Northern route only sixty miles, at most, are as high as 4,000 feet; and the corresponding distance of nine hundred miles, extending from the mouth of the Yellowstone to the Valley of Clark's River, is, on an average, about 3,000 feet lower than the Union Pacific line. Then, allowing that 1,000 feet of elevation causes a decrease of temperature only three degrees, there is substantial reason for the circumstance, now well authenticated, that the snows on the Northern route are much less troublesome than they are on the Union and Central route. At the same time, it should not be claimed that there will be no trouble from snow on the Northern line. The impress I wish to create is this: That a line can be so located, between the Valley of the Missouri and the mouth of the Columbia River, and to Puget Sound, that, for the greater portion of the distance, it will not encounter any serious trouble from snow; and that, in the passage of the Belt Range, between the Yellowstone and the upper Missouri, and the crossing of the Rocky Mountains, at Deer Lodge Pass, no greater obstacles from snow are likely to be met with than have already been encountered and overcome on roads in New England States and the States of New York.

The grades beyond the Missouri, along the valley of the Yellowstone, to near the Bozeman Pass, like those East, will undulate within the general limit of about forty feet per mile, although it may be deemed advisable, at a few points, for short distances, to run to a maximum of fifty-three feet per mile.

The height of the country, upon which the line is traced, may be approximately stated thus, beginning at Lake Superior, going westward:

	Miles	Ave. Height above Sea
Duluth to Dakota valley	300	1,200 ft.
Yellowstone River	300	2,200 ft.
Along Yellowstone	400	2,600 ft.
Flathead Valley	300	3,000 ft.
Lewis or Snake River	200	3,000 ft.
Puget Sound	500	400 ft.

Lake Superior to Puget Sound, via Portland, 2,000 miles; direct line, 1775 miles.

The difference between direct and Columbia River route, 225 miles, is more than made up by its lower grades. Compare this with the profits of the finished line of the Union and Central Pacific Roads. Properly, the comparison should be made from Chicago, the terminus on Lake Michigan, of the Omaha line. There are on that route, approximately, as follows

Chicago to Omaha	500	1,000 ft.
Near Cheyenne	516	3,300 ft.
Coopers	87	7,300 ft.
Promontory Point	482	6,200 ft.
Humboldt	406	4,750 ft.
Reno	130	4,000 ft.
Auburn	45	4,400 ft.
Sacramento	39	300 ft.
San Francisco	135	50 ft.
Chicago to San Francisco	2,410	

On the Northern Pacific line there need be but two principal summits, whilst on the other there are four, the lowest of which is about a thousand feet higher than the highest on the Northern route. If, therefore, the roads were the same length between the Pacific waters and the great lakes and navigable rivers East of the Rocky Mountains, the advantage would be largely in favor of the Northern route; but this actual distance is 410 miles less, and the equated distances for the ascents and descents in its favor will be very considerable in addition.

The last remark of the engineer, Mr. Roberts, doubtless applies to the gain of force and economy of low grades, which is equivalent, in the engineer's mathematical estimate, to a definite number of miles. Engineer Johnson estimated 200 miles of gain for the whole route.

As an attesting fact, it is reported from one of the directors of the Central Pacific Railroad, that the cost of wear and tear of their railroad 200 miles over the Nevadas, including machinery and increase of force demanded, is equal to 1,100 miles of expense of the rest of their road on lower grades.

[153]

As another attesting fact, it is reported that the Reading Railroad, of four tracks for transporting coal 44 miles to market, was first constructed along the side of a hill, requiring a great force to carry the trains over such an elevation. On the estimate of their engineer, they found that the road-bed could be lowered about 32 feet, and the four tracks relaid at a cost of about $2,000,000, and the economy of force and wear and tear thus saved would be annually the interest on $1,000,000 above this extra cost. They decided to abandon the old road-bed and build a new one.

The facts and principles thus far adduced from the highest authority of engineers, show that the Northern Pacific Railroad runs through a series of valleys that extend, with but little interruption, across the Continent. Of the remarkable pass at Deer Lodge, well named the Gate of the Mountains, Mr. Roberts says: "The whole 40 miles from Deer Lodge City to the summit of the Rocky Mountains, by this route, can be built as cheaply as roads are built through prairie countries generally."

A remarkable circumstance connected with this pass will convey a clear view of its particularly favorable character. Private parties engaged in gold mining in a gold field, which exists abundantly on both sides of the Rocky Mountains, have dug a ditch across this summit, which is only eighteen feet deep at the apex of the divide, through which they carry the water of 'Divide Creek', a tributary of the Missouri, across to the Pacific side, where it is used in gold-washing, and the waste water passes into the pacific Ocean. This has justly been termed 'highway robbery'.

THE NORTHERN PACIFIC RAILROAD FIXED BY NATURE— These principles and facts must control the Western end of the road. Its course down the Valley of the Columbia is by a natural law as fixed as the flow of the waters that cut this channel to the ocean. It is the natural route for the transportation of freights. If not built there at first, competition will ultimately compel it to this line, as the great transcontinental route for the Pacific and Asiatic traffic.

THE CLIMATE FAVORS IT—The temperate climate conserves the goods in transit. While torrid heats destroy 5 per cent, of the value of teas in transit through them, this route, through a belt of such cool and even temperature, keeps all such goods in perfection. This is also true of fruits, grain, flour, and, doubtless, many other articles of merchandise. It is destined to be the most rapid, regular route for freight and passage across the Continent, as it has the easiest and lowest grades, and the fewest dangers of interruptions from snows and storms.

THE LAW OF COMMERCE DICTATES THIS ROUTE—The demands of its commerce, like that of all railroads, will direct its route through the most prolific part of the basin of the Columbia. The countries that have the largest annual harvests, or power of harvests, will naturally be traversed on its way to the sea. Judging from the contour of this upper basin of the Columbia, coming on its surveyed route by Pend d'Oreille Lake to near the mouth of the Lewis, or Snake River, it will cross that narrow stream; then skirt the foothills around to The Dalles; then through the Cascade Mountains to the Willamette; thence making one crossing, opposite Kalama, below the winter ice on the Columbia, and thence completing its connection with the terminus on Puget Sound. The charter expressly requires the line to be North of the 45th degree of latitude, to some point on Puget Sound, via "the valley of the Columbia River," with a branch across the Cascade Mountains to Puget Sound. On this route it will easily drain the products of the richest agricultural counties of Eastern Oregon and Washington, viz: Stevens, Whitman, Columbia, Walla Walla, Umatilla and Wasco, and will secure its share of the vast and increasing trade of the Willamette Valley. It will largely assure the Oregon & California and the O.C. Railroad traffic, and thus our welfare. It will, indeed, lose half of the land grant for the distance passed in a State, but its gain in freights, and in the route will, no doubt, compensate for this loss. But, whatever may be the opinions and wishes of the different sections interested in this route, we can hardly doubt that the two elements that must, and will decide the question, will be the best grades, and the best and most steady supply of freights. These two laws hold with a force that controls such enterprises.

WHEN AND HOW CAN THE ROAD BE BUILT?—The whole Northwest is more interested in the fact of the completed road than in its route. Hope on this point was blighted when Messrs. Jay Cooke & Company failed. Its construction has, to some minds, seemed less and less probable during all four years of the panic.

OBJECTIONS—Thoughtful men question the possibility of securing funds to build it. Some have distrusted its Board of Directors, and charged its officials with wasting the funds of confiding bondholders. Some complain that its land grant is too large, and that it ought to be restored to the people.

ANSWER TO OBJECTIONS—It is very probable in the flush times of 1871-2, when there was every prospect of selling bonds enough to complete the road, that the expenditures for depots and rolling stock were in excess of the present need, yet they were probably in anticipation of its immediate future. When its bankruptcy occurred, the only legal course was to turn over its assets to its real creditors, who were its bondholders, and not its stockholders. But when this was first proposed, it was objected to by men in high position, even as lawyers, that its corporate life could not be transferred to its creditors, but that its 550 miles of completed road, and its lands earned by their construction, must be divided among its creditors, and that the enterprise must be given up as a failure. Already the sheriff was waiting in New York—hat in hand—to levy on the property and force the sale. But an inspection of their franchise and their rights under their charter led the prudent and hopeful members of the Board of Directors to resist doing this great wrong to their creditors. One plan was to exchange bonds for lands, at fair rates, which would satisfy the claims of those who chose this method. This was done, to some extent, without the wastage of legal seizure and forced transfer. But the comprehensive plan was to transfer the whole property, the completed road, the land subsidy already earned, the corporate life of the company, with its inchoate franchises, to the creditors. They were authorized to do this by virtue of Article VI of their charter, which (as amended by act of Congress, approved May 31, 1870) expressly authorizes and empowers the Northern Pacific Railroad Company to issue its bonds to aid in the construction and equipment of its road, and to secure such bonds by mortgage on its property of all kinds and descriptions, real, personal, and mixed, including its franchise as a corporation. This last clause was construed to mean its corporate life.

Under this ruling by the court, the transfer of all its property and franchise was made by a legal sale to a third party, and by him to the bondholders, who became the preferred stockholders of the road, with all the rights and powers of the original stockholders to hold the property and complete the enterprise.

CAUSE OF DELAY IN ITS CONSTRUCTION—More than a year of diligent effort on the part of the directors was spent saving the Northern Pacific Railroad from overthrow and absolute annihilation, and in securing the creditors all the assets. This was, to all appearance, a transaction most creditable to the head and heart of the directors. The creditors had all their own property for their bonds, if they should choose to accept it. About $24,000,000 of bonds were given up for preferred stock. Some millions were exchanged for lands. Some bonds are still held back, yet provision is still made for their transfer for stock or lands.

VALUE OF THE TWO SECTIONS ALREADY BUILT—The 550 miles of road paid all current expenses and earned $300,000 more, as per report of 1876. Of this surplus the 105 miles of the Pacific division earned $60,000 over its expenses.

NEW SECTIONS BUILT IN 1877—During the last twelve months the directors have built 63 miles of road, connecting its Eastern division at Brainerd with the railroads at St. Paul, Minnesota, and 31 miles, connecting its Western terminus with the vast coal fields of the Puyallup Valley.

ITS OWNERSHIP—The whole line is owned by its present stockholders. It is free of debt, and is paying no interest – unless it be on the sections built this year – while its earnings are increasing annually.

WHAT THE ROAD ASKS OF CONGRESS—As the time of its franchise expires soon by limitation, it earnestly asks an extension of time to complete the through line.

*THE ROAD NOT RESPONSIBLE FOR THE DELAY—*The railroad was not responsible for the failure of Messrs. J. Cooke & Co., its financial agents. It has not been responsible for the panic and the business failures that have swept over the United States and Europe like a hurricane during the last four years. It is not responsible for the unsettled condition of politics or of the currency. It has done nothing to complicate the labor question, or lay unjust burdens on poor workingmen. It has earnestly desired the opportunity to go forward and employ thousands of the unemployed in completing its line from the Missouri to the Columbia and the Pacific.

*IF GRANTED, THE GOVERNMENT AND PEOPLE WILL BE THE GAINERS—*It asks no additional subsidy. It is content with the lands granted, most of which have yet no value, but to which its construction will give value. It expects to give the same value to an equal amount of contiguous Government land, which now has no appreciable value in any market in the world.

*IT IS AN INVESTMENT TO CREATE VALUES WHERE NONE EXIST NOW—*The road expects to earn its subsidy as it goes along, mile by mile and section by section. This is true of every railroad through an unsettled country. It thus does not claim or ask the subsidy as a gift, but only as an opportunity to confer an equal and even greater value upon the Government, for the trust thus long put in its keeping.

*THE ROAD HAS BEEN A SUFFERER—*It shared its measure of loss and suffering and delay, on account of the great failure, and the greater financial disasters that ensued, and the general disturbance of public affairs. All those things were unforeseen and beyond its control. They have caused the road an unavoidable loss of money and time. The money can be earned again for the completed road for its creditors, if Congress will merely grant an extension of time to do it. This privilege will not cost the Government a dollar. As a business principle it is not withheld, but promptly given by man to man in all the circles of commercial enterprise. To refuse it is like the old law of putting a debtor in jail in order to compel him to pay his debts. It is a demand for "money or the pound of flesh." When understood, men will not do this unkindness. We must hope and

[158]

believe that Congress, urged by the voice of the people, will grant the Northern Pacific Railroad an extension of time to complete its road under the charter.

ITS PLAN OF COMPLETION—A plan has been proposed and earnestly advocated by several of its directors to hasten its completion by commencing next year on the Missouri, working Westward, and on the Columbia near the mouth of the Snake River, working Eastward as rapidly as possible until the two sections meet in Montana. In order to do this it is proposed that the company sell their lands at the Government land offices, get the minimum price of $2.50 per acre, give titles to purchasers, use the proceeds, with the prospective earnings of the roads, to build the line East and West, and also to give credit and a good sale to new bonds which may be issued to perfect the scheme. The object of the directors is ostensibly to build the roads, and not to speculate in the lands. For this object the subsidy is entrusted to them. They want settlements and steady business along the whole line.

This plan to put their lands in the common market with the even sections held by the Government will, no doubt, satisfy all the demands of the settlers, and win a just commendation from all the people. It is to be hoped that it will meet with the approbation of the entire Board, and be placed on their records and in the provisions of the bill for the extension of time.

BRANCH ROAD TO PUGET SOUND—Some objection has been made to their retention of the subsidy for the branch road from the Snake River, through the Yakima Valley, to Puget Sound. It is evident that such a branch is needed. The surveys show easy grades. The main valley and its affluents are rich in resources, and if allowed time, there is little doubt but that the Northern Pacific Railroad will ultimately build this road. But if not, let some other company do it.

INTERCOMMUNICATION ESSENTIAL—Rev. Dr. Field, a recent observer in Greece, where he is still, remarks that the interior of that country is less advanced than the capital. The great want is that of internal communication. "Greece is a country made by nature for commerce and agriculture, and if a few short railroads were opened to connect the inland valleys with the sea, so that the farmers and peasants could send their produce to market, the exports of the country might be doubled. A line of one hundred miles would connect them with the railroad system of Europe. Such a road would give them new life."

Dr. Field here reveals the secret also of their historic provincialism. It is intercommunication which makes a people one in interest and thought. The lack of the former defeats the latter. By quick and free intercommunication we become one people. Without it we are only a company of provinces, feebly bound together, apt to be jealous, and without enterprise. Every argument urges the completion of this direct means of intercourse and this bond of connection with the great body of our Nation.

VIEWS OF THE DIRECTORS—In a conversation with Captain J.C. Ainsworth, one of the directors of the Northern Pacific Railroad, he says distinctly that it is the judgment and purpose of some of the directors of the Northern Pacific Railroad, with whom he fully agrees in the plan to urge the sale of their lands in the Government land offices, at the minimum fixed price of $2.50 per acre, and to use the proceeds, with other funds, at once, to connect the Columbia and the Missouri Rivers by railroad, and thence to extend the road Westward, on the south side of the Columbia, to Portland, on the Willamette, and thence to Puget Sound.

THE COLUMBIA RIVER AND ITS TRIBUTARIES – COMMERCIAL STATUS AND IMPORTANCE—It is a maxim of commerce, both terrene and marine, that the wagon must meet the ship, and the ship the wagon. Facts illustrate this axiom from the earliest times to the present in all countries, whether goods have been moved to the sea by the long caravan of camels, as in Asia, or by the slow wains of Central and Northern Europe and America, reaching first the rivers and shallower bays, thence on light boats and barges to the ship; or whether, as in recent times, the vast and varied products of the country reach the sea by the swifter railroad trains. The exchange of the products of the sea must go inland by these return trains. This is the problem of transportation. This is the key to the busy hum of seaport cities. It is now the motive of railroad and steamship lines, as it was a few years since of canals and river steamboat companies. It is the chief question that enters into the merchant's estimate of his profits, and into the farmer's account of his income.

THE IMPORTANCE OF THE HIGHWAY—For example, when wheat sells in San Francisco at $2.25 per cental, and only at $2.10 per cental in Portland or Astoria, the difference is 15 cents per bushel against the farmer of Oregon or Washington. His loss is 15 per cent, as rated by the bushel, or 25 per cent, per 100 pounds. On 100 bushels he loses $15; on 1,000, $150; on 10,000, $1,500; on 100,000, $15,000; on 1,000,000 bushels, the community of farmers lose $150,000; and on 5,000,000 bushels, the estimated export of wheat the present year, their loss is $750,000. The commission merchants of the state lose a large per cent of profit in the transfer of business to the market below. Yet, the fact is established that ships can come from any port of Asia or Europe to the entrance of the Columbia River as easily, and as quickly, and as cheaply, as to the entrance of the Golden Gate.

OFF SHORE SOUNDINGS—The late off shore sounding by the United States Coast Survey steam cutter *Hassler*, Captain George W. Coffin commanding, which occupied two months, July and August, 1877, gives the following facts, which are kindly furnished from the official records:

1st—Extent of Survey—From Cape Disappointment Northward to Yoke Point Lighthouse, 26 ½ miles of coast line, and about 13 miles out to sea.

From Cape Disappointment Southward to False Tillamook Head, 31 ½ miles of coast line, and 15 miles out to sea.

Total square miles surveyed, 812.

Lines of soundings were 1 ½ miles apart by ship. Lines of soundings were traversed in to 9 feet by boats.

SOUTHERN SHEET—2nd—Ratio of increase of depth to distance off shore—Off North Channel, due West line, it is 5 fathoms to the mile; off Port Adams, due West line, it is 5 fathoms to the mile; off Tillamook Head, due West line, it is 3 ½ fathoms to the mile; off False Tillamook Head, due West line, it is 5 ½ fathoms to the mile.

NORTHERN SHEET—Off Stout's house due West line, it is 4 fathoms per mile; off point midway between Cape Disappointment lighthouse and Leadbetter's Point, due West line, it is 3 ½ fathoms per mile; off Leadbetter's Point, due West line, it is 3 ½ fathoms per mile; off Yoke Point lighthouse, Shoal water Bay, it is 3 ½ fathoms per mile. 3rd—Increase of depth to Seaward in a direction off the South channel (main ship channel) it is 4½ fathoms to one mile. 4th —Increase in depth to Southward. At 2 miles to seaward from Point Adams, West, is found 5 ½ fathoms; at 2 miles to Seaward from Grimes' house, West, is found 11 fathoms; at 2 miles to Seaward from Tillamook Head, West, is found 30 fathoms; at 5 miles to seaward from midway between Tillamook and False Tillamook Head. West, 20 fathoms; at 2 miles to seaward from Falso Tillamook Head, West, is found 32 fathoms.

CURRENTS—5th—Outside of 4 or 6 miles are Coast currents parallel to the shore line, to the Southward in summer and Northward in winter, whose velocities are dependent on local winds, which, when strong, often reverse the current.

Inside of 5 or 6 miles the currents seem to be governed by the outflow and inflow of the Columbia River (South of Cape Disappointment). North of Cape Disappointment Shoalwater Bay affects the current in shore more than the Columbia River, Shoalwater Bay being of large area and almost dry and bare at low water. The inflow causes a strong set in shore to the Northward almost always; the outflow apparently not running down in shore, but joining the Coast current further outside. This is apparently due to the conformation of the land above the entrance to Shoalwater Bay.

DISCOLORED WATER—6th—The distance outside of the bar at which discolored water may be seen varies with circumstances. Good signs to the navigator are the strong tide rips met with off the bar, and to the Northward and Southward of it, sometimes as far as

10 or 15 miles, but rarely more than five or six miles to seaward of the bar.

PRECAUTION—7th—Vessels in doubt as to position would do well to keep outside of 25 fathoms in bad weather, fog, etc. The boats of the survey developed deep water between Tillamook Rock and the Head, and probably large vessels may pass through in case of necessity or to avoid other dangers, though the passage is not recommended.

INFERENCE—The Columbia River has probably cut a channel through this vast bed. Those official statements assure the navigator approaching the bar of his mode of safety, and furnish him many hints to find his position by the lead and by the currents, even if the land marks are hidden. If they are seen, his course is plain.

CHANNEL—The South channel averages a half mile in width, and 20 ½ feet at mean low water, and 5 fathoms at high water; with smooth, hard bottom, free from rocks, well buoyed and mainly direct, with few alterations of the ship's course into the river channel. The shifting sand form the Clatsop Spit and Point Adams on the south side of the channel, and Sand Island and its spits, extending Westward on the north side of the channel, are broken and moved by tides and currents, which sweep through the channel, keeping it open in full measure of depth and width.

If the North channel grows shallower, which the last survey indicates, the south channel will doubtless deepen to the same extent.

DRAFT OF VESSELS—Vessels drawing 22 and 23 feet loaded, have passed and repassed the bar at high tide. Present surveys show that vessels drawing 21 feet of water can always, on half tide, come to Astoria, with a pilot, but better with a pilot and tug. Vessels drawing 17 feet can always pass and repass the channel to Portland, with a pilot.

TIDES—Tides rise from 6 to 10 feet on the bar, and from 6 to 10 feet at Astoria, and from 1 to 2 feet at Portland, 120 miles inland.

RIVER AND HARBOR IMPROVEMENTS—The United States, in accordance with its liberal policy, has kept efficient superintendents of survey and of lighthouses and buoys, and furnished these materials and erected these structures for the benefit of commerce for several years past. Of late, dredgers have been added, and fresh parties have been kept at work on coast and river. Charts have been made with more minute and accurate measurements. The river and adjacent ocean bed are becoming perfectly platted, so that when these maps and charts shall be issued to mariners from the Government office, the safety of navigation, with ordinary care, will be assured more definitely.

It is also reasonable to expect larger Government outlays and increased efficiency, to observe changes, to plant more buoys and shore signals, and to employ dredgers of more power and capacity, thus turning the vast body of river water into the deeper and thus deepening channel. We have no reason to think that the Columbia River will ever have less capacity of commerce, as furnished by nature, but more, as guided by skillful engineers, authorized and supported by the Government.

DISASTERS ON THE BAR—The facts of navigation above considered affect commercial insurance, but absolute wreck at the entrance of harbors is a greater terror to underwriters than the perils of the high seas. Report of such disaster renders the insurer timid and stamps a bad fame upon the entrance to harbor or river mouth. The evil reputation increases as it becomes current. An article published in the *Alta California*, March 19, 1873, from the pen of Captain William Tichenor, of Port Orford, and written in February, 1872 remarks: "On the Northwest Coast of the United States, between the Bay of San Francisco and Puget Sound, a distance measured by more than ten degrees of latitude, there is no harbor a vessel can enter in heavy Southern weather."

He adds: "The Columbia River, latitude 46/12, longitude 124/00, has a barred harbor. Among others, I now recollect the loss of the *General Warren*, Captain Thompson, with 52 persons; the *Demarest*, of New York, Captain Collins, with 9; the *Virginia*, Captain Bird, with 10, and the Industry, with most of the officers and crew. Commodore Hudson, of the sloop-of-war *Vincennes*, told me, I think in 1852, that he had visited most of the ports on the globe, and that none presented such terrors to him as the entrance to the Columbia River. He lost the sloop-of-war *Peacock* there, I believe, in 1846 [July 18, 1841 is the correct date.] Captain Hudson had no pilot. The *Shark* was lost at the same time."

[Captain Tichenor continues] The dread in which the bar was held by mariners in earlier years had, in a great measure, disappeared, under the influence of a better acquaintance with it, and by the aid of the thorough and efficient pilots engaged upon it. But it is not one of those dangers the familiarity with which will ever breed contempt. There is not much detention in getting to sea in the summer months, but during the heavy gales of winter, vessels dare not approach the bar, and are compelled to lie off and on, sometimes for weeks, waiting for the sea to run down. From 1812 to 1851 the Hudson Bay Company had navigated the Columbia. Some of their pilots had, in 1851, been in their employ on the bar and river for over thirty years.

The editor of the *Alta* remarks: "It is to be regretted that it is impossible to improve the entrance to the Columbia River which, inside the bar, has a large, deep and secure bay, and has a thousand miles of channel suitable for navigation by large river steamers. We say that improvement is an impossibility—at least it is improbable. The breakers are so fierce, and the sands at the bottom of the entrance so treacherous, that no breakwater could stand.

To complete this gloomy picture, the *Alta* published a list of disasters North of San Francisco, from the pen of T.B. Shannon, under the direction of the United States Treasury Department, from January 1, 1861 to December 31, 1869—nine years. Yet, in this list of 198 disasters, 110 were small coasting vessels, plying upon shore, and only three occurred on the Columbia River bar, viz.:

In May, 1861, Brig *Woodpecker* stranded	Loss $30,000
In March, 1865, bark *Industry* wrecked	Loss $75,000
In May, 1867, bark *W.B. Scranton* wrecked	Loss $225,000
Total amount of losses	$330,000

This is a relative loss of only 1 ½ per cent, in nine years, or of one sixth of one per cent, for one year. But the impression made by such statements, massed together, is to damage the reputation of the Columbia River bar.

Hon. D.C. Ireland, Clerk of the Board of Pilot Commissioners, attests that only nine vessels have been wrecked at or near the Columbia River bar in the last twenty-five years. Five of these were coming in without a pilot, and the loss of the others was due to the loss of wind and the lack of a tug. Since the tugs have been put on there has been no loss, except the *Architect*, coming in without a pilot. These nine disasters, in about 12,500 crossings of the bar, during twenty-five years, is about .007, or 7-100 of one per cent.

Honorable Wm. Reid, Secretary of the Board of Trade of Portland, has compiled, among others, the following:

TESTIMONY OF MARINERS—Captain Maginn, when President of the New York Board of Pilots, was instructed to report his opinion as to the merits of the entrance to the Columbia River, compared with the entrance to New York. He says:

There is deep water on the bar, it having four and one-half fathoms without the addition of the tide, while New York Harbor has on the bar but four fathoms, without the addition of the tide, which is six feet. The bar in the Columbia is about half a mile across, while that of New York is three-quarters of a mile.

The channel of the bar at the mouth of the Columbia is about six thousand feet, while the channel of the bar at Sandy Hook is about six hundred feet, and shoals rapidly; the channel across the bar is straight at the Columbia; that at New York is crooked. In accessibility to the sea, the Columbia River is the best, as it is immediately at sea, and ships can get out of the sea into the harbor at once, and also get out at once into the high sea. The winds at the mouth of the Columbia are marked regular and steady, while the winds at New York are entirely variable, and cannot be calculated upon by the mariner for any time. The mouth of the Columbia is free of ice and great heat.

The *San Francisco Commercial Herald* of May 21, 1874 says: "The bar at the mouth of the Columbia River, Oregon, has been made the ground of a very unjust and unreasonable discrimination of rates of insurance on vessels bound into the river. The number of casualties that have occurred there is fewer than that of any other barred river known to commerce."

OPINIONS OF GOVERNMENT OFFICIALS AND MASTERS OF VESSELS—The Commissioners of the General Land Office at Washington, in their annual report to Congress for 1870, at page 156: "By the use of a steam tug, in crossing the Columbia Bar, the entrance to the harbor is rendered as safe as that of the Golden Gate, or the Straits of Fuca."

Captain G.W. Harris, of the United States revenue service, who has crossed the bar some thirty times, says: "The crossing of the bar at the mouth of the Columbia River, with the ordinary precautions, is as safe as the entrance to any bay or harbor in the United States."

Captain Hughes, master of the British ship *Montgomery Castle*, 1,300 tons burden, says: "There is no more risk in entering and leaving the Columbia River then there is in coming into or leaving any port or harbor that I have ever visited."

Captain D. Evans, of the British ship *La Escocesa*, who is well known, writing on the 13th of April, 1875, says: "I consider a vessel is as safe, with the use of a steam tug or pilot, in entering the Columbia River and going over the bar, as in going into any harbor in ordinary weather."

Captain George White, writing on the 8th of May, 1875, says: "It is absurd to say that the Columbia River bar is a very dangerous entrance."

Captain Francis Connor, now commanding the steamship *G.W. Elder*, has crossed the Columbia Bar more than one thousand times during the past fourteen years, without a serious accident.

[167]

PRESENT EXTENT OF THE COLUMBIA RIVER COMMERCE, AS SHOWN BY THE FLEET OF TWO YEARS—The report of the Board of Pilot Commissioners to the Legislative Assembly, at the ninth regular session—1876, gives:

Total arrivals and tonnage, 1874-75	Vessels, 233	Tonnage, 161,539
Total arrivals and tonnage, 1875-76	Vessels, 241	Tonnage, 192,750
Total exports for 1874-75 were	Tons 148,141	Value $4,392,272.26
Total exports for 1875-76 were	Tons 162,830	Value $7,453,318.01

PROPORTION ARRIVING IN BALLAST—The number of vessels arriving in ballast in 1874-75 was 71, and in 1875-76 it was 75—a total of 146, or about 33 per cent.

THE AVERAGE DRAFT OF VESSELS—The draft of incoming vessels varied from a small coasting schooner of 4 feet to an ocean steamer of 17 feet. The average draft of 474 vessels arriving was 12 feet. The draft of the entire fleet of vessels departing from the Columbia varied from 6 to 23 feet. The average draft of 474 vessels on departure was 14 ½ feet. The average draft of the whole grain fleet to Europe on departure was 18 feet. The average draft of 60 of that fleet loaded was 19 ½ feet. This draft of loaded vessels is declared by the largest European shippers, to indicate the tonnage of the most profitable ships for general commerce at the present time. For example, the British grain fleet going to the Black Sea is composed of this class of vessels, registering from 900 to 1,400 long tons, and drawing from 14 to 19 feet. It is found that the larger classes of ships, built twenty-five years ago, and carrying immense cargoes, have long delays in loading, with large risks of navigation and more difficulties to find markets.

These facts of practical experience both test and settle the question of the permanent commerce of the Columbia River. It has been supposed that the larger and deeper draft vessels were essential to the most profitable commerce, especially for long voyages, like those to Europe. It has been often said that when a larger population and more capital came to our Northwest, and productions became quadrupled for export, the Columbia River commerce must seek San Francisco in small vessels, and be transferred to larger ones, to be borne to its European markets, or else be transported by railroad to Puget Sound for the same purpose.

San Francisco shippers and merchants nourish this sentiment, and make a strong pressure to control the large and increasing exports of the Columbia River. The most absurd part of the scheme is that the same classes of vessels will transport this produce from the Golden Gate or De Fuca Straits to Europe that now transport it from the Columbia River to Europe. This double shipment—now partly in process—of produce from our ports to San Francisco, and thence to Europe and Asia, is a loss in freight which falls chiefly on our farmers, of $500,000 or $750,000 annually now. It is also a large loss to our business community, and thus to the enterprises which invite and encourage immigration. If we continue to export our raw material for food, wool, hides, iron and lumber, instead of adding home labor to make finished products for the world's markets, as other communities do, we only get a profit on the mere work it requires to collect these raw materials for the use of laborers in other countries, while we thus exhaust virgin soil and nature's resources, and rapidly diminish our own capital in building up this sort of commerce. This is bad enough, as starving fields and weed-covered prairies already show. But when we pay our neighbors below a bonus of a half to three quarters of a million dollars annually, for the privilege of letting our goods pass through their port under their California brand, thus discrediting our own productions in the world's markets, and dishonoring our region and our climate in the view of the intelligent—since we can send off the whole from our own ports cheaper and in better order—we show a degree of folly which will be sure, soon, to bring us shame and greater loss; for every act of folly in business, as well as in morals, surely brings its reward in their own coin.

THE INTERESTS OF ALL CLASSES OF THE COMMUNITY ARE IDENTICAL AND NOT DIVERSE—Some division of sentiment has existed and been fostered, as if a city is a foe to the country, and that the country must watch and defend itself again mercantile frauds and overgrown monopolies. These prejudices confuse trade by diverting it from its natural channels. They also taint and pervert legislation. We try various methods of relief. At one time we work hard for railroads as the sure means of general prosperity. Next we try schemes of immigration. But the former do not come on call, and the latter find little certainty of profitable business for their welcome, and so may turn back in disappointment and disgust.

OUR PRESENT NEED—Both the home born and the stranger want the solution of the commercial problems of the Columbia Valley and its tributaries. Is it, or is it not, an inviting home? Can we and our children, and many thousands and hundreds of thousands more of intelligent and industrious people, abide here, or come and make good homes here? Is all we make and all we bring destined annually to be drained off to pay for imports, or shall a fair part of our income circulate, like healthy blood, through our own body politic? In other words, have we a sure future in our vast Columbia basin, inclosing, as it does, the most of Oregon, Washington and Idaho, and a part of Montana—an area, according to the census, drained by the Columbia River of 250,000 to 300,000 square miles, or four times the area of all the New England States, whose products will drift as naturally to the Western seaboard as its waters flow to the Pacific. We know that the natural resources are as valuable and various to its area as vast and adapted to multiplied industries and mode of living. We know that its climate is health-giving and harvest-giving, having been attested by many of us for thirty years past, without failure.

We learned that immigrants, merchants, mechanics and farmers from Great Britain and France, both the almost exact analogue of our Northwestern Coast in climate and productions, discover the homelike similarity, and take enlarged views of its present and prospective development of resources and settlements. British capital comes here freely and confidently. British fleets rapidly absorb our commerce, and we are glad to see them come. British insurance companies already control the maritime part of this business, and much of that pertaining to fire risks. Already they have reduced the price of marine insurance to our ports to the same rate as to the Port of San Francisco, except the fraction of one-fourth of one per cent extra charge on wheat shipment. Cargoes of flour and salmon are now insured at the same rates in British offices.

British wool-growers are moving from Australia and New Zealand to Eastern Oregon and Washington as the best country for this business. British woolen, flax, iron and leather manufacturers are sure to follow, and produce goods here, instead of wasting a rich margin of profit in the double transportation of the raw material home and the goods back. Facts and reasoning evince the certainty that the homes of industry, thrift and intelligence must and will be established all through the basin of the Columbia and its tributary valleys.

INTERCHANGE OF PRODUCTS—The union of all citizens, in city and country, to increase the means of cheap and easy intercommunication, in order to set all the wheels of business in motion, and to give all hands work in village shop and on country farm, on land, on river and on bay, will do much to inspire heart and hopes.

Whatever state and national legislation is needed to improve rivers, build railroads or canals, or redeem waste lands and increase the number and value of the homes of the people, by putting a value upon products that will induce production, ought, of course, to be secured by united votes and efforts, instead of being lost by partisan strife or selfish chicanery.

Much has been done already by men entrusted with legislative power. More can be done on land and river. If the cost of inviting commerce to our river be by a merely nominal price of pilotage and towage, at the cost of the State, it might be a saving of three-fourths of what we now waste on double freights and commissions.

If a few hundred thousands of dollars would clear out the shoals from the Columbia, Cowlitz, Chehalis, Willamette, Snake, Clearwater, Yakima, Spokane, Clark's Fork, and build needed portages, or canals, the profit of one or two harvests would pay the cost, besides inviting thousands of settlers into these vast regions, and bringing those there now out of exile into fellowship with all other sections.

In the wide regions that railroads must do the business of transportation, united effort without delay could soon give us these facilities on a scale equal to local wants and transcontinental needs, freeing us from tribute to distant and hostile corporations.

PROSPECT OF THE INCREASE OF OUR COMMERCE—The average annual gain in the report of breadstuffs from the Columbia to all ports, by seasons, from 1868 to 1877, is 38 ½ per cent, counting eight seasons of shipment from the basis of amount reported in 1868-9.

It is reasonable to estimate the addition to the population of the Columbia basin this year at 25,000, a number equal to one-sixth of the present inhabitants. It is fair to count the gain to commerce one-sixth. At this rate the State Board of Pilot Commissioners may be able to report to the next Legislature, in 1878, the arrival of 550 vessels, with a tonnage of 410,000 tons, and an export of 360,000 tons, valued at $14,000,000, as the business of their two official years. The gain this year indicates more instead of less than those figures.

The gain in the Upper Columbia business—as per Oregon Steamship and Navigation Company apparent exhibit of growth, is a large per cent, in two years. Their plans with others promise more rapid and wider means of river commerce. We venture no estimate of the amount, but the drift of 200,000 or more bushels of wheat to the Western ocean per year, from the Upper Columbia, will not surprise those who watched the progress of the plow and the reaper there.

It is hardly needful to say, yet it is wrong to forget, that this problem of our commerce has factors, which enter into every home of the people; into every factory and store; into every social question; into every school and church of our wide-ranging settlements. It touches us daily, along or in the crowd, in the routine of business and on journeys. It inspires hope and shapes our plans. It is worthy of our thought, while its successes command our gratitude.

Confidence in this railroad revives. It is known that the company turned its assets over to the bondholders at the least cost and delay, giving them the full benefit of their mortgage. The act shows a desire and purpose to complete the road. It stands now in the hands of the new or preferred stockholders—or former bondholders—free from debt, with 550 miles of road finished and furnished with rolling stock, machine shops, depots, and other means of work and progress. The Pacific division has paid all its running expenses, the salaries of its officers, and $30,000 of old debts, without calling for help from the East.

The Eastern division has paid the running expenses and $30,000 or more overplus. The company have also nearly the entire land subsidy for the whole distance completed. With such assets on which to effect new loans, there is hope to raise the funds and extend the road.

Besides these elements there are new factors in the problem. When the Union and Central Pacific were proposed, it was counted a wild scheme to build that long road over a trackless desert. The problem of fuel was not solved. It was not deemed solvable. The supply of water was supposed to depend upon artesian wells. The eminent State geologist of California at that time said: "I know the limited supply of wood and timber on the Sierra Nevadas, and the road must carry this more than a thousand miles for daily use. It is liable to wear out the track and the stock supplying its daily trains with power to run." His thought or fear was that the transcontinental road could not be a success. Many other intelligent and thoughtful men shared his fears. A graver factor in the problem was, how to get way business, which is known to be the most important element in the success of every railroad, As the road progressed every one of these difficulties were removed. The Rocky Mountain coal fields, along and under the very track of the road, furnished the best of fuel for the present, and for the indefinite demands of the future. Streams and wells supply water abundantly. Wyoming, Utah and Nevada have unfolded marvelous mines of precious metals, and untold riches of agricultural and pastoral lands. The united road pays larger dividends, probably, than any other lines of equal length in the world. Similar factors are already solving some elements of the problem of the Northern Pacific Railroad. Hardly had the Pacific division connected the waters of the Columbia with those of Puget Sound, when the remarkable coal fields of Puyallup, 25 miles from Tacoma, were discovered. The coal has been tested by A. Campbell, Esq., of Portland, and by others in Washington Territory, Oregon, and California, and pronounced by them all equal to the Cumberland and Blossburg coals for all the use of their shops. One of them pronounces it the best for welding steel of any he has ever tried in thirty years' experience.

President G.F. Whitworth, of the Washington Territory University, has examined the fields, and found the veins very numerous—scores of them—from one foot to three, five, and even seventeen feet of thickness. They are cut through by several mountain streams, which permit a series of self-draining shafts to be run at different levels into every vein, all above the shutes, while these are above the natural railroad cut or bed which the streams have made. The Puyallup Valley—a garden in itself—is level for twenty miles, leaving only from five to eight steeper gradients into the mountains. Several engineers of the Northern Pacific corps have declared the route easy to make, and capable of immense traffic. The outlet for coal into shutes on the bluff at Tacoma permits its shipment without rehandling. Professor Whitworth finds it a choice cooking coal, with a large per cent of fixed carbon, hard, compact, and not easily broken by handling, or disintegrated by the weather. Four hundred and ninety pounds of this coal, as tested by the Portland Gas Works, produced 2,250 feet of superior gas, and 400 pounds of coke. The best test of Nanaimo coal gave 2,000 feet of gas from 500 pounds of coal.

Besides the fact that Tacoma Bay is a safe harbor, inviting the largest vessels and fleets from all parts of the Pacific and of the world, so that every product of the region can at once be put into the currents of commerce, these beds of choicest coal, which are in so great demand for steam and mechanical purposes, will at once assure business at this Northwestern terminus of the road. Good and abundant coal is a factor which will ensure any railroad that terminates on tide water. These coal fields invite the completion of the Northern Pacific Railroad at the earliest possible moment. It will save the immense transportation of Sydney and other foreign coals to our Coast and a growing interior. It will save the great cost of transporting Pennsylvania and Maryland coals to this Coast. It will develop the iron industry, in foundries and furnaces, preventing the costly importation and transportation of this product. It will employ artisans and laborers, and build up the homes of an industrious population, and by reaction stimulate the fisheries, the shipbuilding, the agricultural and pastoral pursuits.

Another factor in the problem of the Northern Pacific Railroad is the food supply of this Northern region through which its survey is made. It is a known fact that the most productive and enduring wheat lands of our Continent lie between the Cascades and the Rocky Mountains. They have the largest proportions of the potash and phosphates which nurture the cereals. It has been stated by a well-known geologist that during the six distinctly noted volcanic overflows the ashes, which were carried largely by the prevailing winds eastward into the bays and lakes which formerly occupied the great interior basin, mingled with other sediment to form the deep deposits which now constitute the soils of those valleys and high prairie lands. It is easy to infer that the excess of alkali in spots results from the drainage of this substance from the hills. But the wheat harvests of Walla Walla, Whitman, Umatilla and Baker Counties prove the wonderful fertility of this region. Every year the crops seem to increase in value and amount. The hills and dry sage brush plains have rewarded the cultivator. It is known that every acre touched with water becomes luxuriant with cereals and fruits. The drippings and overflows of that long miners' ditch constructed by the Chicago Company through Baker County has produced many oases in the hitherto dry plains. It is known that an ocean of aerial moisture floats over these regions from the vast Western ocean. It needs only a cooler to deposit the dews. Every field or blade of grass acts as a cooler.

The fields of winter grain, started by early rains or melting snows, provide the vegetation, which in summer deposits enough of this moisture to perfect their growth until the harvest. The deep plowing loosens the soil so as to absorb the air loaded with moisture, which grows cool enough to leave its moisture about the roots of the plant. Thus the lands that have for ages abounded in the bunch grass, which is now wasting away before the increase of flocks and herds, can be restored by the plow, and the choice cereals, wheat, oats, barley and corn, with orchards about every farm house.

Thirty-five, forty, and even sixty-five bushels per acre of wheat are said to be frequently harvested in the counties named. Their need is not food, but transportation to market. Their cattle, and sheep, and wheat, and corn abound far beyond all the wants of their present population. It is claimed that two or three of those counties can produce as large a surplus for foreign markets as the whole Willamette Valley. This factor enters into the problem of the Northern Pacific Railroad. It opens a vast business of transportation from the interior to the ocean, and from our forests and coal fields a large return to supply the treeless interior. Every year also gives steadiness and surety to the mining of gold and silver, and other metals, in the Blue Mountains, as well as those of Montana. Unknown resources are as likely to appear along the Northern Pacific Railroad line, in its progress, as along the Union Pacific. The delay of construction has caused the intelligent to study the problem more intently, and to feel sure that home interests demand it more than ever. Worthless regions will have known values when it comes, and the finest visions promise to be realized by it.

FULL TEXT OF THE HOUSE BILL AS REPORTED BY THE COMMITTEE ON PACIFIC RAILROADS—In the House of Representatives, Feb. 5, 1878; read twice, recommitted, and ordered to be printed.

House Record 3066 Report no. 120. A bill to extend the time to construct and complete the Northern Pacific Railroad.

Mr. William W. Rice, from the Committee on Pacific Railroads, reported the following bill:

Be it enacted by the Senate and House of Representatives of the United States of America in Congress assembled, That the grants, rights, privileges, corporate powers, and franchises, including the franchise to be a corporation, conferred upon the Northern Pacific Railroad Company by its charter, and the various joint resolutions of Congress amendatory thereof and supplementary thereto, be, and the same are hereby confirmed, granted and continued to the said Northern Pacific Railroad Company as now reorganized; and ten years' time from the passage of this act is hereby granted to said company for the construction and completion of its main line, subject to all the terms and conditions prescribed by said charter and joint resolutions, except as changed by this act; provided, however, and said extension of time is granted upon the following express conditions, namely:

First: That said company shall, within one year after the passage of this act, commence the work of constructing its main line at or near Umatilla, in the State of Oregon, or some suitable point between there and the mouth of the Snake River, as the said company shall determine, and shall complete not less than twenty-five miles of its road Easterly per year thereafter, and shall complete, in addition to the road already completed, at least one hundred miles of its main line within two years after the passage of this act, and at least one hundred miles of said main line each year thereafter, including in each said one hundred miles the twenty-five to be completed eastwardly, as aforesaid.

Second: The main line of said railroad between Portland and a point as far East as Umatilla, in the State of Oregon, shall be located and constructed on the South side of the Columbia River.

Third: Actual settlers on unsurveyed agricultural lands within the limits of the grant to said company, if said lands, when the Government surveys shall be extended over them, shall be found to be embraced in said grant; and actual settlers on any agricultural lands within the limits of said grants, who shall have settled thereon at a distance of one hundred miles or more beyond the completed portion of said road at either end; and actual settlers on any agricultural lands within the limits of said grant remaining unsold at the expiration of eight years from the completion and acceptance of the road opposite thereto; if said last mentioned lands shall be then surveyed by the Government, and if not, then within eight years after the Government surveys shall be extended over the same, shall be entitled each to purchase from said company one quarter section, or a legal sub-division thereof, on which they have settled, at the price of two dollars and fifty cents per acre, excepting coal and iron lands within the right-of-way of said railroad; provided, however, that this section shall not apply to lands already earned by said company.

SEC. 2. That all the lands heretofore withdrawn for the branch line of said road, be, and the same are hereby restored to the public domain, to be disposed of as other public lands, except for the distance twenty miles North of the portion of said branch now constructed from Tacoma to Wilkeson, in Washington Territory. And the said company shall receive patents for a quantity of land equal to twenty sections per mile on each side of said constructed portion of said branch, such land to be selected from odd-numbered sections on each side of said constructed branch, but on the North side, not farther than twenty miles therefrom; but the said company may select and receive patents for lands to make up the deficiency in said quantity from any of the public lands within the limits of the grant for the main line.

SEC. 3. That where pre-emption or homestead claims were initiated, or private entries or locations were allowed, upon lands embraced in the grant to said company, prior to the receipt of the order of withdrawal at the respective district land offices, the lands embraced in such entry or location shall be patented to the parties entitled to the same, as if said grant had not been made, and, in the case of abandonment by them, shall be open to settlement by pre-emption or homestead only; but the said company shall be entitled to indemnity therefore, as now provided by law.

SEC. 4. That entries remaining unadjusted and suspended in the general land office, on account of an increase in price of the even sections within the limits of said grant, where the same were made or based upon settlement price prior to the receipt of orders of withdrawal of said lands at the district land offices, shall be relieved from such suspension and carried into patent; but nothing in this act shall be construed to affect existing adjustments, or to authorize the refunding of any moneys received for such lands under existing laws.

SEC. 5. That the said company be, and is hereby authorized to issue its bonds from time to time, to aid in the construction and equipment of its road, and to secure the same by mortgages on the whole or any part or parts of its railroad and property and rights of property of all kinds and descriptions, with the rights, privileges and franchises thereto appertaining, including the franchise to be a corporation; and as proof and notice of their legal execution and effectual delivery, such mortgages shall be filed and recorded in the department of the interior.

SEC. 6. That in case any of the lands heretofore granted by Congress to aid in the construction of sail railroad shall become forfeited to the United States, and be restored to the public domain, by reason of the failure of said company to perform the conditions herein set forth, or any of them, the actual settlers on such of said granted lands as shall not have been earned by said company, who shall have settled thereon under the provisions of this act, or by license from said company, shall each have the right to obtain title to such lands, not exceeding one quarter section, under the homestead or pre-emption laws, as if said grant had not been made.

SEC. 7. That when said company shall sell, or contract to sell, or shall convey, except by way of mortgage or deed of trust, to aid in the construction of its railroad, and of said granted lands, the lands so sold, contracted or conveyed, shall be subject to taxation, according to the laws of the State or Territory within which the same may be situated.

SEC. 8. That this act shall not be construed to affect existing property rights, except as hereinbefore expressly provided; and Congress may, at any time, having due regard for the rights of said Northern Pacific Railroad Company, add to, alter, amend, or repeal this act, or the charter and resolutions hereinbefore referred to, and may provide bylaw against unjust discriminations and excessive charges wherever the same shall be made by said company.

SEC. 9. That the said Northern Pacific Railroad Company shall file with the Secretary of the Interior, within six months from the date hereof, its assent to, and acceptance of, the provisions of this act, or be forever debarred from taking or receiving any benefit from or under the same.

REPORT ACCOMPANYING THE BILL—The Northern Pacific Railroad Company was incorporated by act of Congress, approved July 2, 1864.

By section 8 of that act it was required to complete its road by July 4, 1876. Joint resolution of the Senate and House of Representatives, approved May 7, 1876, extended the time for the completion of the road two years.

Joint resolution, approved July 1, 1868, and entitled "A joint resolution extending the time for the completion of the Northern Pacific Railroad", amended section 8 of the original act by changing the time for the completion of the road to July 4, 1877.

The company claim that joint resolution of May 7, 1876 applies to section 8 of the act of July 2, 1864, as amended by the joint resolution of July 1, 1868, and, consequently, that its time for completing the road does not expire until July 4, 1879.

On the other hand, it is claimed that joint resolution of July 1, 1868, although by its title extending the time for completing the road, in effect, diminishes that time, and that it really expired at the date fixed by that resolution, to wit, July 4, 1877.

The Department of the Interior is reported to have adopted the more liberal construction, and to have assumed that the company has the longer time for the completion of the road.

Equity and generous dealing seems to justify this conclusion, and, in view of the impossibility of the completion of the road even within the longer time, we do not deem it necessary to express an opinion as to the technical effect of the foregoing resolutions. At all events, further time must be granted, or this great enterprise, as at presented organized, must be abandoned.

Up to 1873, the company was in default. It has constructed its main line to Bismarck, in the Territory of Dakota, a distance of 450 miles, and on the Pacific Coast, from Kalama, on the Columbia River, northerly to Tacoma, on Puget Sound, a distance of 105 miles. The financial disasters of 1873 suspended its operations, frustrated its resources and forced it into bankruptcy.

By joint resolution, approved May 31, 1870, Congress authorized the company to issue its bonds, and to secure them by a mortgage of its property. Under this authority the company had issued bonds to the amount of $29,199,400, and has secured the same by a first mortgage on all its property, including its franchises.

In 1875 this mortgage, the company being in default, was foreclosed, and all the property of the company passed into the hands of a committee appointed by the bondholders, for their benefit.

In the summer of 1875 the bondholders, all concurring, either actively or tacitly, adopted a plan for reorganizing the company; preferred stock was issued in exchange for the bonds, and in September of that year a Board of Directors was chosen, which was put in possession of the property of the old company covered by the mortgage.

The stockholders in the company thus reorganized, are between eight and nine thousand in number, and are scattered through more than half the States of the Union. Their money made the property they now seek to save and enhance. They ask no subsidy, no additional grant or privilege, only an extension of time in which to complete the enterprise in which their money is invested, and which has been delayed and hindered by causes over which they had no control, and which occurred by no fault or omission of theirs.

The question for the consideration of the committee is, whether the public interests require the completion of this road, on the route and terms provided in the act of 1864, in the same, or in a greater, degree than at the time of its passage; and, if so, whether additional time should be granted to the company now engaged in the enterprise for its completion.

The arguments, pro and con, on the subject of National encouragement to transcontinental railroads are too familiar to require recapitulation. This discussion was ably and stoutly maintained on either side by statesmen whose intellectual strength and comprehension of the subject have left little or nothing to be added. The result was in favor of promoting, by public aid, the construction of Northern, Central and Southern roads from the Mississippi Valley to the Pacific Ocean.

In pursuance of this policy, thirteen years ago, 47,000,000 acres of public land were granted for the construction of the Northern road. Its route lies through a fertile country, rich in all physical characteristics necessary for the support of a vast and prosperous population. Its grades are easier than on most of the roads in the Eastern States, and where the line diverges from a straight course, to avoid impossible mountain ranges, it opens to settlement the fertile valleys of the rivers whose banks it follows.

Settlers have proceeded in the faith of its construction, and prosperous Territories, all along its route, are only waiting for the additional population, which its completion would speedily bring, to claim their places among the States.

The committee are of opinion that a due regard to the interests of these Territories, and of the hardy pioneers who have settled them, demands liberal action on the part of Congress to complete this road, to which, in a measure, the public faith was pledged; that the lands originally granted are held, as it were, in trust for the benefit of those settlers; and that, even if, strictissimi juris, advantage might be taken of the failure to meet the requirements of the charter in point of time, still, good policy, if not good faith, requires the waiver of that advantage and a reasonable extension of time to secure the accomplishment of this great national work.

[182]

It further appears that the present company is composed of those who have contributed whatever money has thus far gone into the work, and that nobody else proposes to undertake it.

It is operating at the present time nearly six hundred miles of road, in good condition and under excellent management.

In 1874 its net earnings were	$22,876.49
In 1875 its net earnings were	$152,140.00
In 1876 its net earnings were	$202,062.31
In 1877 its net earnings were	$392,698.47

Its property has actually cost about $20,000,000 in money. It is free from debt, and its directors are confident that they can complete the road upon the credit of this property and the land grant, if sufficient time is allowed them. The distance from Bismarck to the Columbia River is 1,205 miles, and the construction of the road for that distance gives a continuous route by rail and water from the Lakes to the Pacific Ocean.

The committee are of the opinion that, under the circumstances, the company is entitled to the favorable consideration of Congress, and that there is reasonable assurance that it will be able to finish the work during the next ten years.

By the original charter of the Northern Pacific Company, it was authorized to construct its road by two routes through Washington Territory, the upper being designated as the main line, and the lower as the branch line. By subsequent acts, these designations have been reversed, so that its main line now tends southwardly from Lake Pend d'Oreille to the Columbia River, and thence, through the valley of that river, to Portland, Oregon.

It is the desire of Oregon that the last division of the road should be constructed on the southerly side of the Columbia River, and the committee have so provided in the bill.

The company has changed the location of the branch line to one more southerly, and it is doubtful whether even the new location is practicable, owing to the difficulty of crossing the Cascade Mountains, which divide the Territory, running northerly and southerly across almost its entire width. The representatives of Washington Territory oppose the grant for the construction of this branch, as keeping the lands tied up against settlement, and the committee, in deference to their wishes, report in favor of the restoration of the land, withdrawn on that branch, to the public domain, excepting about 793,000 acres, earned by construction of the road extending thirty-one miles easterly from Tacoma.

By this change of location more than 6,000,000 acres of land in Washington Territory, covered by the original locations, will be restored to the public domain.

A proposition was considered by the committee to declare forfeited by the Northern Pacific Company all lands in Washington Territory withdrawn for its branch line, and to grant an equal amount to the Portland, Salt Lake, and South Pass Company, a corporation of the State of Oregon, organized to construct a railroad from Portland, through the Columbia Valley, to Umatilla, and thence, by a southerly route, through eastern Oregon, from 450 miles, to the Union Pacific and Central Pacific at Ogden.

This seems to your committee to be a scheme to obtain from Congress an endowment for a new, independent road, and one which, if constructed, would be a rival road to that of the Northern Pacific.

These reasons, without passing upon its merits, seem sufficient to the committee to prevent its incorporation in a bill to promote and encourage the completion of the Northern Pacific Road, and they leave the lands restored to the public domain, by the discontinuance of the branch, unencumbered by any new appropriation.

While reporting in favor of extending the time within which the company may finish their road, the committee are greatly impressed by the necessity of withdrawing, as far as possible, all obstacles to the settlement of the lands covered by the grants to this company.

The marketable value of the lands will, of course, be enhanced as the work of construction progresses, and the company should be allowed some control of that enhancement, and some advantages therefrom.

At the same time, the public advantage to be derived from the early settlement of these lands should not be sacrificed.

The committee have, therefore, enlarged the rights and opportunities of actual settlers, while reserving to the company the control over the land already earned on the line of the finished road, and over the surveyed lands within the limits of one hundred miles from the progress of its construction.

All of which is respectfully submitted,

VIEWS OF THE MINORITY—To accompany the report of the Committee on the Pacific Railroad, on the bill extending the time to construction and complete the Northern Pacific Railroad:

The undersigned disagree to the report of the committee, and oppose the passage of a bill for a renewal of the grant of lands made by it, which is in substance and principle a new grant, to which we are opposed. Such grants are not now warranted in the public interest, and are condemned by the public judgment.

WM.R. MORRISON
J.K. LUTTRELL
G.M. LANDERS

Two telegrams and their resolutions from one of the directors, and the word of another, who was at the meeting April 25th, declare that they cannot build the road under the provisions of the bill, which passed the Senate April 23rd. It has been hoped that the House would amend this bill, and that the Senate would concur, and thus assure the road.

But this hope is fallacious. This bill cannot be reached in the House, and the proper House bill, if reached, is likely to be complicated and defeated by this Senate bill. But the point of chief trouble is that for four months the original Senate bill was held in the hands of their Railroad Committee in order to enforce restrictions which the company could not accept. Mr. Mitchell said in the discussion of this bill in the Senate, April 22nd: "And because I have during the last four months contended with all the zeal and energy I could command for terms that would induce, or, if you please, compel, the Northern Pacific Railroad Company to concede in this proposed legislation conditions which, as one of the representatives of the State of Oregon and the great Pacific Northwest, I regarded as but just to that section of our common country, and which conditions I did not then, and do not now, regard as materially embarrassing to that company, etc. Mr. Mitchell assumes with obvious propriety to represent in this question "the State of Oregon," "the great Pacific Northwest," and "that section of our common country. He was thus holden to his peers in the Senate to the argument upon that high and comprehensive trust. His just and eloquent exordium upon this "great life artery of the Continent," was calculated to inspire further confidence in his zeal and his purpose to secure the early completion of the road.

The progress of the discussion shows that Senators were ready to aid the enterprise.

RESTRICTIONS—What conditions did he, as Chairman of the Railroad Committee, try to enforce upon the Northern Pacific Railroad during four long months? On page 5 of his speeches, April 22nd and 23rd, he says:

First—"Such provision as would compel at an early day the building of so much of their road as would be necessary to open up the monopoly-bound Columbia River to free navigation."

Mr. Mitchell professes friendship for the Northern Pacific Railroad, as a National transcontinental road, shorter and of better grades than others; a road needed for interior commerce, needed to check the monopoly of the Union and Central Pacific Companies; needed by the struggling people of the Pacific States and Territories; needed for the commerce between Asia and Polynesia; needed for the sure growth of the great Northwest, etc. He sees and declares the necessity of this National road as others see it. He is not in any fog at this point. He claims to represent its broad interests. He knows the original purpose of the Government in the survey of this route and its plan in the large grant of land to induce capital to build the road. He knows that $30,000,000 have been invested in it by ten thousand honest, confiding men and women, from twenty States, on their faith in this Government subsidy. He knows that a general bankruptcy, for which they were not responsible, has compelled those creditors to take the property of the unfinished road and become its stockholders. He knows they are compelled to ask for more time to complete the road, and that this is all they ask. He knows that they must do it to secure more funds. He knows that the measure as stated by Mr. Lamar—page 14—"Is demanded alike by justice, propriety and policy," and that, as Mr. Lamar says, "there is objection to loading this bill with other conditions than those which provide for a simple extension of relief."

He knows that their claim for more time was equitable, and that their investment on the previous pledges of the Government had given them vested rights in the whole original land grant for the road.

He knows that no act of these creditors has vitiated these vested rights, and that Congress cannot justly, and that probably it has no disposition to compel these people who have received little or no interest on their investment, to make a new and harder bargain.

He knows that they have never surrendered their franchises; that no quo warranto writ has been issued against them; and that by common law "the privileges and immunities, the estates and possessions of the corporation, when once vested in them, will be forever vested, without any new conveyance to new successions."

He knows that the pioneer settlers from the great lakes to the Pacific Ocean, along this Northern route, have also made large investments on the pledges of the National Government in their original contract with the Northern Pacific Railroad Company.

He knows that these investments of the hardy, self-sacrificing founders of new Territories and States have in equity rights in the nature of contracts, which, on their part, are in progress of fulfillment, and that they wait with intense anxiety along the whole line for the Government to fulfill its part.

He knows that the whole Nation will gain largely by this investment of its lands, which now have no value, but which will at once sell for cash if the road is assured. He knows that the Government expenses along the route will diminish, and Government receipts will increase millions annually, if the road is completed.

He knows that many millions ($50,000,000 or $60,000,000) must be borrowed by the Northern Pacific Railroad to proceed to finish their enterprise, and that capitalists in our own country, and more so now in Europe, are shy of American railroad bonds, and that it will be hard to place bonds of first-class railroads even in any market of the world; and that it will be impossible to place the bonds of any railroad that is cut down in its land franchises, and not allowed to sell its own lands—when earned—at market rates, and those lands are shaded by the indefinite claims of others.

Mr. Mitchell has a clear mind and sharp sight of the main issue in question.

CASH TO COMPLETE THE ROAD THE FIRST GREAT NEED—He has been aware, and he is now conscious, as appears by his own argument, that the chief object of the company is to get funds to complete the road. For this, they ask an extension of time on the original contract. The bankers to whom they apply demand time to complete the enterprise, and put it in condition to par interest before they will open their vaults and issue cash on the bond.

LOSSES BY DELAY—Mr. Mitchell knows that the pioneers in Dakota, Montana, Idaho, Washington and Oregon suffer great inconvenience and loss by every month's delay of the road, and that its completion will add one hundred to three hundred per cent to the cash value of every acre of land in these States. The Union and Central Pacific Railroads have, as per statistics, added from one to four hundred per cent to the value of lands in States traversed by them. "The sales of the Union Pacific Railroad land grant, to December 31, 1875, were 1,193,942 acres, for $5,336,044, at the average price of $4.47 per acre. An equal value, surely, was given to the same number of acres on the even sections retained by the government. The average price per acre of lands granted to and sold by the Central Pacific Railroad Company was $4.58 to January 30, 1875." Many of these lands had no cash value before the railroad was built.

LOSSES BY RESTRICTING THE NORTHERN PACIFIC RAIL-ROAD—Oregon, Washington, Idaho, Montana and Dakota contain 546,271 square miles, which amount to 349,613,440 acres. Suppose they are worth one dollar per acre now, the Northern Pacific Railroad and its tributaries, which would traverse and tap them in all directions, would add one dollar to every acre, or three hundred and fifty millions to the whole.

The average value added by the other transcontinental line is four times as much, which, in this case, would amount to fourteen hundred millions. No one doubts that the Northern Pacific Railroad would add this sum to the property, if not the land, of these States, within five years after its completion.

PROOF—The assessed value of property in California alone rose from over $180,000,000, in 1864-5, when the Central Pacific Railroad was begun, to $237,483,175 in 1869, when the overland railroad was done. The assessed value in 1874-5, five years later, was $611,495,000, a gain of $374,012,000, or about 150 per cent, in five year, or 34.6 per cent per year.

If one State gained in assessed property value three hundred and seventy-four millions of dollars in five years after the completion of the overland road to it, and fifty-seven million in the previous five years, while waiting for its completion, it is fair to assume that the five Northern States, if traversed by the Northern Pacific Railroad, which contain three times the area of California, will gain three times that sum of assessed property value, which would amount to twelve hundred and ninety-three millions of dollars. This sum of assessed valuation falls short of the previously estimated land or property valuation only one hundred millions. We know that assessments fall below real values more than one dollar in fourteen, which is the rate in this case.

THE PUBLIC KNOWLEDGE OF THESE FACTS—Senator Mitchell has reason to know, or keep in mind, all these facts, as the watchdog and sworn guardian of these great National interests, and the special representative, according to his own confession, of this "great Pacific Northwest."

If, in the burden of his other duties, he has not had time to make these simple calculations, or even to read and note the published statements of them, yet the great and intensely anxious public, whose eye has been fixed on him as their representative in his place, at the head of the Senate Railroad Committee, has read them again and again, and weighed and measured them, having confidence in their Senator, have invested their homes and their money on the assurance of this overland road.

THE PEOPLE ONLY WANT WHAT IS JUST AND FAIR—As reasonable men, the people along this whole route would far rather grant an extension of time to the company on the original franchise and contract, as the bill for extension of time passed the Senate, in the session of 1876-1877—Senator Mitchell, himself, then favoring it —than to lose this overland road, or than hinder it by restrictions to kill it. Reasonable settlers prefer to buy their lands of the company, at their market rates, varying with their quality and location, rather than get those lands as homesteads and thus be deprived of this transcontinental road. They can afford to buy and pay for the lands with the road. They cannot afford to take them and hold them as homesteads far on the route without the road. In this case most of the region must remain pasture ground.

THE ISSUE—In the face of all these facts and the collateral interests of the vast section of our common country which he represents, Senator Mitchell, as he says, tried for four months, in his place as the head of the Railroad Committee, "to compel the Northern Pacific Railroad to open up the monopoly-bound Columbia River to free navigation."

[190]

In other words, they must agree to borrow $400,000, or perhaps $900,000, as engineers estimate, mortgaging their completed road, in order to build twenty miles of portage road to compete with a local yet rich portage transportation company. In other words, they must lose the entire grant of the overland road unless they will fight what he styles a local monopoly. Mr. Mitchell admits, page 9, that "there are obstructions to navigation at these two portages, which cannot be overcome except by the construction of a canal and locks, and that the General Government has commenced those at the Cascades, though a work of this character will require considerable time." He knows that the Oregon Steamship Navigation Company can afford to take freight across their portages free, or so low as to break an opposition railroad portage company that has no continuous railroad line from tide water to the interior. He may know that the company cannot borrow money on this end, along the Columbia River, until their railroad connects this river with the Missouri. Yet he insists on forcing the Northern Pacific Railroad into conflict with a rich corporation.

They must fight with borrowed money and run the risk of losing both interest and principal. They must do it while depending on that hostile company to do the freighting for their own main line eastward from the Columbia River. Senator Mitchell, as he confesses, sought to force the local issue from December to April upon the Northern Pacific Railroad Company, which wasted time, and made capitalists more shy of the investment in their bonds, and so far defeated this great National overland road. He knew that if they could not afford to borrow money to build and run these opposition portage railroads, no other company could do it, and that the only possible way for the free navigation of the Columbia was by canal and locks.

SECOND ISSUE—By constraint he admits that after April 1st, he yielded his restriction of uniting the Salt Lake branch with the Northern Pacific Railroad, yet, insisted on complicating the two roads as a common road. Sections 8 and 9, with their numerous provisos, darken the prospects still more in the way of securing funds to complete the enterprise.

*THE ESSENTIAL THINGS TO THE NORTHERN PACIFIC RAIL-
ROAD*—A fixed purpose to have this road built, demanded that the
bill be as Senator Lamar said (page 14) without 'other conditions
than those which provide for a simple extension of relief.' This was
Senator Morrill's view (page 24). He thought the loss of eleven
million acres a burden for the road, and the combination of roads
another burden. Success required that every provision of the bill
be made after its review and acceptance by vote of the directors.
Success required the report early in the session.

Defeat of the enterprise is the logical result of months of delay; of
lack of harmony with the Board of Directors; of new restrictions
upon the grant and fruitless local hardships upon its construction.
These have triggered it, and probably switched it off the track,
entailing a deep disappointment and loss upon multitudes, and
gain upon only a few.

Senator Mitchell had the courtesy to send me a copy of his speeches,
April 22nd and 23rd, upon this Senate bill, and I have felt at liberty
to note what have seemed to me the fatal restrictions upon the
enterprise. Sharing the pain of this defeat with large numbers of the
pioneers of Oregon and Washington, who have waited long in hope
of this overland road, I submit these views, with the more cheerful
ones of the past few months, to the public.

THE LABOR MARKET—The bankruptcies, from 1873 to 1878,
stopped many home industries and crippled others. Laborers
have been thrown out of employments and been compelled to
use up their savings. Many, out of work and out of funds, have
suffered. Families have suddenly been reduced to want, and some
to beggary or starvation. No wonder that industrious men ask for
work. They may not all see that the Civil War compelled the issue
of two thousand millions of Government notes and bonds, which
were called money, and taken as coin—though at a discount—and
that this great increase of what seemed to be money, caused prices
of goods, food, lands, flocks, herds, manufactories and ships to go
up; which, in turn, bred excessive speculation, that has ended in
bankruptcies and the stopping of work. Such has been the fact. He

may not see that these things always follow great wars. A few get rich, but the multitudes get poor by war. Yet, our country is rich in resources. It recovers rapidly. The Government can and will repay its debts.

LABORERS HAVE JUST CLAIMS—Government owes a debt to its own laborers. If it was a duty to protect the Nation for the sake of the people, it is no less a duty to protect the people for the sake of the Nation. If it is fair—and it is—to pay the Government bonds, according to contract, whether held at home or abroad, it is also fair to help the industries of the people, who must earn the money by their toil to redeem those bonds.

LEGISLATION APT TO BE PARTIAL INSTEAD OF NATIONAL— After the war the re-construction raised new and grave questions, difficult of solution. The passions of the hour gave occasion for ambitious partisans to mount the rostrum, and secure the confidence and suffrages of the people on the specious pleas of overflowing patriotism. When in power the partisan sacrifices the public interest to his private ambition.

While the State and National Legislatures have done many noble things to harmonize conflicting opinions and interests since the war, and all branches of Government have deservedly won the gratitude of thoughtful citizens, yet, they are open to criticism for neglecting to use the means within the province of legislation to revive the industries of the people.

EFFECTIVE LEGISLATION—A most effective system of finance is to open the way for the miner, the artisan, and the manufacturer to earn the money to pay the expenses and debts of the Government. Instead of this, little has been done for five years by Congress to start the iron furnaces of Pennsylvania, Ohio, Tennessee and Missouri, or develop their coal mines, or to restore the workmen to the ship-yards of Maine and Massachusetts, or open new ones in Oregon and Washington. Upon the farmers and stock raisers, and cotton-planters, and lumbermen, and oil producers, has been laid the chief burden to furnish their raw products for foreign commerce, most of which has been carried in foreign ships, and used to pay the supplies and the interest of our debt abroad.

It is true that some manufacturers, of late, under the pressure of sharp competition, have won their way into foreign markets with their cotton fabrics, their machinery, their agricultural implements and military equipments, and have turned the balance of trade in our favor. But these triumphs of trade have not been gained by the aid of Congress, but in spite of its party strifes and adverse or uncertain legislation. The true policy in the United States, as in England and in France, is to furnish manufactured goods, as well as food, to Nations, and to carry these goods abroad and find or develop markets for them.

England holds the trade of China, South America, Africa, Southern Asia, and most of Polynesia for her manufactured goods.

The leading men of the South today assure us that "they are looking for its future welfare, not to politics, but to industry." A delegation of them, headed by Senator Gordon, recently visited Boston to learn more about the manufactures of New England. Some time ago the cities of Charleston, Savannah, New Orleans, Galveston and others designated General Gordon to represent the industrial interests of the South in Europe, during the coming season, by presenting to capitalists and others, who might be interested, the facts in regard to its natural resources, with a view to investments for their better cultivation and development.

"Speaking of the extension of foreign trade," says the Boston Advertiser, "especially with the countries nearest to us, it is always to be remembered that the first condition of success is a prosperous and vigorous home industry."

HOME INDUSTRIES, NOT PARTISAN POLITICS, OF MOST VALUE—The strife between the North and the South and the East and the West is to be not which shall produce the most of the raw materials to be manufactured and sold by other Nations, but which shall imitate England in employing the labor of the people, and thus reap the profits on both raw materials and finished goods. New and

[194]

quick routes of commerce must be opened and new markets for goods developed.

The Pacific States front the shores of populous Asia and Australia. We have the advantage of space and time, and immense but partially used resources to ultimately run a large share of that commerce.

THE THREE OVERLAND RAILROADS NEEDED FOR THIS PURPOSE—The eminent statesmen who projected them in 1853, and secured the act of Congress to make the surveys, foresaw their importance. The acts of incorporation of the Northern and Southern, requiring that American iron be used in their construction, aimed to employ American labor and promote our industries.

Those unfinished roads wait for Congress—in one case to merely extend the time of completion, and in the other to grant about one-sixth the aid extended to the Central and Union Pacific Railroads.

AMOUNT OF LABOR AT ONCE EMPLOYED—In the mere construction of the present transcontinental railroad "A total force of 20,000 to 25,000 workmen all along the lines, and 5,000 to 6,000 teams had been engaged in grading and laying out the track or getting out stone and timber. From 500 to 600 tons of materials were forwarded daily from either end of the lines. The Sierra Nevadas suddenly became alive with wood choppers, and at one place on the Truckee River twenty-five sawmills went into operation in one week. Upon one railroad 70 to 100 locomotives were in use at one time, constantly bringing materials and supplies. At one time there were 30 vessels *en route* from New York, via Cape Horn, with iron, locomotives, rails and rolling stock, destined for the Central Pacific Railroad.

The labor employed in building these roads has opened vastly larger fields of labor on the routes and at both ends. Labor employed increases its own opportunities. The completion of the Northern Pacific Railroad would employ many thousands of workmen on the routes, and as many thousands more of artisans in the mines and shops. All industries would revive and would increase.

The Texas Pacific would produce the same effects. Both are legitimate, reasonable enterprises, sure to enrich the builders, the States and the Nation, and to expand foreign trade, as they would build up our own industries.

The success of one line is proof of that of the other two, running at such distances North and South.

THE FOLLY OF RESTRICTIONS—Who can tell the evil of hindering the completion of either of these roads? We feel most keenly the defeat of the Northern Pacific Railroad.

Workingmen feel it in their pockets, at their tables, in their lack of power to provide comforts for their families. Pioneers have been waiting twenty years for these overland roads, and politicians, by their acts, coolly tell them that the time has not come for these roads to be built. Our Nation runs behind in the race with those who have fewer resources. Our artisans who ask for work are compelled to linger on street corners to get small jobs for the support of life. Shops are closed and fires die in the furnaces because, forsooth, Legislators spend their time in planning for new elections.

Shame on American statesmanship! Other nations mock us for our folly. Holding the key for the grandest progress across the Continent and on both oceans, the partisan neither uses it for the relief of his suffering countrymen nor for the honor of his country!

POSSIBLE FORCES TO SECURE THE NORTHERN PACIFIC RAILROAD EXTENSION BILL IN THE NEXT SESSION OR IN THE NEXT CONGRESS—The defeat of the Northern Pacific Railroad bill this session, says the Sacramento Record-Union, "diminishes its chances of becoming a law at the next session." This would be true with the same conditions. But failure in one mode of a right cause turns true friends to another mode. Grant, for the sake of argument, that the Union Pacific and Central Pacific Railroad will try to stop every rival transcontinental railroad North or South of their line, or buy its controlling stock. If it wins its way, then the first step is to measure the force of that combined opposition. It is folly to blink such a fact. It is wisdom to count its full measure. If it is a vested capital of $200,000,000, with a net income of $20,000,000 —two hundred millions of dollars, with an annual income of twenty millions of dollars—opposing the Northern Pacific Railroad and the Texas Pacific Railroad, the friends of the two rival roads ought to keep that fact in sight.

LARGEST FORCES CONFRONT THE VAST CAPITAL—This wealth created and represented by one railroad is only a sign of what can be created by one or two or three other lines across the Continent. One store in a good location invites two or three or five others. They come and win their share of the trade and profits, and thus the village grows into a city. Suppose the first store fights the second and the two combine against the third, the contest will end in planting all three stores. If the present overland railroad develops business and pays better every year – which is the known fact – then the rival roads can, and will be built. The force of the existing line, however rich and mighty, points to a twofold or threefold force to be developed in the other lines. We can count that force at twice twelve hundred millions, that will be the real property in the market in ten years after the other two lines are built.

CASH VALUE OF ONE OVERLAND ROAD—The capital of the Union Pacific Railroad, in 1876, was $116,220,212. That of the Central Pacific Railroad, in 1876, was $140,440,188. Amount of both, $256,660,400.

The assessed value of property in California alone, in 1874-5, was $611,495,197.

Its value during five years after the overland railroad was done had risen over three hundred and seventy-four millions of dollars. This testimony from the assessors' books is a good affidavit in the case. One hundred and fifty per cent gain in assessed property in California, in five years after the overland was completed, is an argument that will move capitalists to enter upon like enterprises. Thirty-one and three-fifths per cent per year will rouse the bankers, small and large, in our country and in Europe, to again secure the prize. Every man's acre shares the gain. Small landholders in California are made rich by the overland railroad, who were poor before its completion. Large landholders there have gained the wealth of princes, without effort on their part, simply by the completion of that railroad. San Francisco has more than doubled its population and its property valuation at the same cause. Sacramento has lifted itself up out of the swamps, dyked itself with high and solid lines of embankment against floods, and laid itself out with inviting homes for its increasing population of industrious artisans and merchants from the impulse given by the completion of this road. San Jose, Santa Cruz, Los Angeles, Marysville, Chico, and many other cities thrive and grow from the life imparted by this overland road and its branches.

GAIN TO STATES AND TERRITORIES—Other States, through which this road passes, have gained a large per cent by its completion. They have received millions from this enterprise without investing one dollar in it.

The productions of Utah, mineral, agricultural and miscellaneous, in 1875, amounted to $17,314,337. The increase of land cultivated in 1875, over 1874, was 60,250 acres. The Surveyor General reported lands sold in the year 1875, 49,956 acres.

The imports and exports of Utah, during 1875, were $9,150,851. The large business of that interior Territory is due almost entirely to the completion of the overland railroad.

Such facts apply to all the States and Territories on the line, and adjacent to the line, of the completed road. Nebraska, Kansas, Iowa and Missouri and Illinois have received like increase of property values. The unsold millions of acres of Government land on the line, and for hundreds of miles on either side have been made salable by that finished road.

PRODUCTS MADE AVAILABLE—The miscellaneous products of Utah consist of pig iron, iron ore, coke, fire clay, granite, ice, wool, tallow, hides, pelts, which, in 1875, amounted to 3,276,499 tons, worth $860, 384. They represent similar classes of products developed in other States and Territories by the Union Pacific and Central Pacific Railroads.

These freights were moved and these goods were made marketable by means of the overland railroad and its connections. Such an interior commerce was impossible until that highway was opened. Such productions are impossible from the vast interior of our Continent without such transcontinental roads.

UTAH MINERAL PRODUCTS, 1875

Base bullion, tons	16,330 at $250	$4,082,500
Lead bullion, tons	44 at 100	4,400
Silver lead ore, tons	312 at 100	532,000
Copper bullion, tons	349 at 250	87,949
Silver bars		35,800
Gold dust		750 ,000
Ore on dumps at mine, smelters' tons	10,000	
Tons	27,319	$6,145,21

These mineral values were, in fact, mostly created by the railroad, which transports the crude ores and base bullions to the smelters and then to market. The ores of Idaho, Montana, Dakota, Arizona and New Mexico lie buried and useless, waiting for the railroad cars and engines to put them into the life currents of business.

UTAH MANUFACTURES IN 1875

Railroad tie, 200,000 at 50c.	$100,000
Lumber, M 8,000 at $45	360,000
Founder works, boiler, etc.	175,000
Boots and shoes	75,000
Leather	5,000
Lime, bushels, 100,000 at 40c	40,000
Soap	3,000
Flour, pounds, 40,000,000 at 3c	1,200,000
Charcoal, bushels, 400,000 at 22c	88,000

Fire brick, M 500 at 80c	40,000
Building brick, 155,000 at 10c	155,000
Ale, porter and beer barrels, 15,914 at 15c	238,710
Cigars, M 375 at $65	24,375
Woolen goods	300,000
Total	$2,803,985

These products were mostly created by the influence of the overland railroad. They represent like products in ten other interior States and Territories, which must depend mostly on transcontinental railroads for their development. Of these seventeen millions of Utah productions in 1875, it is fair to set ten millions as the effect of the overland railroad. Multiply that gain by ten other such States and you have one hundred millions of yearly products waiting for such railroads.

The rise in the value of lands, and other real property, exceeds three hundred per cent, in ten years, as per the census tables in California. Count the gain one dollar per acre in Oregon, Washington, Idaho, Montana, Dakota, and the proposed Territory of Lincoln, as the result of the completed Northern Pacific Railroad, and count it as much in Western Texas, New Mexico and Arizona, in case of the completed Texas and Southern Pacific Railroad—the whole making an area of five hundred million acres—and that sum will at once be added to the permanent value of those states and of the Nation.

Unless both roads are built, those values cannot be created. This argument is effective now. In view of it the Central Pacific Railroad has pushed the construction of the Southern Pacific Railroad.

The Southern Pacific Railroad has

Authorized capital stock	$90,000,000
First mortgage bonds authorized	46,000,000
Twelve million acres land grant, valued at $2.50 per acre	30,000,000
Total	166,000,000

This immense preparation and outlay imply faith in a completed Southern overland railroad. The 500 miles built from San Francisco to Fort Yuma, on the Colorado, on the Western end, and about 450 miles Westward through Texas on the Eastern end, are proofs of a set purpose to complete that entire line. The strife of the two companies to secure special grants and advantages from Congress adds the evidence of their intense desire to win the greatest benefits from the enterprise. In fact, that transcontinental railroad has been a foregone conclusion in the minds of thinking observers of the facts.

THE SIGNS OF HOPE FOR THE NORTHERN PACIFIC RAIL-ROAD—Its defeat in Congress, this year, was evidently due to its restrictions. But the public in the great Northwest, from the lakes to the Pacific, has become aroused to its importance and its danger. The press of Chicago and New York is awake on the subject. The plottings of its foes, in and out of Congress, are watched and exposed. The merits of its claims and the injustice of neglecting or denying them, are seen and felt by larger numbers in the House and Senate. Business men and capitalists in city and country in the North, and many in the South, from the Atlantic to the Pacific, are believed to favor the enterprise as an act of justice to its creditors and of necessity to the unity and welfare of the whole country.

Its certainty and value to Oregon are assured by the present narrow gauge railroads built and in process, and the plan of construction to transport the products of the smaller valleys of the interior Columbia basin to the river. These branch lines anticipate not only water carriage to the sea, but a trunk line of railroad to tide water. Otherwise, they would be idle three or four months every year while the upper Columbia is blocked in ice. Every railroad branch system implies a trunk line.

A CLEAR SIGN—The increase of business on its 600 miles of road; the quick sales of its lands in Dakota and Minnesota; the growth of settlements along its proposed route; the proofs of its vast resources of choice coal, lime and iron mines, and timber forests on and near Puget Sound, besides its agricultural lands, furnish evidence that it will pay expenses and the interest on the capital needed to finish it.

[201]

ITS NEED—More than all, it needs friends from Oregon and Washington in the House and Senate. Faith, hope, courage and diligence in a man who sees and feels its absolute necessity to our region can win the case. An open, earnest, broad-minded hearty plea in private and public, with untiring zeal, will secure the simple extension of time to the Northern Pacific Railroad Company to finish their road. Divided counsels, partisan efforts and doubtful restrictions, will defeat it in the future as in the past.

The late Oregon election hinged upon this question. Oregon has instructed her Representatives in the Legislature to send her ablest, truest, and most faithful citizen to the Senate, to work for the completion of the Northern Pacific Railroad as a National enterprise; and as an act of justice to the 10,000 creditors, who invested $30,000,000 in its good faith eight years ago, and who have received no interest on their investment, as an absolute necessity to the welfare of this great Northwest, and to thousands of hardy pioneer settlers, who have, with faith in the Government pledges to the road, invested themselves and their property in homes on this exposed frontier, and as a most efficient means of protection from Indian wars along this Northern belt of our country. The voice and vote of Oregon emphasize every one of these reasons at this moment.

THE BASIN OF THE COLUMBIA—The upper country gives signs of becoming a vast area of grain fields. The stock ranges, rich in bunch grass, are fast changing into richer fields of wheat, which check the hills and valleys like a carpet. It is a marvel that the high hills produce all the cereals as abundantly as the plains. Its solution is due to a two-fold fact. First, the soil of this whole interior of high prairies was once the bed of a system of lakes, as appears from the lectures of Professor Condon, and illustrated by many fossils of former lacustrine and tropical life found embedded therein. It is also attested by the wonderful system of drainage carried on for ages by the Columbia River and its affluents. Those waters have not only cleaved dykes of basalt, miles in length, and scores, and even hundreds of feet high, as with a knife, 3,500 feet down to tide water. Uncounted numbers of ravines, in all directions, indicate the extent and magnitude of the drainage, which has left its records on the rounded hills and deep canyons. The volcanic overflows, traceable in the Cascade Mountains, that formed, on cooling, their basalt dykes and cliffs with their peculiar columnar crystallizations, added much to the mineral elements of the soil. Immense quantities of volcanic ashes doubtless were blown by winds, or carried by streams, into those ancient lakes, giving like valuable deposits.

Some of our rivers, as the Sandy, flowing from Mount Hood, and the Nisqually, flowing from Mount Rainier, are now often made milky white in summer by these volcanic ashes, loosened by heat from their beds under the ice, and borne down by the rains and melting snows. The Sandy has thus for a long time been forming some of the alluvial soils, like the Columbia Meadows. The soils of the Willamette Valley owe much of their power to these sources, which become more apparent as the higher prairies and hills are cleared and sown with wheat or set with orchards.

In like manner, these old volcanoes furnished the abundant mineral elements in the upper country, on which all the cereals feed and thrive, viz.: the potash, soda, lime, magnesia and phosphorus and silicic acids. The basalts are largely Feldspathic, which consists of silicia, alumina and potash and are easily disintegrated by frost, thus adding large annual increments to the soil.

These high table lands, under the plough, exhibit the finest tilth from one to twenty feet or more deep, and alike through the whole mass. Unlike the dark vegetable mold of the Mississippi basin, the soils of this Columbia basin are whiter and more highly charged with the alkalis and fixed acids.

Western farmers are astonished that such whitish lands there, and in the Willamette Valley, can produce the cereals; but they are more astonished to gather a harvest of thirty or sixty bushels of wheat per acre from these high tracts. It is also a surprise that the berry of all kinds of grain is so plump and large, and that the straw is so tall and strong. The wild rye grass of the Yakima Valley is like a withe for toughness. The bunch grass on the hillsides bends before the wind and bends back like a bow of steel. The willow and the poplar, and other soft woods, take on a kind of robust, oak-like strength.

[203]

The analysis of mineral elements required for grain, published by Professor P. Collier, of Vermont, suggests the reason, as was intimated in an article in the *Commercial* a few weeks ago. For example, the berry of wheat requires the following proportions: ash, 2.07 %; potash, 31.1%; soda, 3.5%; magnesia, 12.2%; lime, 3.1%; oxide of iron, 0.7%; phosphoric acid, 46.2%; sulphuric acid, 2.4%; silicic acid, 1,7%; chlorine, 0.5%; or ten mineral elements, ranging upwards in the proportions of five-tenths of chlorine and seven-tenths of oxide of iron to thirty-one and one-tenth of potash and forty-six and two-tenths of phosphoric acid.

These are factors mathematically fixed. The soil which has these elements will produce wheat, other things being equal. Soils destitute or exhausted of them cannot bear wheat. Rye requires very nearly the same proportions of the same substance. Oats require about half of the proportions of the same, with the addition of forty-six and four-tenths of silicic acid. Barley requires about two-thirds the same as wheat, with twenty-seven and two-tenths of silicic acid, instead of 1.7, required by wheat. But wheat straw requires ash, 4.26%; potash, 11.5%; soda, 1.6%; magnesia, 2.1%; lime, 5.8%; oxide of iron, 0.7%; phosphoric acid, 5.3%; sulphuric, 2.5%; silicic acid, 69.1%; chlorine, 1.1%; that is, it demands the same mineral elements in the proportions, 0.7% of oxide of iron up to 69.1% of silicic acid, which gives the tube of straw its firm, glossy quality. E.L. Youmans remarks: "Silica is necessary to the growth of vegetations, and exists abundantly in many plants, particularly in the stalks of grains and grasses. It is this which communicates stiffness and strength to their stems, as the skeleton does to the bodies of animals. If there is a deficiency of soluble silica in the soil, the grain stalk will be weak, and liable to break down or lodge."

We may suppose, by observing the growth of the grain in the upper country, that those soils contain these elements in abundance. This supposition is confirmed by their geologic origin. The final proof will be a qualitative and quantitative chemical analysis rigidly tested.

While these elements remain abundant in the soils, the cereals can be produced. Exhaust them by successive crops, as in Western New

York, and in many Western States, and crops will lose in quality and in quantity.

The second fact, which solves the problem of reclaiming this interior basin from mere pastures to farm lands, is that the invisible ocean of vapor, constantly borne inland from the Pacific over these high plains, can be cooled and deposited in the form of dews, mists and showers, so as to furnish all needed irrigation. The complaint was made for thirty years that they were practically deserts. It is only a few years since the plow has moved up the hillsides. Now, fields of wheat, oats, barley and rye wave luxuriantly by the side of dry bunch grass tracts, even on the higher ranges.

The plow proves to be the cooler. It opens the light, porous soil to the air, which enters it freely and parts with its heat and its moisture at the same moment to nourish the plants. The higher the hill, the quicker the cooling process occurs in still air, so that the night dews and mists water the plants there best every evening when the wind dies away.

Some persons have tried to explain the growth of grain on the upper plains by a sort of capillary attraction, drawing up the moisture. It has also been explained by electrical changes, caused by the telegraph. But whenever the plow is freely used, and the seed planted, though scores of miles away from the telegraph, the growth of grain and vegetable becomes luxuriant.

Orchards, groves and fields increase the cooling surfaces, giving more moisture and more summer showers in all that region that had been rainless. The practical benefit already is a larger variety of productions, and a grand harvest of cereals for home and foreign markets.

Granting that these two facts are true of the upper Columbia basin; that the soil abounds in the constituents to furnish various and most valuable harvests, and that the climate is favorable to their production, it is reasonable to expect a wider area of cultivation every year. The day of doubt is past. The experiment has been made. The plow, the reaper and the wagon of this season must be duplicated the next, and so on while the markets demand supplies.

Forecasting the future, the country that can possibly be thus cultivated stretches from one range of mountains to the other, East and West, and from the high plains of Nevada into the British possessions.

It is reasonable to expect more springs from the hillsides and larger streams in the valleys with the increase of population. Instead of stock ranches and settlers' cabins widely separated, we may look for farming communities and thriving villages in sight and not far from each other. Such is the process now in Umatilla, Walla Walla, Columbia and Stevens Counties.

The facilities for transportation furnished by the Oregon Steamship Navigation Company, and by the railway from Wallula to Walla Walla, completed by the skill and energy of Dr. D.S. Baker, will, perhaps, stimulate the early completion of a railroad from Umatilla to La Grande, and one from Dayton to the mouth of the Tucannon, on the Snake River. There is need of lumber and fuel all over that region. Every reason urges the completion of the Northern Pacific Railroad to the Columbia and the ocean waters, that the exchange of commodities on the Coast may be made at all seasons with those of the interior.

INVISIBLE VAPOR—Air absorbs and retains a certain amount of moisture, at a given temperature. Heat it one degree and it will hold more. Cool it a degree and it will hold less and deposits dew. A glass of ice water in summer will cool the surrounding air and form drops outside the glass. It has simply reduced the power of the air to suspend the vapor. Let the glass stand a few minutes and the drops will evaporate. Warmer air carries them off.

TRADITIONAL FARMING—The custom to hoe corn in New England three times rested on a scientific principle, but our fathers did not tell us boys forty years ago what it was. Perhaps they did not know, yet their common rule, that it did the corn good to stir the ground often, insured a good crop.

[206]

The older men now work their gardens as long as the hoe can touch the ground between the plants. The result is thrifty growth and the finest vegetables.

The stirred soil presents a larger cooling surface, which quickly tests a dew point in a still night, and waters the plants with a gentle mist. Science now unveils and extends the benefits of the old traditions.

THE EXACT AMOUNT OF VAPOR IN THE AIR IS KNOWN— Tables of figures show the weight of vapor that the air can sustain at the various degrees of temperature. This power of suspension increases from 2.13 grains at 32 degrees—the freezing point—to 18.84 grains at 100 degrees, a gain of 16.71 grains per cubic foot.

*WEIGHTS AND MEASURES OF AIR IN SUSPENSION—*A column of air 10 feet square, 1,000 feet high, if saturated at 32 degrees sustains 30 pounds of water, which equals four and five-sevenths standard United States gallons. At 5,000 feet – the base of Mount Hood – the same column, at 32 degrees, will sustain 197 pounds, equal to 23 and three-sevenths gallons. A column of saturated air covering an acre, 1,000 feet high, at 32 degrees, contains 13,068 pounds, or 1,568 gallons of water. The same column, 5,000 feet, holds 65,340 pounds, or 7,940 gallons.

*AMOUNT OF SUSPENSION IN OUR FOUR SEASONS—AVERAGE IN A WINTER SEASON—*Our average winter air, 39 degrees, saturated in a column ten feet square and 1,000 feet high holds up to 39 and three-sevenths pounds, or four and five-sevenths gallons of water. The same column 5,000 feet high holds up 197 pounds, or 23 and three-sevenths gallons. A column of saturated air at 39 degrees, covering an acre, 1,000 feet high, contains 17,175 pounds, which equals 2,061 gallons. This column, 5,000 feet high, contains 85,875 pounds, or 10,305 gallons.

*AMOUNT IN SPRING—*Western Oregon in spring averages 52 degrees. A column ten feet square and 1000 feet high, saturated, holds 62 and five-sevenths pounds, or 7.5 gallons. At 5,000 feet —the highest of the lower clouds—it contains 313 pounds, or 37.5 gallons. Such a column, covering an acre, 1,000 feet high, contains

27,318 pounds, or 3,278 gallons. At 5,000 feet it contains 136,590 pounds, or 16,390 gallons.

AMOUNT IN SUMMER—Oregon air in summer averages 67 degrees, and if saturated, a column of it, 10 feet square and 1,000 feet high, suspends 104 pounds, or 12.5 gallons of water. At 5,000 feet, the column suspends 520 pounds, or 62.5 gallons. A column an acre in size, 1,000 feet high, holds up 45,702 pounds, or 5,484 gallons. The same, 5,000 feet high, holds up 227,510 pounds, or 27,420 gallons.

AMOUNT IN AUTUMN—Our air in autumn averages 53 degrees. A column of it saturated, 10 feet square, 1,000 feet high, suspends 65 pounds, or 7.8 gallons of water; and 5,000 feet high, it suspends 325 pounds, or 39 gallons. A column covering an acre, 1,000 feet high, suspends 28,314 pounds, or 3,398 gallons. The same column, 5,000 feet high, suspends 141,570 pounds, or 16,990 gallons.

UPPER COLUMBIA BASIN—We are not able to get the average temperatures for the four seasons in Eastern Washington and Washington, as the United States Signal Service is not yet extended thither, as it needs to be.

Assuming 70 degrees as the summer average of the upper Columbia basin, and assuming that the air, blowing constantly from the ocean by day, is well saturated with moisture—which everyone feels as he stands facing those sea winds—it holds 8.01 grains of watery vapor. A column of it 10 feet square and 1,000 feet high suspends 114.75 pounds, or 13.25 gallons. The same column, 5,000 feet high, or about the height of white clouds that hover near Mount Hood in summer, suspends 572 pounds, or 69 gallons of water. Such a column, covering an acre, 1,000 feet high, suspends 49,864 pounds, or 5,983 gallons. At 5,000 feet high it suspends 249,320 pounds, or 29,915 gallons.

Cool that air to 50 degrees—which is done, usually, every night all over Oregon and Washington, and it loses 3.91 grains per cubic foot, or almost half its vapor. Vegetation drinks it. Heavy dews cover the grass. Soils deeply plowed and broken up into fine tilth absorb it and give abundant food to plants. Professor Brockleby remarks: "The air over the ocean is always saturated, and upon the Coasts, in equal latitudes, contains the greatest possible amount of vapor; but the quantity decreases as we advance inland, for the atmosphere of the plains of Oronoco, the steppes of Siberia, and the interior of New Holland is naturally dry." But the interior of Oregon to the Rocky Mountains cannot be called very dry, as its vapor comes fresh with every sea breeze.

OCEAN OF INVISIBLE VAPOR OVER US—There is such an ocean of vapor covering all of Eastern Oregon and Washington, from the Humboldt to the Fraser River Valleys, and extending Westward to the Pacific, 5,000 feet deep from the bed of the Columbia, enclosing an area of over 300,000 square miles.

FEARS OF LACK OF MOISTURE—The climate east of the Cascades has been called dry and the land arid. The question of assured moisture in summer is often discussed and weighed by comparing seasons. The last was better than former years. Showers were common in Walla Walla and other lower valleys. But will showers increase and extend with cultivation? Will springs break out on the hillsides as the high prairies are plowed and filled?

AN EXAMPLE OF RAIN WITHOUT CLOUD—Standing in Dayton (WA), Columbia County, near the Touchet, July 12, 1877, at 5 o'clock A.M., as the sun rose before me, I noticed a fine rain falling from a cloudless sky and wetting the grass in Mr. Matzgar's garden. Mr. Matzgar had noticed the same fact often. Its solution was, that the trees and grass and garden had cooled and compressed the column of air and deposited part of its vapor. As the sun rose higher in the clear sky the same moisture was re-absorbed by the re-expanding air, as a sponge takes up water and gives it out on pressure and re-absorbs it when the pressure is off. Cooling the air acts like pressing the sponge. Heat expands it and increases its capacity to hold vapor. Professor Brocklesby attests several instances of showers occurring when the sky was clear. This phenomena was several times observed by Humboldt; and Kametz says it happens in Germany twice or thrice a year.

NATURE'S IRRIGATION—Grant that an acre of air at 70 degrees and 1,000 feet high suspends 59.83 gallons of water, and when reduced to 50 degrees, on a still night, gives out about half its supply, or 2,900 gallons, sprinkling it in finest dew over every inch of the land, and you have an irrigating process superior to any number of streams or system of artesian wells. Suppose the column 5,000 feet high, the deposit at 50 degrees may be 14,500 gallons.

OBJECTION—Do you object that a far less amount seems to be deposited? Only approximates can be given. Air cools one degree every 243 feet high, about three degrees per 1,000 feet. This reduces the vapor. Every degree of heat, with the ascending sun, re-absorbs the moisture until all is gone that was not drunk up by the leaves and grass, or by the soil, and very soon the soil gives back what it received, unless its web of rootlets have drunk it up. If the soil is baked, never plowed, and never set in cereals, or shrubs, or trees, it gets very little good from its nightly drenching and, at the earliest sunrise, the blessing flies away to its treasure in the skies.

GOOD CULTIVATION GARNERS THE VAPOR ABOUT THE PLANT ROOTS—On the high hills of Columbia County, Washington Territory, wheat grew luxuriantly in July, 1877, while four feet distant the bunch grass was drying up. This was the first plowing for the wheat, while the other land had never been plowed. That upland soil has a fine mixture of the mineral elements or alkalies, and thus a spongy lightness, which easily absorbs vapor and gaseous foods. Hence its marvelous productive powers.

IT NEEDS THE PLOUGH, THE SEED AND THE TREE—Those high prairies, that now seem so dry in summer, need to be broken up, sown, set with shrubs and trees. The soil, once open and set with wheat, will absorb its full supply of moisture every cool night, which will carry its load of nutriment to rootlets, or drip away to form springs. Trees and shrubs also become coolers and deposit moisture.

FALLOW GROUND AN INJURY—Rotate crops, as in Great Britain, for best results. No fields need be left fallow for many years. Sown, or planted and tilled, they will increase the deposit of moisture and then assure the coolness and crops on other fields.

[210]

WHEAT IN ROWS LIKE CORN—If wheat or oats become too dry, as happens in the lower Walla Walla Valley, run the light plow or cultivator through the grain every three or four feet, leaving it in rows like corn. Do it once or twice in the summer.

The section harrow and clod crusher made by Messrs. Carter, in Albany, will make a fine, light tilth, that will absorb moisture. This process will give a larger product of wheat from the rows of grain than from the entire field, left crusted and dry.

EXAMPLES—A gentleman raised a fine field of corn two and one-half miles from Walla Walla, ten years ago, without a drop of rain. He simply plowed the land, planted the seed, and used the plow or cultivator between the rows. Two years ago, another farmer raised over 40 bushels per acre, of corn, back of The Dalles, without a drop of rain. His plow kept the ground loose and spongy, and it absorbed all needed moisture from the air.

In 1877, L. Patterson, of Hillsboro, planted three rows of new kinds of wheat in his garden two and one-half feet apart, dropping the seeds about eight inches apart in each row. From thirty to sixty stalks grew from each kernel, carrying as many heads, which had from fifty to one hundred grains each. The ground was kept light and spongy, and was always moist a half inch below the surface. The wide spaces gave room for the plants to feed and grow well. The stalks sprouted from the center stalk like a currant bush. This proves that every wheat plant must have room and a fine tilth to give the largest products. Mr. Patterson thinks four quarts enough to plant an acre. His field of wheat, a few rods distant, looked fair, but it was crusted over and dry and impervious to moisture, and thus in part a failure, as every field of grain, sowed broadcast and left to turn over, must be.

Rev. O. Dickinson had a field of wheat near Salem last year, which became so foul with wild oats that he ran the plow through every three feet to kill the oats, leaving rows of wheat three feet apart. The result was a larger crop of wheat than the entire field would have given. This year he proposes to cultivate some land on this plan, using the Carter Excelsior Combined Section Harrow to break the clods and reduce the tilth between the rows.

THIS PLAN IS APPLICABLE TO FLAT PRAIRIES—The yellow patches of grain on some of the flat prairies of Marion, Linn and Lane Counties are an eyesore. It is stated that Linn County raised only half a crop in 1877, owing to late excessive rains, followed by hot, dry months. The ground baked and the plants were choked and stinted. Had farmers run their plows through the fields, about two or three feet apart, in June, as the soil began to crust over, and then followed in July with the cultivator, or section harrow and clod crusher, between the rows, the evidence is that they would have had a much larger crop. The plan is worth trying this year, as the continued rains may keep those lands soaked till late.

THE PLAN APPLIED TO VINEYARDS—The vineyard connected with the San Gabriel Mission, near Los Angeles, I am told, is cultivated of late entirely without irrigation. The plow, spade and hoe prove entirely sufficient to keep the ground moist and give an abundant crop.

IT APPLIES TO DRY LAND ELSEWHERE—A gentleman has raised fine fields of corn, ten miles south of Los Angeles, without a drop of rain, simply using the plow and the cultivator freely.

A Baker County farmer, I am told, plowed up the sage brush, outside of an old field, and raised seventy bushels of oats per acre, without rain. The soil is mineral, light and spongy. Once open, it absorbed moisture enough for fine growth and product.

The plains of Kansas were marked on the old maps, 40 years ago, as a part of the "Great American Desert." The plow and cultivator have caused luxuriant fields of corn and wheat to replace those once parched lands.

ITS EFFECT TO PRODUCE SPRINGS—Rev. C. Eells and J.A. Perkins, of Colfax, noticed stock water on a side hill near the Touchet last fall, where ten years ago there was only a slight sign of moisture. A dozen farms have been opened ten miles around within ten years. Others report springs since the hills have been cultivated where none existed before.

Suppose the rich bunch grass plains and those eaten off, which lie on the route from The Dalles to Umatilla, are plowed and sowed or drilled in wheat, the excess of moisture deposited will probably produce springs where none can now be found. Add trees and shrubs, and the result will at length become a certainty. Instead of depending on costly artesian wells, it is better to draw a water supply from the air.

EFFECT ON THE STREAMS—Doubtless the increased acreage now cultivated in the upper basin of the Columbia has added volume to the smaller streams. The limit of increase will not be reached so long as the plows and wheat fields and gardens and groves extend over those high hills and deep valleys. Grand and beautiful will be the panorama when the whole interior, not a treeless region, shall be dotted with farms, orchards and dwellings. The plow will hasten that day.

DROUGHTS PREVENTED OR MODIFIED BY SUCH CULT-IVATION—A traveler sent a letter to one of the Puget Sound papers last year, describing his rough, dusty journey Northward from Southern California. One morning his stage started at 3 o'clock, and he found nothing to note but the ascent of a hill about 1,500 feet through a fog bank as many feet deep. As the sun rose, the same dry plains and hills greeted his eye on every side. That fog bank was Nature's store house of water for the thirsty ground. The San Francisco Bulletin reported later fine fields of wheat in the upper counties without a drop of rain; but a wise use of plow and harrow opened the soil to absorb the invisible vapor. One farmer is reported to have planted wheat in rows and tilled it, raising as per his test over 60 bushels per acre. It is cheaper to raise 60 bushels on one acre than on four acres.

Probably a wise use of the plow in cultivating wheat, instead of the poppy, would have lessened the famine in the high plains of Hindostan last year, or have possibly prevented it. The Northern

Provinces of China may possibly be saved the same desolations by using horses and American plows instead of hoes and spades. Shallow cultivation gives too little cooling surface to the heated air of those high plains. It is certain that there is moisture enough in the air, but it must be cooled to the dew point in order to be used. The protection and assurance of crops every year is the deposit of invisible vapor suspended in the air.

THE PUGET SOUND BASIN—SHORE LINE 2,000 MILES—This network of deep land-locked bays, inlets and sounds, opening to the Pacific through the DeFuca and Georgian Straits, is the wonder of navigators and the joy of commerce. Fleets of lumber, coal, lime, vegetables, hops, grain, fish, oil, fruit, staves, hoops, furniture and furniture woods, water pipe and pump stocks, ship knees and spars, and the products of several other new industries, already glide through these ample water ways to the ocean and world marts.

Freights are cheaper from Puget Sound to Liverpool than from Lake Michigan to Liverpool. The harvests now annually gathered from the forests and mines, from fields and orchards, from rivers and sea waters, all are mere signs of vastly greater and more harvests yet to be gathered.

LUMBER—MILLS—The great mills are improving and increasing their machinery, using late inventions to economize force and perfect their lumber for the demands of builders and shipwrights, and other wood workers, while adding twenty to eighty per cent to their average daily product. This draws more ships to their wharves, loads them quicker and oftener, and sends them in search of new markets.

COAL—The Seattle mines of coal are a type of a vast series of veins which enriches this entire basin. These extend in sections Northward into British America, and Southward into the Columbia River, and along the foot hills and spurs to the Cascades and Coast Mountains into California. The Seattle Coal Company will export over a hundred thousand tons the present year of good domestic which is sold readily in San Francisco. The Seatco mines are

[214]

sending an equally good domestic coal to Olympia, at lower rates on the Oregon & Transcontinental Narrow Gauge Railroad. A short side track from the Northern Pacific Railroad can put the same coal cheap into the Portland markets.

LIME—The San Juan and Orcas Island lime have already become known as choice brands in our markets, displacing those from Santa Cruz, as the latter did the Oahu lime 15 years ago. The Puyallup lime beds now bid fair to rival those of San Juan, as their hops do those of more Southern climes.

COAL—Coal, lime and iron beds near together and near the sea make blast furnaces and rolling mills and machine shops both possible and profitable. The same vegetation which produced the coal veins also formed the deposits of iron ore. Their common laboratory was in the vast morasses of the carbonaceous period. Finding the coal outcroppings, you may expect to find the iron ores nearby, and probably the lime rocks in some form. All these mines are found near Tacoma. The branch Northern Pacific Railroad, up the Puyallup Valley, now opens the coal and lime to market, and touches the outcroppings of iron ore that indicate both the quality and quantity needed for home use and export. Once developed, the savings in freights alone will furnish a large margin of profit for this home industry and a chance for export also to the vast marts of the Pacific Coast, worthy of the attention of the prudent capitalist and manufacturer.

LUMBER—During twenty-five years the mill companies of Puget Sound have been exporting their products of fir and cedar to all the markets of the Pacific, while many cargoes of their spars and ship knees have gone to the maritime ports of France and England. Their annual export now exceeds two hundred millions of feet of sawed lumber. Yet they have only penetrated the forests from one to three miles from the shores of bays and rivers, and only culled the timber so far. Single trees often make from 12,000 to 15,000 feet. Their average, as estimated, is 10,000 (feet) per tree, and 50 trees, or 500,000 feet, per acre. When cut close, as in Eastern forests, this amount, in many places, will be doubled. In the valleys, curly maple, alder, ash, cedar and some other furniture and fine cabinet woods, are found for a growing market.

FISH—The waters of Puget Sound are the home of the salmon and salmon trout, the halibut, the herring, the rock and tom cod, the flounder, the sea perch and smelt, with other varieties of food fish, besides extensive clam beds and oyster beds. The dogfish and others are taken for oil. The fisheries have only just begun to enlist attention and capital, but they promise a large reward to enterprise.

FRUIT—The apple, pear, cherry, plum, and even the Isabella grape flourish on the shores and islands of this archipelago, while the currants, strawberries, raspberries and blackberries grow luxuriantly, and give large and delicious harvests for the reward of every faithful gardener.

VEGETABLES—The potato, turnip, tomato, beet, carrot, parsnip, squash, pumpkin, cabbage, cauliflower, celery and onion are raised easily and beyond home market demands. Nearness to the sea offers a profitable market for their exports.

THE GRASSES—Timothy, red and white clover, and orchard grass, blue grass, indeed, every variety tested thrives in this soil and climate, whether on lowland or highland.

THE CEREALS—The specimens of these were shown by Mr. Bush at the Centennial Exposition, for which he received a well deserved medal of honor. His fine exhibit can be matched by any careful farmer in any of the valleys of the Puget Sound basin, and on all the wooded plains that trend toward the hills and mountains, and on the islands and dyke lands of the Skagit and Swinomish flats. These latter often yield one hundred bushels of oats or barley per acre.

THE SOILS—It has been thought, at the first glance, that the only good lands are the river bottoms and tide flats, and that the light and more sandy bluffs and slopes, and forest-covered hills, will be worthless to the farmer after the lumbermen have culled their grand treasures of lumber. But look at the grass plots and gardens and orchards of Olympia, and the farm near by; or of Seattle, of

Port Madison, or Port Gamble, or Port Ludlow, or Port Townsend, or Dungeness, or Coupeville, or Seabec, or any spot in Whatcom, or Snohomish, or Island, or Mason, or Kitsap, or King Counties, and you will see a luxuriant vegetation, a strength of tube and stock, a breadth of leaf, a rich coloring of flower, that give token of a soil and climate remarkably rich in all the mineral, vegetable, gaseous and vapor elements needed for garden and field, as well as forest.

The difficulty of clearing is more than matched by the cost of transportation from the distant though rich plains of the interior. The gain of nearness to the sea is found in the greater variety of products for use and export. The lack of alluvium and the deep, black mold of the low valleys is more than compensated by the richer mixture of the mineral, alkaline and silicious deposits in these upland soils. They will last longer, make better and stronger tubes, holding up the grain heads firmly, proof against rust and storm, and probably a surety against insect foes.

This soil, opened deeply by the plow, and often stirred deep in the summer afternoons, will absorb the air saturated with vapors, and furnish the finest irrigation to all sorts of plants, and yield the largest harvests. Nearly every city, village and hamlet of the Puget Sound basin are open doors to abounding resources from the Creator's hand. The need is of thought, toil, patience and economy to enrich that whole region with homes and farms abounding in comforts, health, luxuries and wealth.

TRANSPORTATION—When the Northern Pacific Railroad shall be completed, opening the vast grain fields and pastures of the interior to the sea, and carrying inland the lumber, coal, iron and ocean commerce; and when the narrow gauge railroads, like the S. & W.W. R.R., and the O. & T.R.R., shall extend the exports and imports through all the valleys, there will be ample occasion for an increase of enterprise on land and sea.

WESTERN OREGON AND WASHINGTON—CLIMATE AVERAGE
Winter: 39 degrees; Spring: 52 degrees; Summer: 67 degrees; Fall: 53 degrees.

REMARKS GIVING PARTICULARS OF WIND, SEA, WEATHER, TRIM OF SHIP, KIND OF CARGO, ETC.—The weather since leaving Esquimalt has been favorable. Ship's draft leaving Esquimalt,[i] forward 19 feet, 2 inches; aft 19 feet, 3 inches. Cargo consisting principally of produce. The coal received at Tacoma has been exposed to the weather for months, which, nevertheless, has done good work corresponding to the power exerted. I would recommend all steamship companies, or large corporations, to give it a fair trial and test. In order to do this, it is necessary to have a good grate surface and good draught. I would rather use this coal, from what I have seen of it, than any other on this Coast. The mine is new yet, and the coal not at any great depth, and I am positive it will improve rapidly as they go into the mine. [Editor: One page chart appears here, of consumption of coal on Pacific Mail Steamship *Alaska*, voyage from Port of Esquimalt to San Francisco, Oct. 21-24, 1878] I have tried all other kinds of coal, except Seattle, and that, I am informed from good authority, is very sooty; while, on the other hand, Puyallup coal makes no soot whatever—therefore, no sponging of tubes is necessary. I would say to all, try it, and I will substantiate my statement."

Very Respectfully, (signed) John Stewart, Chief Engineer

---

[i] Esquimalt is a port west of Victoria, B.C.

SEVEN

Writings about Native Americans

Atkinson's earlier correspondence and publications say little about Native Americans, but the three years from 1877 to 1880 produced five *Oregonian* articles devoted to various aspects of the subject. This fits with the time (1874-1880) when Gen. Oliver O. O. Howard served as Commander of the U.S. Army's Department of the Columbia.

Gen. Howard is best known for his work as the first Director of the Bureau of Freedmen, Refugees and Abandoned Lands (popularly known as the Freedmen's Bureau), which he headed for five years, beginning in May 1865. In 1872 President Grant sent Howard to the Southwest to negotiate treaties with Indian tribes, most notably Geronimo, a Chiricahua Apache leader.[i] From that work, Howard moved to Fort Vancouver for his assignment in the Pacific Northwest.

Howard, a lifelong Congregationalist and committed Sunday School teacher, had become acquainted with Atkinson at a national meeting of Congregationalists in 1871, where the two men were elected as vice-Moderators. While at Fort Vancouver Howard taught Sunday School at First Congregational Church in Portland, and helped to organize a YMCA in the city. He also led in the establishment of the Indian Training School, initially placed adjacent to the Pacific University campus in Forest Grove but soon moved to Chemawa, just north of Salem, Oregon, where it is still located. Atkinson's writings include several references to conversations with Gen. Howard about Native Americans.

---

[i] Howard, *Indian Chiefs I have Known.*

The last of these articles recounts a personal visit to the Warm Springs Reservation, in Oregon, where Atkinson reviewed its schools and farms, concluding with a serious, enlightening dialogue with the tribal council.

Native Americans

Source:
The Oregonian Archives
Multnomah County Library

Dec. 22, 1877

Indian Homesteads

To the Editor of the Oregonian:

T he endorsement of the very able letter of Mr. A.J. Cain upon securing land to Indians in severalty will doubtless meet a like response from many readers. The people of Oregon, Washington and Idaho want to be just to the Indians as individuals. Mr. Cain's plan is fair to both parties. His idea is to ignore the tribe and give every man and every family a right in the soil. Mr. Cain shows that the more intelligent Indians want a title to a farm the same as a white man has. The 14th and 15th amendments to the constitution permit him to give up his tribal relations and become a citizen and take his homestead. A partial enabling act, it is said, has been passed by Congress to encourage it. The reservations and tribal treaties complicate the question, by precluding those on the reservations from taking homesteads within those limits and by restricting them at the same time within those limits. A few Indians like Timothy and seven other families at Alpoowai on the Snake river have ventured to assume their recognized rights, to take land, to fence and till farms, pay taxes, submit to the law and claim its protection. They have gained the respect of their neighbors and confidence of officials, and an abundant support for themselves. Under this new regime they improve year by year. Mr. Cain's report of an Indian village near the upper Spokane bridge under Stylome as head man and business manager, is another suggestive facts in the same line. The fact itself commands respect and wins confidence.

Allow Indians on the reservations to *own* farms there, as Mr. C. and many others testify, the system of Indian homesteads will displace that of 'Indian reservations'. If government surveys follow up this policy, the whites and Indians will choose their locations with little if any conflict. The vast areas of valuable lands within and without the reservations, now merely roamed over, will be occupied by peaceable settlers, white and Indian, subject to the same laws, and enjoying the same privileges. From Mr. Cain's long acquaintance with the Indians of the upper Columbia, his testimony is the more valuable on this point. It confirms the growing sentiment that it is both safe and wise to treat the Indian as a man. Give him his rights and hold him to his duties under the law. Interest will more and more bind the better class to this policy. Anchored to the soil by title he will expose and defeat any Indian league against the white settlers whose laws protect his own rights. So strong is his conviction of his title now, that enforced removal breeds war. That was the key to the war with Chief Joseph. This will arouse war again. Its opposite will promote peace, and help to save and civilize a much larger per cent of the Indians than the mixed policy has done.

Secretary Schurz' report of Nov. 1, 1877, just received, commends 'allotments of small tracts of land to heads of families on all reservations, to be held in severalty under proper restrictions, so that they may have fixed homes."

Those who support their families he would admit to the benefits of the homestead act, if they are willing to detach themselves from their tribal relations, to the privileges of citizenship.

He adds, "To protect the security of life and property among the Indians, the laws of the United States, to be enforced by proper tribunals, should be extended over the reservations, and a body of police composed of Indians, and subject to the order of government officers, should be organized on each of them. It is a matter of experience that Indians thus trusted with official duty can almost uniformly be depended upon in point of fidelity and efficiency.

These views accord with the experience and judgment of Mr. Cain and many other gentlemen who, like him, have been agents, or have become acquainted with Indians in their own country. It is to be hoped that this policy will be distinctly adopted by the government, and carried out promptly by the interior department in its conduct of Indian affairs both on and off the reservations.

Yours, respectfully,
G.H. ATKINSON

June 27, 1878

The Indian Question: Its Hopeful Signs

REPORT OF THE CONGREGATIONAL ASSOCIATION OF OREGON AND WASHINGTON AT OREGON CITY, JUNE 22, BY REV. DR. ATKINSON

E very element of a problem in its process of solution must be weighed. The public have long been considering the problem of the Indian. It would be strange if no progress had been made toward solution. The two policies stand out in sharper lines by their effects. That of force tends rapidly to extermination. Treated as tribes, any man can cause an Indian war, filling them with the terror of utter ruin—they foresee that end—and ourselves with shame.

"Three young Nez Perce of Chief Joseph's tribe left their camp on Camas prairie where they were digging their annual supply of roots in June a year ago and went over to Salmon river. One of the young men, whose father was killed on Salmon river by a white man, on coming to the man who killed his father, killed him and three others with him. This is the first murder the Indians committed. The next day they returned to the camp and it is said they openly told what they had done at Salmon river, and induced young men to join them and kill more whites on Camas prairie, although the chiefs tried all they could to prevent further depredation, but all was to no purpose. The next night many more Indians joined and killed more white men at Camas prairie. Thus the war with Chief Joseph and his band commences."

This is the account given to Mr. Barstow by James Reuben, assistant teacher at Lapwai agency school, and a scout under General Howard until those Indians fled to Montana. It bears the marks of truth and agrees in substance with other accounts given at that time.

Had such murders been committed in the British territory the civil government, employing both a white and an Indian police, would have seized, tried and punished the murderers, first the white man who slew the Indian's father, and then the Indian who slew the white murderer and his friends. This process of municipal law in holding every man responsible for his own acts, would have prevented other murders and saved the community from disturbance and even from alarm. English law deals with the individual without regard to race, color or condition. It does not recognize the tribe, and it cannot come in conflict with the tribe. This is understood by both parties. Both assent to it. Justice is done. An Indian war cannot occur in the British dominions.

The American policy loses sight of the Indian and holds the tribe responsible for his crimes. It fails to arrest and punish the white man for his crimes against the Indian. It prepares for war and excites other tribes into hostile confederation; prolongs the conflict for months as last year at a cost of hundreds of lives on both sides, and $800,000 in cash, and general alarm and suspense of the white community.

The commissioner of Indian affairs testifies that: "During the forty years prior to 1868 the cost of Indian wars—without including the destruction of private property—was not less than $500,000,000, or an average of $12,500,000 per year. The great Sioux war of 1852, 1853, 1854 cost the government $40,000,000, without improving our relations with those Indians. In 1854 and 1855, the cost of quelling disturbances by the army in Oregon alone was $10,000,000. The Cheyenne war, caused by the barbarous massacre at Sand Creek, besides the immense loss of property and life, cost the government $35,000,000 and the lives of many soldiers. And the war that broke out again in 1867, by reason of an unprovoked assault of our troops upon peaceful Indians, was continued two years at a cost of $40,000,000."

A blunder in our policy is like a misplaced switch. The wreck and death and losses are prolonged the whole length of the train. So our national blunder of dealing with Indian tribes, instead of individual Indians, has been a prolonged series of disasters, wars, death and losses for more than two centuries, and the present year, even this hour, continues its long train of horrors. The Bannacks [*ed.*—the Bannock tribe] were starving at their reservation agency in April last. They hurried off to their old camas grounds. A conflict doubtless ensued with herders on those plains. The result is a costly war of extermination.

Hopeful Signs From Another Quarter

In 1853-5 treaties were made with many tribes of the interior and with all in Oregon and Washington, with provisions for the survey of their reservations and the allotment of small farms to Indian families, with the pledge of patents of inalienable title to individuals in severalty. A part of these surveys and allotments were made. The law is still in force. Steps are taken to secure the patents. Special attention is called to these treaty stipulations by the general commanding the department of the Columbia. Their completion is urged as a war measure, in order to satisfy the just claims of those Indians who have improved their farms and who desire peace, and who will thus become a strong barrier against any and every hostile band.

Another fact is the right of every Indian under the amended constitution. The Fourteenth and Fifteenth amendments to the constitution gave every 'American', without distinction of race or color or previous condition of bondage all the rights of citizens. The judiciary committee of the Senate affirmed that the Indian can become a citizen by abandoning his tribal relations. The negro became a citizen at once by the act itself. The question arises whether the American Indian did not also become a citizen by the act itself? If he may do it by simply taking oath before a magistrate, viz., "I renounce my tribal relations and claim my rights as an American," What is there in the amendments to forbid the census-taker or assessor from counting him as a citizen as it does the negro? In either case, *his citizenship is placed in his own hands by the constitution*, and beyond the reach of all policies or Indian laws. These amendments at one blow broke the yoke of negro slavery and of the Indian tribal bondage. It is a strange anomaly that continues the latter bondage in national legislation since it is possible for the entire population of the Indian territory and of every state to assert their freedom from tribal relations and to claim their individual rights as citizens.

The 15th and 10th sections of the act of congress of March 3, 1875, extends the benefits of the homestead act of May 20, 1862, and the acts amendatory thereof, to the Indian and his family if he will accept them. The point may be taken, why put the burden upon the Indian to abandon his tribal relation, which requires in him more courage than to go to battle? Why not declare the tribes a nullity and void in law by judicial decision or by act of congress, under the late amendments, instead of asking the poor Indian to make it a nullity and void by abandoning it? The power given him to do it is very much like saying it is done already in fact. The area of citizenship has taken in the negro and Indian alike.

The board of Indian commissioners in their ninth annual report January 10th, 1878, declare that, "The ultimate solution of the Indian question is the absorption of all Indians into the body politic, and their endowment with all the rights and duties and responsibilities of citizenship." To this end they recommend four things:

1. Government of Indians by law.
2. Division of reservation lands and homestead rights.
3. Larger appropriations for the support of schools.
4. Consolidation of agencies and reduction of expenses.

The secretary of the interior in his annual report to the president Nov. 1, 1877, recommends that Indians who support their families be admitted to the benefits of the homestead act, and that those who abandon their tribal relations be allowed the privilege of citizenship, that the laws be extended over the reservations, and an Indian police, subject to the orders of the government officials, be organized on each of them; that the attendance of their children in school be compulsory, that boarding schools be established, and that the English language be taught, and that they carry on their own reservation farms instead of depending on white employees. These are advanced positions tending to solve the Indian problem justly and humanely.

A more favorable sign is the census table which illustrates some fruits of the policy during nine years past.

The number of Indians in the United States (those in Alaska not included) is 278,000.

	1868	1877
No. who wear citizens dress	-	112,903
Houses occupied	7,470	22,194
Houses built last year	-	1,703
Schools	111	330
Teachers	134	437
Scholars	4,716	11,515
Money spent for education	-	$337,379
No. who can read	-	40,397
No. who learned to read in last year	-	1,206
Church buildings on reservations	-	207
Indian church members	-	28,000
Acres cultivated by Indians	54,207	292,550
No. male Indians who work (Indian Territory not included)	-	31,612
Bushels of wheat raised	126,117	688,278
" corn	467,363	4,056,952
" oats and barley	43,976	349,247
" vegetables	236,926	656,975
No. tons hay	16,216	148,473
Horses and mules owned	43,950	216,286
Cattle "	42,870	217,883
Swine "	29,890	127,358
Sheep "	2,683	587,444

These results, say the commissioners, in industry, education and Christianity in the short space of nine years confirms our belief, often expressed in former reports, that the peace policy is the only right policy.

But the most hopeful sign of the solution of this problem is the Indians' own action. They begin to know and to desire titles to their lands as homesteads. They plead for their rights under the law. The moment is opportune to win many of them from the tribe to the homestead of citizens.

It is our duty to help them to attain the position and rights awarded to them by our constitution and laws.

June 29, 1878

THE INDIAN WAR. CAN IT BE STOPPED?

We are in the midst of an Indian war. It has signs of being more extensive, costly and bloody than any of the past wars with them. This arises from the fact that the treaty Indians, the peaceable and industrious, as well as the non-treaty, idle and nomadic, have come to believe that the government does not mean to keep its faith with them or to redeem its treaty pledges to give them titles for their allotments of farms on their reservations. They learn that congress and the commissioner of Indian affairs propose to force them from their homes to new, strange and rugged reservations, or to mass them on one or two large reservations.

THEIR FARMS ARE THEIR HOMES

Many of them have made small farms, built houses, bought agricultural equipment and stock and other means of comfort. All these have cost them much labor. They love and cling to their homes as we do to ours.

CAUSE OF WAR

They know that the war with the Nez Perce chief, Joseph and his band, arose from this purpose to force him and his band away from their own—never-sold lands—in the Wallowa valley, and drive them on the Nez Perce reservation. This was felt by many to be unjust in principle and impolitic in practice. Those Indians felt it more

[231]

keenly. All the tribes sympathized with them. Runners have passed from tribe to tribe during twelve or fifteen months past, discussing their grievances among themselves, and trying to bring all to a common purpose not to go to the new reservations, and not to give up their homes. The result is that a general distrust of the word of the whites and the honor of our government prevails among them. They will not furnish General Howard with scouts for this war. They will if pressed fight and die in defense of their homes.

AN INJUSTICE TO THE INDIAN GIVES HIM GREAT POWER

Treat any man unfairly and you put a mighty weapon in your hand that will smite yourself. The avenging Nemesis will find and punish the guilty. Word has come that a white man has filed on the farm of Charley, a Nez Perce of Timothy's band, at Alpowai, also a faithful scout under General Howard last year. The white man now alleges that the Indian has not taken his land exactly according to the forms of law. But we know that the law giving Indians homesteads off the reservations was not passed until March 3, 1875, and that these Indians have lived several years as citizens at Alpowai, and that their rights began as citizens with their occupancy of the claim, either by pre-emption or homestead. They can and must hold in chancery these homes in which they have lived ten or fifteen years. It will be a fine opportunity for a generous-minded attorney to go into court and defend the case and secure the rights of this faithful scout.

The general land commissioner ordered the farms of those Indians to be kept for them. The Coeur d'Alenes, whose farms are probably on unsurveyed lands, will doubtless present similar cases in equity. Meanwhile the attempt of white men to jump that Indian claim will be like a lighted match to powder. It will destroy the faith in us of the best Indians, our longtime friends. It will fire their hate and expose the guilty and innocent alike to revenge. Such a deed published among the other tribes will incite them to deeds of blood. The meanness of the act will arouse sympathy for the Indian, who is striving to do all his duty as a citizen. Every one of that band gave their property under oath to the assessor to pay their taxes. How base the deed that will strike an Indian down and cast a firebrand into the homes of the settlers.

The injustice of withholding titles to homesteads on the reservations, of not securing to the Indian his home in law, causes the same peril to communities on the frontier. In fact there is no safety to any man, white or black or copper colored, except under the protection of law. This flag of law, instead of war, ought to have been thrown over the Indian long ago. The cost and difficulty of doing it now, of turning him from war, will be great; yet it must be done, and that soon, or the next offer of the Sybylline leaves of wisdom will come with added losses and costs.

EXTENT OF THE DISTURBANCE

General Howard said to me the day before the outbreak of the Bannacks: "I expect war at any moment. I have been in constant communication with Gens. McDowell and Sherman for several weeks. The ferment is widespread. It is among many once quiet tribes. It seems to extend across the continent."

Understanding that titles to Indian homesteads on the reservations had been pledged to them by treaties, and that they had long desired these titles, and that they knew the recent plan to move them to new reservations, and that they would not go unless forced to do it, but would be quiet and friendly, if the patents were given to them, Gen. Howard, in view of these facts, sent a telegram to the president, asking him to issue those patents at once as a war measure. No reply has come. Meanwhile, the war has begun with its usual murders, raids, uncertain movements, alarms, vexatious suspense, costly traversing to and fro by long marches and slow trains over the arid plains of the interior, 600 miles away southeast of the headquarters of the department of the Columbia, on whom the responsibility has again fallen to quell the disturbances.

Distrust of the whites and the government turns friendly Indians into foes. Telegrams today give signs that the Umatillas, the Warm Springs and Klamaths are hostile. Gen. Howard strives to prevent the union of those now at war, with those on the reservations. The duty of the hour is to redeem every pledge and win back their faith to the government. The president and the commissioner of Indian affairs can do this by fulfilling the treaties. Life, property and the welfare of the frontier settlements are at stake.

When this is over and peace restored, not the war policy or the peace policy, but the *citizens policy* should be enforced.

G.H. ATKINSON

Aug. 8, 1878

SETTLEMENT OF THE INDIANS

A THOUSAND INDIAN HOMESTEAD FARMS ON THE RESERVATIONS IN OREGON, WASHINGTON AND IDAHO

This is possible under the treaty pledges made in 1855. Suppose the allotments of 40 to 320 acres each to 150 Nez Perces, 150 Umatillas, Cayuses and Walla Wallas, 150 Yakimas, 100 Spokanes and Coeur d'Alenes, 100 Warm Springs or Wascos, 100 Puyallups, 100 Skokomish, Clallams and Makahs, 100 Tulalip and adjoining tribes and 100 on Grand Ronde and Klamath reservations, the quote of 1,000 would be filled. Suppose that these Indians receive their patents from the president as the treaties provide, and that the titles to these farms legally vest in them and their heirs, on condition that they occupy and till a portion of same, and that a majority or all of them get the idea of ownership which no changes of agents or Indian policy can make void; and suppose a majority of these Indians shall within two years have houses, gardens and fields of grain, horses and cattle on these homesteads, and begin to have some of the comforts of a settled home life, suppose that several hundred of their children attend school, and that some of them are learning to work on the farms or in mills and shops, would such a class of facts offend the whites in any degree or injure the country?

Suppose the Indians have begun their farm life under these pledges, but have lost courage and hope by the long delay to grant them patents or certificates to an acre, and hence have felt no motive to work on lands not their own, would such a class of facts be strange, or wrong on their part, or unnatural even for white men? How long and how hard will a white man work on a farm not his own or on a claim to which he can get no title?

How would he feel to be called a lazy, worthless wretch, fit to be kicked and chased out of the community or shot because he will not build a house, till a garden or cultivate a field without pay or ownership?

Suppose the Indian department of government begin to look at this matter and assign to Indians their pledged homesteads and to grant patents to them on the reservations as fast as these can be made out, in due form, with well-defined limits, according to the U.S. surveys, will it be a means of quieting the ferment that has every year prevailed among the Indians as the white settlements have crowded more and more upon them?

Will a thousand Indian owners of farms upon these scattered reservations act as a constant barrier to war parties, outlaws, and the hostile runners who pass from tribe to tribe every season to stir up strife?

Suppose the board of Indian commissioners authorize every Indian agent to appoint an Indian police to detect and arrest every criminal and bring him before a legal tribunal for trial, and thus act with white sheriffs and constables to preserve the public safety and peace instead of our annual Indian war, and would the people be glad to have this done?

Suppose the board of Indian commissioners should urge all the Indians to take homesteads at once, and should open the reservations to public sale and use the funds for permanent Indian schools, or for mills and shops, and to pay for head mechanics and farmers to instruct them, as the treaties of 1855 provided, would the present public sentiment approve and sustain this policy?

These questions are practical at this moment. We can hardly doubt that the answer will be in favor of such measures from every part of our Pacific Northwest.

G.H. ATKINSON

Apr. 17, 1880

WARM SPRINGS INDIAN AGENCY

Indian Farmers

It is well to study every subject in sight of its examples. The rule of the Great Teacher, 'by their fruits shall ye know them', is as true in business and in education as in religion. 'Every tree is known by its fruit'. This test will always be applied, and its results must be accepted. A public journal stands upon its merits, or fails for lack of them. So a public man—and every citizen is in a degree a public man—wins that measure of respect, confidence and esteem, which his general conduct deserves. His race, or nationality or color adds no weight to the decision. A watch, whether made in Waltham, Lyndon or Geneva, is valued at its worth, and not for its trade mark. A bushel of wheat rates in market by its quality, not by its producer, whether a Russian or an American, or whether his skin is white, or black, or copper colored.

In like manner a man will be judged by the use of his talents and opportunities, and not by their number. The fact that Indians whose habits for generations have been to hunt and fish and dig camas and pick wild berries for a living, and roam about and build wigwams of poles and mats where nature supplied their wants best with the labor, have now become farmers with fixed houses and board houses with doors and windows, chimney and fireplace, stoves, tables and chairs, lounges and beds, pantry and dishes, flour and vegetables and meat, books and papers, clocks and mirrors, combs and brushes; and that husband and wife and children are clad in the garb of a civilized people, command respect for them and for their instructors and for the present policy of the Indian department.

[236]

The plan of Dr. Whitman and Rev. H.H. Spalding and Rev. E. Walker and Rev. C. Eells of the A.B.C.F.M. in eastern Oregon from 1836 and 1838 and thereafter, to keep their tribes from annual trips to the buffalo ranges for meat, and the camas prairies for roots, by furnishing them with hoes and plows and axes and teams and teaching them how to raise food at home, was a credit to their wisdom and their piety.

This missionary idea was the germ of the 'Peace Policy'. It means Indian homes on farms which they till and own. It means the school and the church. It means the six days of labor and the Sabbath of rest for them and for their households and their beasts of burden. It means the quiet domestic life in fixed dwellings which stimulates industry and insures a more intelligent responsibility and a nobler manhood and womanhood and childhood.

PRODUCTS OF INDIAN FARMS ON THE WARM SPRINGS RESERVATION IN 1879

These consist of the cereals and vegetables and hay for the most part. Of wheat they raised 10,000 bushels; of oats about 500 bushels; of hay, about 150 tons; of potatoes, about 3,000 bushels; of turnips, several hundred bushels; pumpkins, by count, several hundred.

MODES OF FARMING

On a trip of four or five miles up and down the Tenino valley, on both sides of the brook, I saw eight or nine small farms, fenced and in process of cultivation. Some were ploughing, others harrowing, another was rolling a field of oats, just sown, broadcast, as whites do it. They had ploughs, harrows, wagons, harness gear and tools, purchased of agricultural merchants.

Their methods of using them were like our methods. The present superintendent of agriculture, James Luckey, Esq., and his predecessors, had taught them these methods. Formerly they sowed grain in spots, hills and patches. Now they clear the land of bushes and make way for the plow. Their fences are of pine rails of good size and length, and well laid up zig zag. The bottom rail rests on stones put in order along the line. Among the willows they make a kind of pole or wattle fence with stakes and thongs. They show the same kind of skill, economy and industry as other farmers. Their corrals for stock are strong. Their barns and sheds are low, but convenient for mowing hay and grain and for shelter for work horses and calves. They learn to feed work horses with hay and oats, and to take care of cows and sheep and fowls. In a word they find work enough about home and on their farms to keep them busy, and they are glad to do it for the profit and comfort which it brings.

TULLUX HOLLOQUILLA

This man's farm lies up the creek, about 3 miles from the agency. His house is built of sawed lumber with windows, doors, floors, apartments, sitting rooms, bed room and kitchen; with stove, table, chairs and stools, crockery on shelf or in pantry, fire place, lounge, bedstead and beds, bedding and clothing like that of white people. His wife died last year leaving him three bright little children. His sisters, Mrs. Orville Olney and Miss Nettie Holloquilla [ed.— modern descendants use the spelling Holliquilla], keep house. The children attend school about eight months in the year. He was in the corral, branding yearling ponies when we drove up. His manner has the marks of intelligence and self respect. His words are few, and his replies are given with a trace of caution common to his people. While three of us—Messrs. C.H. [ed.—Cyrus] Walker, clerk and teacher and also acting agent in the absence of Capt. John Smith, Hon. I.N. Smith, who is abiding here for health, and myself called at the house. Tullux, as he is familiarly addressed, continued his hard job of lassoing, throwing and branding his wild colts. Mr. Ramsby, the stage driver, helped him finish the task of branding about thirty, and got very weary and worn by it, in addition to his all day and night ride from the Dalles.

These incidents show the mutual respect and confidence which exist and increase between the resident whites and Indians on the reservations.

The next farm above belongs to his father, Holloquilla Senior, a man about 65 or 67 years old, whose rather grave, dignified way appears in his son and daughters. A fence divides their farms. They have similar fields, houses, stables and barns, not large or costly, but convenient for present needs.

Other farms taken along the brook, as the farmers elsewhere have done, are like these two. Some have five or ten acres under fence, and some perhaps thirty or forty. Farm wagons and ploughs unused were under shelter.

The bench lands and low buttes, and hill sides up to the rim rock on both sides of the valley, and all the level, grassy upper plains between the numerous valleys are stock range and timber regions, whence logs are cut and drawn to the mill at the agency and sawed by the Indians for their lumber and for sale.

Their wheat is ground by an Indian miller at the agency flour mill, which furnishes all the flour used by whites and Indians on the reservation.

NUMBER OF INDIAN FARMERS

There are between eighty and ninety of these farms. The number of houses built of sawed lumber is eighty-one and of logs only two. They gradually increase, by marriage and the settlement of young people, and by the change of others from the chase and from the camas prairies to the surer harvests of their own fields.

LAND TENURE

The reservation is about thirty-six miles square. Yet the east line meanders along the De Chutes river, the south line along the Metolius, which rises on the northeast side of Mt. Jefferson, the west line along the Cascade mountain summit, and the north line meanders eastward along the Mutton mountain range to the De Chutes. This irregular boundary implies the loose and uncertain lines which must limit unsurveyed districts. But surveys and allotments have been made of farming portions within the reservation, according to treaty. The Indian farmers usually live on these allotments. They consider them their own. They are surprised when told that they each need a deed, signed and sealed like those of the white man. I met them in council, and after commending their progress in agriculture and in the comfort of their homes, I spoke of their uncertain land titles, and suggested to them that a bill is or will be before congress to give deeds of farms to them in severalty on their reservations inalienable for 25 years. They know or they ought to know that they can take homesteads off the reservations under the law of March 3, 1875, and become citizens at once. Wm. Chinook [ed.—commonly known as Billy Chinook], who went to Washington in 1844 or '45 with Gen. Fremont, replied in a general way that they kept faith with the whites and found my words good. Py Nuse [ed.—usually spelled Pinouse], the head chief, in a dignified speech, related their history, dealings, and wishes, and wanted time for counsel on the subject of deeds in severalty for their lands. Both held that they own the whole reservation now. Why, then, they asked, get deeds? They recall the sale of other large sections, which they had deeded to the whites and given up to them. Why take deeds of what they had never sold, i.e., the reservation? My reply was that Tullux Holaquilla and his father, and Wm. Chinook and Py Nuse, and every other man who had land, had no records on the books, and no one could tell where their bounds were, and that others could get their farms away unless held by legal limits and written titles. These ideas seemed new and strange and somewhat startling.

AN OLD FRAUD COMMITTED AGAINST THEM

Wm. Chinook said that Agent Huntington talked good and said he was their friend and made promises to deal honestly with them. He drew up a paper and asked them if they would like to have a pass from the agent every time they left the agency? He told them it would be a good thing to protect them. He got them to sign the paper by which, they thought, they were to have passes.[ii] After he was gone, they learned that the paper contained the sale of their fisheries at The Dalles for $10,000. They were thus cheated out of their rights to fish, which was a large part of their living. They now have to pay a rent every year for fishing there, to white men who claim the land and fishing ground. It makes them afraid to sign

---

[ii] See "Fraudulent Huntington Treaty", *Oregon Historical Quarterly*, Winter 2007, 108:721

papers. It makes them want to know more about these deeds. This deed of the salmon fishery at The Dalles was new to me. I could make no reply. On inquiry, I learned that such a conveyance had been made years ago, and that the $10,000 had not come to the Indians, but that they had the hardship to pay a yearly rental for the use of that fishing ground which was their heritage by birthright.

After the council was over they waited in little groups around the agency for an hour. Some came to shake hands. The former hereditary chief of the Warm Springs, who had come fifteen miles to attend the council, wished to know more about the deeds. He said the words were good, but he wanted to understand it better. I referred him to Mr. Walker and to others who had it better explained. Another cluster sent Charles Pitt, the excellent interpreter, to know why the deeds would give them any better title than they now had? I went over to the group and explained the facts to him and to the young Pi-Ute [ed.—Paiute] interpreter, who talks English well, and to the others. As the Indian cook, Charley, came to call me to supper, the little bands began to leave for their homes up the valleys and on the hills. Tullux Hollaquilla, who had listened in silence with close attention and an occasional nod, collected his three little children and two sisters in his farm wagon and drove off home, like any regular farmer leaving town. Hollaquilla Senior mounted his pony and rode away with his family. Wm. Chinook lingered a little longer. As night came all were gone to their homes.

THEIR SCHOOL

The records show over a hundred children of school age, among the four tribes, whose total resident population is about 550. There were 18 deaths and 21 births last year, making about one per cent gain. Eighty-eight are enrolled in school. The last term roll gave an average attendance of 81.[iii] They learn to read and study in English, beginning in the primer and advancing like other children, step by step, into higher grades. They study geography and arithmetic,

---

[iii] Fifteen of these students would be taken to Forest Grove and enrolled in the Indian Training School there just a few months after Atkinson wrote this letter, on July 13, 1880, including the children of Tullux, Pinouse, Olney, Chinook, Pitt, and the Paiute interpreter.

and learn to write and sing. They do chores at home and about the school room. The matron, a very capable Indian woman, prepares them a plain noonday meal, which favor somewhat depends upon their prompt attendance and good conduct. The school term had closed, but the plans and reports commend the agent, Capt. John Smith, and the teachers, C.H. [ed.—Cyrus] Walker and Miss Smith.

THEIR RELIGIOUS ACTIVITIES

All the men, women and children who could sing followed their leader, Komar, a sprightly young farmer, in singing several of Roupes' version of the psalms.

A short sermon from John 3:16 on the word 'life', and what it does and is, was first interpreted into the Wasco language, sentence by sentence, by Chas. Pitt, and next into the Warm Springs language by another earnest interpreter. This process sometimes passes into a third interpretation into the Pi-Ute language, of whom some fifteen were present. It is slow, but seems to satisfy their craving for bible truth. They gave close and unwearied attention to every word, and joined heartily in the doxology and response 'Amen'. Capt. Smith or Mr. Walker leads their services every Sabbath and gives them a short practical sermon. Life and property are safe on the reservation. The doors are not locked day or night. Lost animals or goods are restored if in their bounds. Order prevails. Whisky is neither sold or allowed within their limits. Ten of their number are enrolled as a police force, with C.H. Walker, whom they respect, trust and esteem as their chief and captain. All dress in uniform on Sabbath or council, or gala days. They have little to do except to keep children quiet, and seat the congregation or show authority. But they will serve well for sheriffs or constables when state and U.S. courts are held among them.

The evening closed with an hour of singing "The Gospel Songs," led by Mr. Walker at the organ and joined by Mr. Charles Pitt and his two daughters, whose voices are clear and strong. I asked him, where or how he learned so many languages so well? He speaks four, the Wasco, Warm Springs, Pi-Ute and English equally well. He said he was born in Pitt river. When taken in war and made a slave among the Wascos, then among the Warm Springs and was bought by a white man, and was kept in a white family for several years. Even now some of the older Indians call him a slave and dislike to have him as interpreter, but his merits keep him in this service.

It is plain that Capt. J. Smith, whom the Indians trust and esteem, and his employees have done well for these Indians and well for the government, and they deserve the esteem and confidence which they have won.

THE CHANGE OF INDIAN POLICY SUGGESTED BY THESE FACTS

Certainly a transfer to the military is not wanted. The gain thus far is in the line of personal rights, personal manhood and womanhood. They have proved the fitness of Indians to support themselves in a civilized way. They can and will be industrious and economical, if entrusted with farms deeded in severalty, if protected by law and made amenable to its obligations. The outlook for them is forward, not backward. They are no longer to be called "Siwashes", and their women to be called squaws, and their children "papooses". That policy degrades them as it degrades those who use such terms. The manly and honorable policy is to treat them as men and women with rights and duties under law, and to establish the laws of the state and the nation among them. Let this be the next step in the Indian department and the Indian problem will be solved. Indian wars will be arrested by courts of law. Troops on the border for the sake of protection and peace, will be superseded by an efficient corps of Indian police, who will cooperate with state and municipal police, and be part of them, and who will ensure safety and order in their own precincts. The need of large Indian subsidies and appropriations—so long and so often depleted in passage to them—will also cease. Frauds will cease also for lack of motive. The Indian question will then appear in its true light, as one of manhood and citizenship among us, and not that of tribes under government, but outside the scope of law. The blunder of two and a half centuries will thus come to an end.

EIGHT

Histories of Pacific University

On two occasions, separated by twelve years, George Atkinson wrote a history of Pacific University. Although the second contains considerable duplication, there are substantial differences in style and content, which warrant reproduction of both documents in this volume.

The first of the two was prepared for, and forwarded to the U.S. Centennial Exposition in Philadelphia. On Jan. 24, 1876 State Supt. Rowland, asked three men from Pacific University (trustee Atkinson and faculty members G.H. Collier and Horace Lyman) to prepare and provide a history of Tualatin Academy and Pacific University for the Exposition. It appears to have been written in some haste, appearing in the *Oregonian* on Feb. 9, just sixteen days after Rowland's letter of request. A note at the end of the published report, from Profs. Collier and Lyman, tells us that they had asked Atkinson to write the 'historical sketch'.

The second history was written by Atkinson and presented to the Fortieth Annual Meeting of the Trustees, on June 19, 1888. It would be Atkinson's valedictory to the school, his death occurring the following February.

The first history was written at a time of public tension between Pacific's President, Sidney Harper Marsh, and some of the faculty and trustees. This is particularly evident in the penultimate paragraph, where Atkinson declares:

"The divorce of such a school from the warm heart of the Christian church is a calamity which no golden endowments can compensate." That sentence suggests that the college was growing away from its church roots, and seems to speak critically of Pres. Marsh's exceptional success in raising funds for the school, a record documented in detail in a preceding portion of the article.

The writer continues by defending the trustees, and the Oregon Association of Congregational Ministers and Churches, against charges of interference in the affairs of the school. Two years later President Marsh, in reviewing with the trustees his twenty-five year tenure, expounded at some length about inappropriate ecclesiastical efforts to influence the affairs of the school (see *Atkinson: Pioneer Oregon Educator*, p. 160).

In the interests of historical clarity a sustained investigation of Marsh's differences with the Trustees might well be warranted, to determine which things other than church interference were at issue, thus providing a clearer rationale for their challenges to Marsh.

The lengthier second history (1888) takes a more leisurely pace through the founding years, in addition to discussing the tenures of Marsh's two successors, J.R. Herrick and J.F. Ellis. Marsh's leadership is applauded, and the controversy over ecclesiastical interference is not mentioned.

History of Pacific University: 1876

Source:
The Oregonian Archives
Multnomah County Library

Feb. 9, 1876

CENTENNIAL: HISTORY OF TUALATIN ACADEMY AND PACIFIC UNIVERSITY

Office of Superintendent of Public Instruction
Salem, Oregon, January 24, 1876

Prof. G.H. Collier, Rev. Prof. H. Lyman and Rev. G.H. Atkinson,
D.D., Forest Grove, Oregon

G entlemen—You are hereby appointed a committee to prepare the history of Tualatin Academy and Pacific University, to be forwarded to this office by next February 15 where will be compiled Educational and Scientific Reports for the U.S. Centennial Exposition for 1876.

Very Respectfully Yours,
S.S. Rowland, Chairman, comm. E. & S. Reports.

The undersigned in fulfilling this service premise that the frequent mention of several persons connected with this history has been essential to its truth and completeness. The sources of history, as of a river, are like hidden springs, hardly known, until the tiny rivulet marks its own course.

We can trace the rise of this institution to only two distinct and apparently independent sources that united opportunely, or as we prefer to say, providentially. What thoughts had been germinating in other minds before are concealed from us.

The American Home Missionary Society in September 1846, within a month after the treaty on the Oregon boundary had been made public by President J.K. Polk, having planned to begin their mission work on the Pacific Coast with Oregon as a field, requested Rev. G.H. Atkinson to be their pioneer missionary, with a commission to aid in planting churches, schools and diffuse Christian knowledge. Dr. Badger, the Secretary, directed him in May 1847 to call upon Rev. Theron Baldwin, Secretary of the then new Society for Promoting Collegiate and Theological Education at the West. The interview was brief, ending in these incisive words: "You are going to Oregon. Found an Academy that shall grow into a College, as we founded Illinois College."

Two weeks after his June 21, 1848 arrival in Oregon City George Atkinson shared Baldwin's message with the Rev. Harvey Clarke, who had come from Vermont and New York with his wife as self-supporting missionaries to the Indians of Eastern Oregon and thence to West Tualatin Plains, now Forest Grove. The Oregon Association of ministers to churches was there planned and partly organized to meet at Oregon City Sept. 1848. The subject was presented to that body, and the following minute was made of their action.

"At the meeting of the Association of Congregational and (New School) Presbyterian brethren Sept. 21st, 1848, it was resolved that it was expedient to found an Academy under our patronage. On discussion it was resolved that the Tualatin Plains is the most favorable location. After continued discussion it was resolved to appoint Trustees, who shall locate an Academy, become incorporated, and attend to its interests." Rev. Harvey Clarke, Hiram Clark, Esq., P.H. Hatch, Esq., Rev. Lewis Thompson, Wm. H. Gray, Esq., Alvin W. Smith, Esq., James M. Moore, Esq., O. Russell, Esq., and Rev. G.H. Atkinson were appointed Trustees, who organized by choosing Rev. H. Clarke, President, Rev. G.H. Atkinson, Secretary, A.T. Smith, Esq., Treasurer and Hiram Clark, Esq., Auditor and by adopting a constitution and by-laws.

Another mind had been moved to a similar purpose. Mrs. Tabitha Brown, a lady of 68 years, formerly from Brimfield, Mass, the widow of an Episcopal minister, had followed her children and grandchildren from Illinois in 1846 to Oregon. Her heart had been moved by the sight of many orphan children, left on the Plains, and in 1847 she said to Mr. Clarke "I wish I was rich." Why?, said he. In order to found an orphan asylum and build up an educational institution to furnish a home and instruction for these children. The two formed the plan and collected the means to erect a log house for a home. Mrs. Brown gathered in 40 or 50 children, boarding them for a dollar per week. They employed a teacher and the enterprise was launched at West Tualatin. This Orphan School was offered to the Trustees of the proposed Academy that should grow into a college, and accepted by them.

Rev. Harvey Clarke pledged 200 acres of his claim, taken and held under the then existing Provisional Government of Oregon, for the site of the Academy and school village which was expected to grow up around it. The old log church with mud chimney on the outside, and puncheon floor and seats within, was offered and accepted as the temporary schoolhouse, and L.D.C. LaTourette was chosen 1st teacher. Rev. C. Eells was next employed as teacher, and a contract was let to build a more commodious house of hewn logs, a few hundred dollars having been subscribed.

The Trustees secured an act of incorporation from the first legislature of the Territory, called by the authority of the U.S. Sept. 26, 1849, "establishing in Washington County a Seminary of learning for the instruction of persons of both sexes in science and literature, to be known by the title of 'the President and Trustees of Tualatin Academy', empowering them when it shall be expedient to do so, to exercise all the privileges as President and Trustees of a college, or University, as the case may be, that should be exercised by the President and Trustees of other colleges and universities that may hereafter be created in this Territory."

The land was laid out into blocks of four acres each, an acre to a lot, with streets 4 rods wide, and 20 acres were set apart for a campus; 10 of land pledged by Clarke and 10 of land pledged by Mr. Stokes and Rev. E. Walker.

Meanwhile the gold mines of California had been discovered, and, though gold dust in some hands was plenty, prices ruled high for labor, materials and food for all classes.

The school grew in favor and the need for more rooms led to the erection of what is now called the Old College Building. The Orphan \

House was sold for $1,000 to be paid in the labor of the contracts, rated at $10 per day. Lumber was bought at $50 to $60 per m., lots were sold, which with other collections, paid $5,000 of the $7,000 which the building, enclosed with one or two rude rooms had cost.

The changes of teachers, the growing demands of this work, and the increasing debt laid a heavier burden upon Rev. Mr. Clarke and his family and other trustees & friends than they could bear. Grave questions had called for frequent councils of the trustees during these early years and you might see them coming on horseback by trails & roughest roads, through the woods, to spend days and nights in anxious search and earnest prayers for wisdom to guide and means to execute their original plan. The tides of a changing population were annually flowing to the mines, and it became a more and more difficult problem to know what to do with this and other institutions, and church buildings, that were more or less dependent upon the same men.

At this juncture in April, 1852, at the request of the Trustees Rev. Mr. Atkinson went to New York to enlist the aid of eastern friends and especially of the College Society. A circular reciting our efforts, aims and wants was published with endorsements of prominent ministers and business men in New York.

The enterprise thus begun was laid before Dr. Baldwin, who had given the idea, and then before the College Society with the request to be adopted as the next or 9th on their list, and to have the grant of $600, the interest on $10,000, annually to support a permanent Professor. Both requests were granted, and by public and private appeals $800 in coin and $700 in books were collected for the institution.

A professor was engaged, who after having spent weeks in studying text books and plans for the college course, declined to come, but introduced Rev. S. H. Marsh, a student at Union Theological Seminary. Mr. M. accepted a commission and began to collect a library and funds in order to enter upon the work in Oregon in May 1853. Dr. Eleazar Wheelock, his great-grandfather, had founded Dartmouth College in the woods of New Hampshire. Dr. James

Marsh, his father, had revived and strengthened the University of Vermont at Burlington. The memory of the one, and the many friends of the other, like Hon. Rufus Choate, Hon. Sydney E. Morse, Hon. George P. Marsh, Hon. H.J. Raymond & Hon. E.E. Benedict and others would probably aid the enterprise in which the son was enlisted, which has doubtless proved true.

The institution, thus adopted by the College Society with pledges of interest equal to an endowment of $10,000; having the renewed favor of the A.H.M. Society; with a larger circle of new friends and a professor, whose salary and supporters were assured, had indeed cheering prospects.

With this impetus in 1853 new pupils gathered to the Academy, of which Prof. J.M. Keeler had become the principal, and a few with crude but real college aims formed the first preparatory classes, placed under the care of Prof. Marsh. Prof. E.D. Shattuck, on becoming principal, gave a still greater uplift to the institution. The library of over 1,000 volumes, collected by Prof. Marsh had been placed upon its rude shelves; other rooms had been partly finished; the first Act of Incorporation had been replaced in January 1854 by one styled Tualatin Academy and Pacific University with more distinctive college privileges, Pupils and parents had learned more of the aims and methods of the Institution and though few had ever seen the example of a true college, they were well disposed to it, and in 1854 subscribed in lands and money $6,500, partially pledging $3,500 more. The community shared all the hardships of pioneers, added to the ferment of mining speculations and the terror of the Indian War of 1855. It was a day of trial and sacrifice to teachers, and in part to pupils, but more of a great burden to Rev. Mr. Clarke, who was held responsible for supplies, and debts, and improvements also, and to other trustees, who were toiling to provide for their young families. But all these friends sustained the institution, amid all the clouding proposals and discussions about change of location and subordination of the Academy to the College.

April 13, 1854, Rev. S.H. Marsh was chosen President, and was inaugurated August 21, 1855. E.D. Shattuck, Esq. was chosen professor of languages, but not accepting this office, he continued through 1856 as principal of the Academy.

The ever faithful College Society was relied upon to support the professors, and applications were made in 1855 for $600, in 1854, 5, 6, 7, and 8 for $1,200 per year, the first being granted and paid, the larger sums were granted conditionally and paid as fast as possible by installments. In 1856-7 the faith of the college was tried by the departure of its students to the better endowed Eastern colleges. Our log houses had given way to frame dwellings, shops and churches forming a little village, yet there were no sure endowments. This exigency led to a special effort. Rev. T. Baldwin sent a free pass to Rev. Mr. Marsh to go to New York and help secure the annual salaries needed. Rev. H. Lyman having been chosen as professor of mathematics, April 5, 1857 with Rev. C. Eells, took charge of the declining institution and sustained it three school years. He reported the assets of Tualatin Academy and Pacific University, May 12, 1859, as $18,300 and $3,000 in subscriptions, with $850 debt.

The death of Mrs. T. Brown in 1857, and Rev. H. Clarke March 24, 1858, with other tried coworkers before and since added to the past trials. Yet pupils who had spent a few months, or terms, or years went away with new ideas of study, better fitted for business life and with some preparation for professional study.

Under the auspices of the College Society President S.H. Marsh, by patience and energy raised the general endowment, and reported on his return, May 21, 1861, $21,736.10 in valid subscriptions and $1,200 in books, receiving his expenses and $2,000 salary for two and a half years of collecting service.

With these funds new teachers and scholars came, and new demands for extended instruction. The first graduate was H.W. Scott, Esq., in 1863. The course of study was published to be in substance the same as that pursued in Eastern colleges, covering four years. The usual applications were made to the College Society for yearly aid, but their funds were not equal to their demands. Five young gentlemen were graduated in 1866. President Marsh was again authorized to go East to obtain a larger endowment, under a pledge of $1,500 salary and expenses, leaving Prof. Lyman in charge of the institution. Hon. H.W. Corbett, as treasurer, had given special care to increase and invest the funds, and W.S. Ladd, Esq., having accepted the office and trust, fulfilled it in the same manner.

On June 16, 1867 President Marsh reported new collections and subscriptions for general endowment, $25,228.04 and the appointment of two more professors, viz: G.H. Collier, Professor of Natural Sciences, and J.W. Marsh, Professor of Languages. The report of the treasurer, May 5, 1868, showed a balance of $44,303.60 in invested funds. The library had been increased, by the efforts of Dr. Marsh, to about 5,000 volumes. The cabinets of botany and mineralogy have also been collected by the efforts of the professors in that department, yet the illustrations in philosophy and chemistry have been to some extent made with rude instruments, in part of home manufacture. The classes in the academy and college have been more distinctly organized and conducted, the public school having drawn off the least classified element. Students more patiently pursue the preparatory studies and some form of the collegiate course, either the scientific or classic. New and gifted teachers have helped to raise and sustain the higher standard of the school, while the numbers in all departments have not increased in like proportion.

President Marsh, needing a sure salary, made a third trip East in 1869 and reported May 3, 1870, $20,942.75 subscribed for a presidential endowment fund.

The loss of valuable instructors has often worked harm to the institution, as of Messrs. Eells, Shattuck, Tanner and Anderson. The list of graduates from all the departments, college, scientific, ladies' course and normal course is 33. With the present corps of teachers and facilities much larger classes can be well taught and fitted for life's work, yet there is still need of more funds for apparatus and buildings and special professorships, for which the president is making a fourth trip and appeal among the Eastern donors of the College and Home Mission Societies.

It is worthy of note that no trustee or officer of the board, as such, has received a dollar for his services or traveling expenses to the numerous trustees meetings and more numerous hours of consultation. Only teachers and other employees have been paid. The present secretary having held the office from the first meeting in 1848, and made all the records with one or two exceptions, is able to trace the growth and strength of the institution, and to feel assured of its more abundant and noble benefits to the people for the future. All its records have been transcribed, and all its titles and conveyances of land have been grouped in abstract forms and placed in a fire-proof vault. Its funds and endowments of $65,000, and other property of $20,000, entrusted to the care of its treasurer, Hon. H. Failing, are separately kept for the purposes for which they have been given, without cost for the care.

The village has grown to be incorporated with charter rights and powers, desirable for families and attractive to strangers. The influence of its alumni is felt in the circles of private and public life, in places of trust and of honor. It is no longer an experiment. The trustees have learned by trials its perils and its wants. Its opportunities for greater usefulness are opening every year, while the call for its best possible work is made by greater numbers of youth of both sexes. The steady drill of such men as have been and are in the faculty is its real force, while it also depends upon the vital sympathy of the Association which gave it organic shape and watched its earlier growth.

The divorce of such a school from the warm heart of the Christian church is a calamity which no golden endowments can compensate. Never has the touch of ecclesiastical control been laid on it. Never is it possible for an Association of such churches to control a corporate board who fill their own vacancies. Never has the Association or Board of Trustees attempted to use the Association for selfish ends. They have sought the common benefits shared by all the people in equal degree. The one view of the board has been to do the utmost good to the children and youth of the land and thus to all the people. Any attempt to pervert the funds, or to sequester any part of them to perpetuate personal, or family connections with the Academy of University, beyond the choice of the trustees, by attaching conditions to funds given for the common welfare, will be a root of bitterness like the Dartmouth College case,[i] that had no remedy until it was purged by the highest court in the nation.

The Home Missionary Society and the College Society, which suggested and which have by their large constituency sustained it, deserve our gratitude. The laborious and faithful teachers, and the far-seeing and energetic President, with all other generous friends, deserve well of the public for the constant benefaction of this Academy and College. Its conduct in the past is its assurance in the future, in the hands of its custodians and teachers, whose names appear in the enclosed catalogue.

Respectfully submitted
G.H. Atkinson
G.H. Collier
Horace Lyman

The Rev. G.H. Atkinson, who has been the secretary of Tualatin Academy and Pacific University from its inception to the present time has, at our request, and with our sanction, prepared the above historical sketch.

G.H. COLLIER
HORACE LYMAN

TRUSTEES

---

[i] In 1819 the New Hampshire legislature attempted to make Dartmouth College a state school. Wood, Gordon, *Empire of Liberty*, Oxford, 2009, 464-6. See http://www.american-bar.org/groups/public_education/initiatives_awards/students_in_action/dartmouth.html. Accessed 11/19.2014.

FINANCIAL COMMITTEE

Rev. S.H. Marsh, D.D., Chairman; Hon. G.H. Collier, A.M., Secretary; Hon. Alanson Hinman, Hon. Henry Failing, Treasurer; Prof. J.W. Marsh, Librarian.

FACULTY

Rev. S.H. Marsh, D.D., President and Professor of Intellectual Philosophy; Rev. Horace Lyman, A.M., Professor of Rhetoric and History; George H. Collier, A.M., Professor of Natural Science; A.J. Anderson, A.M., Professor of Mathematics and Pedagogics; J.W. Marsh, A.M., Professor Latin and Greek; Mrs. P.A. Saylor, Preceptress; Rev. Thomas Condon, A.M., Lecturer on Geology; Miss O.A. Haskell, Teacher of Instrumental and Vocal Music.

ALUMNI

1863—Harvey W. Scott, A.M. 1866—Geo. H. Durham, A.M., Rev. Myron Eells, A.M., Edward B. Watson, A.M., 1867—John Q.A. Bowlby, A.M., Rev. J.E. Walker, A.B., D. Raffety, B.S., 1868—Charles C. Hall, A.M., (one or two names indecipherable due to folded page)—1869—(?) Hoover, A.B., Raleigh Stott, A.B., Harriet Hoover Killin, M.S., 1870—Frank L. Stott, A.B., Addison A. Lindsley, A.B., Georgiana Brown, M.S., Phebe Irene Clark, M.S., Candace A. Neal Luce, M.S., 1872—H.B. Luce, A.B., 1873—L.C. Walker, A.B., W.R. Bilyou, B.S., W.D. Lyman, B.S., Mary Goodell, M.S., Sarah L. Lyman, M.S., 1874—E.P. McCornack, H.F. McCornack, W.H. LaTourette, J.G. Stevenson, Hattie Martin, Dora Hinshaw, Ella Scott, 1875—S.B. Putman, 1876—E.M.L. Atkinson, Hatsutaro Tamura.[ii]

[ii] According to "Nose Sakae's Study Abroad", Yatsutaka Maruki, *Oregon Historical Quarterly*, Spring 2014, 115/1/48, Momotaro Sato and Sakae Nose also received degrees from Pacific University in 1876 ("Nose Sakae", "Sato Momotaro", and "Tamura Hatsutaro" are the Japanese convention, with family name first).

History of Pacific University: 1888

Source:
Pacific University Archives

MEMORIAL SKETCH OF TUALATIN ACADEMY
AND PACIFIC UNIVERSITY DURING FORTY YEARS

Read at Fortieth Annual Meeting Held at Forest Grove, Oregon,
June 19, 1888
By Rev. G.H. Atkinson, D.D.,
Secretary of its Board of Trustees

To the Honored Board of Trustees and Friends:

I have taken the liberty to revise the minutes of our Board, of which I have been secretary forty years, and collate salient facts herein as your own memorial.

In giving a sketch of the origin, progress and condition of this institution of learning, we desire to be especially grateful to God for his providential care of it from the first until the present hour. Our own conviction has doubtless deepened with years that his thought gave it being, nourished its infancy, furnished its needful support, guided its course, raised up instructors and watchful friends, and has thus made it a blessing to many youth, to many families, and to many communities.

Looking over its record kept through forty years, and recalling its early, frequent and not finished labors and trials, we find cause for thankfulness at every step in its history.

First, we thank God for its Home Missionary origin.

In September, 1846, the writer was solicited by Rev. Milton Badger, D.D., Secretary of the American Home Missionary Society, to become their first Home Missionary to Oregon. Being then under appointment of the A.B.C.F.M. for their mission among the Zulus of Southeast Africa, the request was declined. It was renewed in December, 1846, and accepted, after an honorable release from the Foreign Board.

On making a visit to New York in May, 1847, for instructions, among other duties, Dr. Badger introduced me to Rev. Theron Baldwin, Secretary of the American College and Education Society, then newly organized to establish a college in every state. Dr. Baldwin's reply was: "You are going to Oregon. Build an academy that shall grow into a college, as we built Illinois college."

Having waited for a ship, we sailed October 24th, 1847, for Oregon via the Sandwich Islands, and arrived at Oregon City June 21st, 1848.

About July 5th, in company with Deacon P.H. Hatch, I visited Rev. Harvey Clarke at West Tualatin, now Forest Grove. He lived in the log house now standing on the road to the depot. Mrs. Clarke, with her infant son of two weeks, commissioned her little daughter of six or seven years to bid us welcome. Her husband soon returned from his camp-meeting at the grove. After expressing his surprise and joy at our coming to help in Home Missionary work, which he and other had done with no help from the American Home Missionary Society, I mentioned to him the plan of "an academy to grow into a college," and the need for an association of our churches and Christian brethren to choose trustees. We agreed to invite a meeting for such purpose, to be held at Oregon City, September 21, 1848.

That meeting was held, the association organized and the board of trustees were chosen and requested to incorporate and establish an academy with collegiate privileges.

A majority of the persons chosen were present and they met and organized.

It was resolved that a majority of the officers, with as many of the trustees as may be present at a regular meeting, be a quorum.

Rev. H. Clarke was chosen president of the board of trustees, G.H. Atkinson, secretary, A.T. Smith, treasurer, Hiram Clark, auditor.

The trustees adjourned to the 25th. They met as adjourned and resolved to solicit subscriptions in two counties, Tualatin and Clackamas, for funds to erect a building, and again met and located the academy, near the orphan asylum, established a few months previous by Rev. Harvey Clarke and Mrs. T. Brown.

They formed and adopted a constitution, which authorized the name, location, officers and duties; provided that in all areas trustees shall be elected who believe and will maintain evangelical principles in conducting the institution. They declared its object *to be the greatest mental and moral improvement of the pupils*; that morning and evening worship shall be held; that the Bible shall always be a text-book in the institution. They required that the annual meeting of the trustees shall be held at 10 o'clock a.m. on the Wednesday preceding the annual meeting of the Oregon association, which then was held on the 2d Thursday in September. The constitution permitted no change in the articles which maintain evangelical principles and the use of the Bible. The by-laws required that every meeting of the board shall be opened and closed with prayer. No pupil is allowed to use tobacco in or about the school grounds.

Eight trustees signed the constitution March 1, 1849.

ITS ACT OF INCORPORATION

ENACTED September 29, 1849, by the legislative assembly of the Territory of Oregon, recites: "that there shall be established in Washington county a seminary of learning, for the instruction of persons of both sexes in science and literature, to be called 'Tualatin Academy'; and that George H. Atkinson, Harvey Clarke, James Moore, Peter H. Hatch, Lewis Thompson, William H. Gray, Hiram Clark, A.T. Smith, and J. Quinn Thornton and their successors be declared a body politic and corporate in law by the name and style of 'The president and Trustees of Tualatin Academy.'"

Among other powers, Article Second recites: "That they shall have the power so to enlarge the operation of said seminary as to enable them, whenever in the opinion of said president and trustees it shall be expedient so to do, to exercise all the powers and enjoy all the privileges as president and trustees of a college or university, as the case may be, that should be exercised and enjoyed by the president and trustees of other colleges and universities that may be hereafter created in this territory."

The previous minutes and these citations from the act of incorporation show that the original purpose and spirit of the institution were assured. The academy had also a college charter of as large powers as any other that should ever after be created in the territory.

Its trustees were men of some experience in life's affairs. They were pioneers, who heartily cherished the educational and Christian aim of this institution, and freely gave their thought and labor to start it, though in the humble log cabin. They accepted the log orphanage, with its groups of boys and girls, then in care of the aged matron, Mrs. T. Brown, and opened the way for their brighter prospects. Plans were laid to secure permanent and choice teachers, suitable books, and in 1851 the present college building was commenced by their agent, Rev. H. Clarke. Other building plans were given up for this object. Very little money was in circulation among the friends of religion and education. Subscriptions were small. Economy was essential at every step.

LAND GIFTS

The gift of two hundred acres by Rev. H. Clarke at first, became the sure basis of the enterprise. The village was platted in four acres blocks, including streets, giving ample space for residences and campus. The additional gifts by Rev. E. Walker and by Deacon T. Naylor extended the village limits to valuable and attractive proportions. Its location and surroundings and scenic views in every direction, were found to be the objects of beauty and more in harmony with its aims as a school center than is usual to find. The gifts of Messrs. Buxton, Catching and others, at a later date, confirmed the permanence of the location. In this confidence families began to buy lots and move to Forest Grove to educate their children, and the growing village became a desirable place for refined and intelligent homes. The original conditions, that the sale of intoxicating drinks is forbidden in the deed of the property and every lot sold, on penalty of forfeit of title, has added to the moral protection of the youth gathered there and to the families as well.

PRELIMINARY PLANS

An educational scheme begun so early had to prepare its own pupils in primary studies for the higher classes, and suffer the loss every term of those unable or unwilling to pursue even academic, much less collegiate, studies. This was our inevitable fortune. Here and there one had the wish to attain and complete an academic course; but the majority of those who were taught by Mr. L.D.C. LaTourette in the fall and winter of 1848 were in primary classes. Rev. C. Eells' classes, from March, 1849, to 1851, and also at a later date, were in the common studies. Those of Rev. D.R. Williams, from January 9, 1851, two terms, were of the same standing with few exceptions. In fact, when the trustees let the contract in 1851 for the first academy building, now styled the old college building, it was said: "You have only a common school." Miss E.E. Miller, now Mrs. J.G. Wilson, coming fresh from a ladies' seminary in New York, found a school with only slight signs of grades and advanced classes. Prof. J.M. Keeler, in 1853, contracted to teach the academy, but its course of study had hardly an outline, although some pupils were up in the advance lines.

The wide-spread mining fever, the haste to take and improve claims, or to engage in business or professions or domestic life, depleted the school term by term of many of its promising pupils. Besides, the ideal academy was indistinct often in the mind of patron and pupil, while the college, with its four years' course in classics, mathematics, sciences, philosophy and history, was far above the average student's thought or purpose. Here and there a young gentleman or lady had listened to the teacher's story of a thorough course, and quietly resolved to pursue it in this school, or in a better endowed institution in an interior or eastern state. Our board had to face this fact, and forecast its issue. What if it should establish the academy and prepare students for the college, could they be held to a full course here? Could we have any graduates? If so, could they rank with the alumni or alumnae of other colleges?

Whence could come the teachers for such a curriculum? How could they be supported? How could buildings be erected and furnished? How could a library be collected? How could apparatus and the most needed supplies of the school room and lecture hall be secured? How could we prepare and provide for these things, forty or thirty-five or thirty, or even twenty years ago, isolated as we were as an extreme state, almost beyond the pale of national recognition, and also isolated from the lines of travel in our own state? Not twenty-five years ago even, our condition was thought to be hopeless and helpless.

This problem was discussed by the trustees in the forties and fifties and sixties with deep and often feverish interest. Many a trip was made from Oregon City and Portland and Salem to Forest Grove, or vice versa, on horseback, or in lumber wagon, or on foot, in summer heat and winter storms and mud, to study and solve the oft-repeated questions of the academy and the college, the instructors and the books, their cost and the funds to pay them. Many an evening was prolonged to midnight and the early hours in conference and prayer and plans and resolutions, only to close with renewed purpose to go on with the enterprise with steady hand, as God in his providence should open the way. *It was all a gratuity* on part of the trustees. Our teachers had also all been in advance of the work before them. They ranked far above the school. They were poorly paid, and their income was not often definite and certain. They shared some of the toil and care of the Board also without pay, except the fine consciousness of aiding a good cause. But the main object, growth, permanence and fruit of the institution, were held firmly in mind.

DEBTS

Building accounts were settled from time to time by balances charged against the corporation. These were foretokens of larger ones on the completion of the academy. To avoid this and protect it against liens, work was stopped within the shell and a partly finished room or two. This was thought to be no disgrace, but an honor to the self-sacrificing president and agent of the Board, from whose gift of land lots were sold to complete the building.

THE AMERICAN COLLEGE AND EDUCATION SOCIETY

Early in April, 1852, it was foreseen by the writer that the institution must be put on a solid basis, by an appeal to the Eastern friends of higher Christian education in Oregon, through the American College and Education Society, whose Secretary, Rev. Dr. Baldwin, had first briefly outlined its plan. It was thought that this Education Society would endorse and place it on their list of colleges, as it had obtained academic and collegiate powers in its act of incorporation, this having been the first act of the kind in the Territory of Oregon or on the Pacific coast, under the protection of the United States.

It was also thought by the writer that the College Society would pledge the interest of a fund for the support of at least one instructor or professor in the proposed collegiate department from year to year, until such a fund could be raised in the East and safely invested. With these objects in view, while still a Home Missionary, he secured a pass to New York by the kindness of Capt. Benj. Knight, agent of the Pacific Mail Steamship Company, and a commission signed by a majority of the trustees to do this service and secure such an instructor or professor for the college.

Endorsed thus with the authority and opportunity, he ventured to leave wife and two infant children with small provision for themselves, and start, April 1852, on the ocean and trans-Isthmus journey of about five thousand five hundred miles, trusting the endorsement of the act and its two objects by the officers and friends of the American Home Missionary Society. (The interests of a female seminary in Oregon City were also included in this purpose, as it had been largely in his care.)

The voyage was favorable, except for a severe illness on the Isthmus, which continued to New York. The return voyage was in a small, crowded steamer, infected with yellow fever, of which disease a large number died, and a larger number were stricken down, myself included.

Dr. Badger's welcome was cordial and assuring. Dr. Baldwin's was equally grateful, with the pledge to present and advocate the endorsement of our academy with its collegiate powers, by the American College and Education Society, at their annual meeting in October, in Boston. Five months of waiting for that event was spent in soliciting aid for both institutions, and presenting their home missionary aspects and needs in sermons in New England, New York, and Brooklyn churches. The result was a collection of over $4,000 in cash and in books, for school and library in both.

The American College and Education Society endorsed our college and put it ninth in its order on their list,[iii] and pledged the interest, six per cent, of ten thousand dollars for the salary of our first college professor. This pledge they continued, and increased, on the application of our Board, the next and following years, and finally in 1856-7-8-9 and 60, on our application, and until a fund was secured in the East and securely invested so as to give an income of a greater amount.

A circular was prepared by the writer, and endorsed by leading ministers and educators, and used widely in every place visited to advertise and enlist friends for our institutions until January 5, 1853, on which date he started on the return trip to Oregon.

TEACHERS

Assured of $600 annual aid in support of one suitable man, the effort made to find such an instructor resulted in the choice of Rev. S.H. Marsh, then a student in the Union Theological Seminary, New York City, in October, 1852. A commission was given to him to collect funds and library under the auspices of the American College and Education Society, and report in Forest Grove, Oregon, in May, 1853, which was done. His appointment was confirmed by the trustees as Professor of Languages and General Science in

---

[iii] The first eight colleges on the list were Marietta College (Ohio), Illinois College, Wabash College (Indiana), Knox College (Illinois), Iowa College (name later changed to Grinnell), Beloit College (Wisconsin), Wittenberg College (Ohio), German Evangelical Mission College (Missouri). Citation: *Ninth Annual Report of the Society for the Promotion of Collegiate and Theological Education at the West.* New-York: Printed by J.F. Trow, 1852., in the Society for the Promotion of Collegiate and Theological Education records, RG 0756. The Congregational Library and Archive, Boston, MA.

the Collegiate Department of Tualatin Academy, May 9, 1853. The agent's reports were received and approved at the same date.

Prof. J.M. Keeler was put in charge of the academy and its income. Prof. Marsh had all the collegiate departments, with its small income and $600 from the American College and Education Society.

THE NEW NAME

One of the earliest plans of Prof. Marsh was to develop the college. At the annual meeting, September 6, 1853, a committee of three were chosen to petition the legislature for new college privileges, and with reference to a new name and place. At a meeting December 6, 1854, on the request of Prof. Marsh, the name "Pacific University" was adopted. January 10, 1854, the legislature considered a bill which became an act of incorporation, with the present title and the same college privileges as the first, and the same official powers and privileges, having eleven instead of nine Trustees in the Board, and the right to hold $500,000 in capital stock instead of $50,000. A change of location was proposed, and offers were made from the East Plain, besides larger offers to retain it at Forest Grove. Prolonged discussions were held upon separating the institutions into three divisions in care of as many special committees.

GRADES

In 1855 E.D. Shattuck, Esq., took charge of the academy and Prof. Marsh of the college. The institution thus had a teaching force far in advance of its own grades of scholarship. Prof. Marsh felt keenly the disparity and so do did Prof. Shattuck. It was hard to find here any semblance to their Vermont academy and university ideals. The names, academy, college, university could not create either. Each term was only a sign. But progress had been made by the faithful pioneer teachers of 1848, '49. '30, '51, '52, and '53. The more advanced and thoughtful students had a sort of prescience and ambition for the higher culture. Three men, who have been prominent in Oregon public affairs for twenty-five years, and whose influence has been widening with age and experience in their several lines of activity, were at an early date attracted to Tualatin Academy and its prospective college. At length they became Academics; fitted for college and graduated; two at Yale, and one became the first alumnus of Pacific University. They were the first fruits of the faithful work of their teachers. They have reflected honor on both instructors and school. I need only name them to verify the fact—President J.W. Johnson, M.F. Mulkey, Esq., and H.W. Scott, Esq., helped to solve the ideal problem of our institution. It was done slowly. While it cheered Pres. Marsh, it made his desire more intense for students in the upper grades with a collegiate aim in view. As a parent's heart is bound up in his child, so President Marsh was bound up in his pupils, for their sake and for the school. Their success filled him with joy. Their failure in the course made his path dark. The next class, in 1866, George H. Durham, Rev. Myron Eells, and E.B. Watson, Esq., gave strength to his conviction that both academy and college had a future of hope.

The following class of three, in 1867, J.Q.A. Bowlby, Esq., Rev. J.E. Walker, and Dr. D. Raffety, confirmed his hope. Later successive classes did the same.

Meanwhile, this slow progress for thirteen years excited and aroused him. He aimed for quicker and larger results. The younger classes that filled the academy pretty well every year gave too few to the college. How to make one build up the other was his desire, care and toil. Few knew his secret struggles. None, perhaps, felt all that he felt on the subject. The trial of the three committees did not make three schools.

FUNDS

Some thought that two teachers would suffice for fifty or sixty pupils of all grades, but there must be a corps or faculty for an academic and collegiate course. This was the herculean task before President Marsh. Rev. Dr. Baldwin sent him a "pass" on the Pacific Mail Steamship line to New York, in 1858, to go East and raise his own annual salary by pledged subscriptions for three years. His effort one year at this task barely succeeded under the aegis of the College and Education Society. Friends advised him to try for a fund of $20,000, and in two years he raised it and returned. Meanwhile,

Rev. H. Lyman, with other helpers, had held the fort. In two more trips he (ed.: Marsh) secured $45,000 more, thus making cash endowments of $65,000. This success prepared the way to support, in part, an able corps of teachers.

FACULTY

The well-invested fund secured the support of a small faculty. The successive professors, Rev. H. Lyman, E.A. Tanner, D.D., G.H. Collier, L.L.D., J.W. Marsh, Ph.D., Prof. A.J. Anderson, Ph.D., Thomas Condon, Ph.D., W.N. Ferrin, A.M., W.D. Lyman, A.M., and other, illustrate the quality and high standard of instruction given. The graduates, men and women, in the successive classes for the second twelve years until his death, were a grateful testimony to the value of his aim and labors in establishing the college. His last statement on record, that "the college may have begun ten years too soon," or that the academy could, perhaps, have done the work, was hardly sustained by the facts. It was his heroic purpose and effort alone to establish the college in *fact*, as well as in name, that could win the crown, and it did. His final statement that the institution is one body, with its various departments, shows the error long pursued of a threefold division.

This brief review of the steps of progress actually made awakens gratitude afresh for the kind Providence that brought him to this work and held him a quarter century in it. He was conscious how incomplete it was when disease obliged him to lay it down. He became aware that the enterprise could not, in the nature of things, have been hastened much more rapidly.

INVESTMENTS

By the faithfulness of our treasurers, especially Messrs. Corbett, Ladd, Failing and Hinman, all the trust funds have been sacredly made up and held. Incomes have been devoted to the current cost of instruction. Nothing has been lost on investments. Rigid economy has been the rule, while prompt quarterly payment to instructors has not only given them confidence, but has won credit to the institution.

In the changes that have occurred during the last decade among the Faculty and the higher standards and more varied courses of study, the aim has been to keep in rank with Eastern colleges, and furnish our pupils a curriculum of equal value, as far as our funds will allow.

PRESIDENT J.R. HERRICK, S.T.D.

During the brief term of our second President, the courses of study in both academy and college were revised and advanced to higher standards. Dr. Herrick saw the need of a Ladies' Hall, and promptly undertook to raise the funds in New England and New York, under the endorsement and aid of the American College and Education Society, to erect the present building on plans prepared by an eastern architect at the expense of Mrs. F. Billings. It is not complete, but it is commodious and a monument of his energy and zeal for the welfare of the institution. It has especially given a high character to the ladies' department.

PRESIDENT J.F. ELLIS, D.D.

During the four or five last years, the plans and efforts have been to bring the academy in closer relation to the college. The classes have been graded and drilled in the line of college work. Prof. Edwards has found it far easier to lead and hold students to this line than it was for either Professors Keeler, Eells, Shattuck, Tanner, Marsh, Anderson, Robb or McMahon, or the lady principals. They all prepared the way in the minds of pupils and parents. Now, the movement is in the higher direction. The present is opportune for personal life plans and their vigorous execution. Help may be given at vital points. Our educational forces may center on the definite aims of the pioneers of thirty and forty years ago. It may be said that every truth and trial in the past has been valuable. The tests in school and home have evolved thought and created an educational sentiment of a higher order and a wider range. The ethical idea and aim of the institution have been kept in steady course by the Christian teachers and by the Christian homes and churches here established, and no doubt supported and diffused by the sympathies and prayers of the same classes everywhere. It has been easy to introduce the aesthetic elements at this later period of our progress. The Conservatory of Music, begun in fact by Mrs. Dr. Marsh and other years ago and now in care of Mrs. Prof. Edwards and her assistants, has become a cheering and more assured factor, because of better facilities and classified courses of study and practice.

ART

The Conservatory of Art, in care of the skillful and well-trained amateur, Prof. Clyde Cook, a native Oregonian, not only invites students in the vicinity, but bids fair to draw them from wider fields. Prof. J.M. Garrison is restoring the almost lost art of penmanship. The Botanical Department, in charge of Prof. J.W. Marsh, Ph.D., only waits suitable rooms and cases to display a well-arranged variety of Oregon's rich and luxuriant flora, collected by himself, and by the enthusiastic botanist, Prof. Howell, of Sauvie's Island.

Other departments of science in care of Prof. W.N. Ferrin, A.M., wait for rooms and cases, funds and time to collect and enlarge the exhibits, easily accessible and accumulating around us, which the hands of experts will readily help to arrange and illustrate.

We dwell among mountains which unfold nearly all the strata of geologic eras. We traverse the glacial moraines of the unknown past and connect them with those in process of formation. We touch the shores of the older oceans and collate their memorials with the later Biology and Conchology.

These open to us abundant sources to enrich the cabinets and form a museum of instruction for pupils in every line of study.

Our library of six thousand volumes only waits for a suitable building to unfold its rich treasures of knowledge, and to collect larger stores where they can be safely kept.

Can we have such a building? Will friends of good learning help erect a library building with classrooms and halls for apparatus and museum?

FEMALE EDUCATION

We have thus far done much to ennoble the quality and range of female education, according to the terms of our original academic and collegiate charter, granted Sept. 9, 1849—the first act of this kind granted under United States law on the Pacific Coast—and under our second charter, granted in 1854, on the same terms, as we have done for the education of males. We have taken for granted that the law of birth of both sexes in the same family, and of home education together, implies the birth-right of equal advantages in the same school-room and lecture hall. We have seen no reason why the self-respect and mutual respect, the dignity, the virtue and the honor cherished in the home, should fail to be cultivated to even higher degree in the school of every grade from the primary department to the academic and collegiate graduation. Our trial and observation of the experiment during forty years have deepened this impression upon our minds.

And we think that as trustees we have voiced the sentiment of our corps of teachers, twenty-three gentlemen—Messrs. L.D.C. Latourette, C. Eells, D.R. Williams, Wm. Adams, J.M. Keeler, S.H. Marsh, E.D. Shattuck, H. Lyman, W.A. Tanner, G.H. Collier, J.W. March, O.G. Harpending, A.J. Anderson, T. Condon, W.N. Ferrin, J.C. Powell, J.D. Robb, W.D. Lyman, J.F. Herrick, J.F. Ellis, J. McMahon, D.L. Edwards, L. Walker—and nine ladies—Mrs. E.M. Wilson, Mrs. Prest. Marsh, Mrs. Prest. E.A. Tanner, Miss Wing, Miss Mack, Miss Carson, Miss Scott, Miss Adams, Miss Pool, and their associates and assistants—who have been the instructors in this institution. Surely, we have heard no dissent from them. Their high standing as a body of educators has not been surpassed in the State. Their judgment is entitled to respect and confidence.

It only remains to express our gratitude to God for the continued existence of Tualatin Academy and Pacific University. We hold in grateful remembrance the two great societies that proposed and have aided it from the first. We inscribe a memorial tablet to Rev. Harvey Clarke for his gift of two hundred acres of land and ten years of service as president and agent essential to its being, and to other like donors and helpers. We owe grateful remembrance to such a body of instructors, who have shared its discomforts patiently while doing its work. We keep in glad memory its eighty-three graduates, Alumni and Alumnae, most of whom still live to reflect honor upon their Alma Mater, but also to realize that their faithful and patient course of study to the end made this academy and this college possible. We rejoice in the prosperity of many hundreds of other students who have remained with us for a few years, or even a few months, only.

We thank God for Dr. Marsh, its first president, to whose untiring zeal and courage for a quarter of a century are due the order of its course and the chief endowment for its support.

We recall the aged matron, Mrs. Tabitha Brown, whose maternal sympathy for the orphan waifs, children of Oregon pioneers, fathers or mothers, who died on the plains, caused her and Rev. H. Clarke to plan and build the log orphanage, collect those children, provide food and clothing for them, and, with others, teach or provide a school for them, and finally, when the number became too large, and the care too great, transfer the building and the school to the Trustees of the Academy. The sacredness of this trust has been a precious aroma in the life of academy and college. We know not whether any one of them long shared the benefits of our school, but they were the first plans in its nursery, and they remember it as their school home. We trust that the Brown endowment fund, left by Mrs. B. and now accumulating in the hands of our trustees as a sacred trust, will at length furnish an income to pay the tuition of many orphans and thus support at least one Instructor *in memory of Mrs. Brown, the orphan's friend.* No purer or sweeter memorial can grace her name and gladden her children and her grandchildren and great grandchildren in the Pacific Northwest, or reflect more honor on her native town and State, Brimfield, Massachusetts.

We recall the devotion of A.T. Smith, and Deacon T.D. Naylor, early trustees, to the well-being of the institution, and many other friends of its infancy by whose help it grew.

We trust that the Marsh endowment fund, begun by his small bequest, and rapidly increased by our treasurer's faithfulness and skill, shall ere many years become the endowed professorship of its author's favorite and chosen studies, mental and moral philosophy. We trust also that the Eells endowment fund, now creeping up into the thousands, may before a third decade closes furnish an income to support a professor of those ancient languages and literature which have done so much to give depth of thought and breadth of influence to college-trained students, and thus extend the benefits indefinitely to future students, according to the wish and aim of the liberal donors, Rev. Cushing Eells, D.D. and wife.

We are well aware that the life of this institution of learning gave life and growth to the village, and a full reward to all the people for whatever they did in its behalf. We know that most abundant blessings return to liberal souls.

Now, as a Board of Trustees, twenty-eight of whom have been thus associated, ten of whom have died, one only of the first incorporators and two only of the second incorporators now remaining in the Board, we can unite in a thank-offering of praise to God that he has called us to the trust and service of this institution of Christian learning. We are well aware that it has been largely a season of preparation. We have aimed and prayed that it might be a constant benediction to the assembled youth and to all the homes of the people. We rejoice that it retains its long-tried friends in the Eastern societies and national societies. For their gifts and sympathy, we have cherished gratitude and hope. With the gains of four decades assured, we now face the future. It is not to rest, but to enlarge our view and our plans. We need and must keep abreast of the inflowing population. The outlook cheers. The door of opportunity opens. The demand for trained youth of the best Christian stamp is urgent. The material is at hand in our homes and churches. The prayers and purposes of the good and true are with us. Ours is vantage ground, more commanding than we could see forty, thirty, or twenty years ago. We need not abate a jot of heart or hope or courage to give up our strength for a longer term and deliver our work to others whom we may trust to extend it to other generations.

Our third president is ready and eager to lead on and up to the highest ideal and broadest culture of the academy and college. The gentleman and lady principals of the academy and their assistants show by the choice quality of their work now done and doing, their ability to bring out even more and better fruits of culture. The faculty of the college rejoice in the real and finer growths of their departments under the improved qualities of the academic grades. They will join heartily in the upward and onward movements of the institution, especially if relief can be given in some lines of study by a division of labor. In manufactories one man is set to do one line of work, and he is expected to do that perfectly. It must be so in the college. One or two men can not do everything. It takes many persons to do everything in an institution of learning, and it pays to have them. This means the investment of more money. This is now the imperative demand of Tualatin Academy and Pacific University. What have we as a ground of hope? The same purposes and plan with which we began forty years ago. These same great Missionary Societies, the American Home Missionary Society and the American College and Education Society, and their friends in four thousand churches! We have the assets and experience of forty years. The institution is an object lesson. We have its site and furnishings. Its endowment. Its faculty. Its graduates. Its students. Its *friends. Possibly its foes,* for every cause *must prove its worth* by its enemies as well as by its friends. We have more and better material out of which to make more finished products. We have larger home resources, and abler and more willing donors. We know our pressing needs. We can utilize our gains more wisely. We have the same Divine Providence and Holy Spirit to safely lead us and assure us the best results.

The present Board of Trustees in the order of their time of election is—Rev. G.H. Atkinson, Hon. A. Hinman, Hon. H.W. Corbett, Rev. O. Dickinson, Dea. G. Shindler, Prof. G.H. Collier, Hon. R.P. Boise, Hon. H. Failing, Rev. M. Eells, Prest. J.F. Ellis, E.M. Atkinson, Esq.

List of trustees deceased—Rev. Harvey Clarke, Rev. E. Walker, James M. Moore, Esq., Hon. Israel Mitchell, Dea. T.D. Naylor, Prest. S.H. Marsh, D.D., Dea. W.F. Abrams, Rev. H. Lyman, A.T. Smith, Esq., Hon. J. Quinn Thornton.

List of former trustees still living—Hiram Clark, Esq., Dea. P.H. Hatch, Hon. Wm. H. Gray, Rev. Lewis Thompson, Rev. Prof. T. Condon, Ph.D., Rev. Prof. J.R. Herrick, S.T.D., Rev. P.B. Chamberlain.

INDEX OF PERSONAL NAMES

INDEX

---

[i] For a more complete description of these societies see Sevetson, *Atkinson: Pioneer Oregon Educator*, pp. 261-5 (Appendix: Congregational Mission Societies).

INDEX

CPSIA information can be obtained
at www.ICGtesting.com
Printed in the USA
FSOW01n2056191215
14423FS